HOW TO

WIN YOUR

PERSONAL

INJURY CLAIM

BY ATTORNEY JOSEPH L. MATTHEWS

EDITED BY BARBARA KATE REPA

NOLO PRESS BERKELEY

YOUR RESPONSIBILITY WHEN USING A SELF-HELP LAW BOOK

We've done our best to give you useful and accurate information in this book. But laws and procedures change frequently and are subject to differing interpretations. If you want legal advice backed by a guarantee, see a lawyer. If you use this book, it's your responsibility to make sure that the facts and general advice contained in it are applicable to your situation.

KEEPING UP TO DATE

To keep its books up to date, Nolo Press issues new printings and new editions periodically. New printings reflect minor legal changes and technical corrections. New editions contain major legal changes, major text additions or major reorganizations. To find out if a later printing or edition of any Nolo book is available, call Nolo Press at (510) 549-1976 or check the catalog in the *Nolo News*, our quarterly newspaper.

To stay current, follow the "Update" service in the *Nolo News*. You can get a two-year subscription to the paper free by sending us the registration card in the back of the book. In another effort to help you use Nolo's latest materials, we offer a 25% discount off the purchase of any new Nolo book if you turn in any earlier printing or edition. (See the "Recycle Offer" in the back of the book.)

FIRST EDITION
First Printing   NOVEMBER 1992
Editor   BARBARA KATE REPA
Book Design   JACKIE MANCUSO
Cover Design   TONI IHARA
Index   MARY KIDD
Proofreading   ELY NEWMAN
Printing   DELTA LITHOGRAPH

Matthews, Joseph L.
    (How to) win your personal injury claim / by Joseph L. Matthews :
    edited by Barbara Kate Repa -- 1st national ed.
    p.   cm.
    Includes index.
    ISBN 0-87337-189-5 : $24.95
    1. Personal injuries--United States--Popular works. I. Repa,
Barbara Kate. II. Title.
KF1257.Z9M37   1992
346.7303'23--dc20
[347.306323]   92-10996
                                                CIP

ACKNOWLEDGMENTS

Thanks go to several people who gave of their time and skills to help make this book happen. Annie Tillery did sometimes dizzying research with thoroughness and good cheer. Stephen Elias gave the manuscript a careful reading at several stages and gave numerous helpful suggestions along with unfailing encouragement.

Special thanks go to Richard Duane, Esq., who took time out from his busy law practice to review the manuscript and give it the benefit of his great expertise in the area of personal injury law. Both the quality and willingness of his assistance came as no surprise, since he is known to trial lawyers and clients alike as a tireless and brilliant advocate for the rights of the injured.

Last and greatest thanks are reserved for Barbara Kate Repa. Far more than merely a skilled and dedicated editor, Barbara Kate vetted this book into the world with her vast talents and compassion tuned equally to the needs of future readers and to the foibles of a wandering and sometimes wondering author. The assistance this book will provide its readers comes in large part from her untiring efforts.

CONTENTS

1

HANDLING YOUR PERSONAL INJURY CLAIM

2

WHOSE FAULT IS IT?
HOW LEGAL RESPONSIBILITY IS DETERMINED

3

INITIAL STEPS IN SETTLING YOUR CLAIM

4

UNDERSTANDING INSURANCE COVERAGE

5

HOW MUCH IS YOUR CLAIM WORTH?

6

PROCESSING YOUR CLAIM

7

NEGOTIATING A SETTLEMENT

8

FINALIZING YOUR SETTLEMENT

9

THE LAST RESORTS: LAWYERS AND COURTS

ACCIDENT CLAIM WORKSHEET

Who Can Use This Book?

You don't need any special training to handle most injury claims—just patience, perseverance and some basic information about how the insurance claims process works. It doesn't matter if you were partly at fault for an accident as long as the accident was not entirely your fault.

You can use this book if you have been injured in any sort of accident that occurred other than at work. And even an on-the-job injury can be compensated by using this book if anyone other than your employer or a co-worker might be partly to blame.

You should use this book if you want to receive up to 40% more in compensation for your injuries than if you hired a lawyer, and if you want to receive far more in compensation for your injuries than if you were to deal with an insurance company on your own while unprepared.

The book sets out all the information you need to get a fair settlement through the insurance claims system and to:

- protect your interests after an accident
- understand what your claim is worth
- prepare a claim for compensation, and
- negotiate a settlement with an insurance company.

It also gives you strategies for what to do if an insurance company refuses to negotiate fairly.

What Kinds of Claims Can You Handle Yourself?

Automobile, cycle or pedestrian accidents

Whether you make your claim against the other driver's or owner's insurance or under your own policy, and whether or not your state has some kind of "no-fault" auto insurance law, you can handle your own claims for accidents that occur:

- while driving or as a passenger, in your own car or someone else's, riding a bicycle or motorcycle, or as pedestrian
- while riding public transportation, or
- while you were at work, whether in a company vehicle or your own.

Slip or Trip and Fall Accidents

- on commercial property—a store, office or other business
- at a private residence or other private property, or
- on a sidewalk, street, park, public building or other public property.

Home Accidents

- caused by a dangerous or defective product
- caused by a dangerous or defective condition of rental premises, or
- caused by a neighbor's careless conduct.

Miscellaneous Accidents

- caused by anyone's careless conduct
- caused by children or animals, or
- work-related accidents caused in part by someone other than your employer or a co-worker.

How To Use This Book

This book helps you understand almost any type of accident situation and most every wrinkle in the insurance claims process. You won't need all of the information here to settle your claim, but it's all here if you do need it.

The chapters are set up both to help you understand how the process works and to give you step-by-step directions for protecting your rights and receiving all the compensation you deserve.

Directories at the beginning of chapters explain what is in it and who needs to refer to which parts. You can go straight to the information you need while skipping whatever doesn't apply to your situation. For example, if you had a slip and fall accident, you don't need to read special rules about auto accidents; or, if you had a car accident but you don't have no-fault insurance, you can skip the explanation of how a no-fault claim works.

Handling Your
Personal Injury Claim

The world's most solitary tree is located at an oasis in the Tenere Desert in central Africa. There is no other standing tree within 31 miles. In 1960, a Frenchman accidentally rammed into it with his truck.

❧

In 1896, there were only four automobiles registered in all of the United States. Two of them ran into each other in St. Louis.

❧

Walking up and down stairs is not usually considered tricky. Yet every year thousands of Americans are injured falling on stairs, often from defects in the stairs they never noticed.

In this crowded, hectic and corner-cutting world, no matter how careful you are, the odds are still great you'll be injured in some accident caused by another person's carelessness.

And what happens after the accident can often be as aggravating as your injury. A whole line-up of profiteers lies in wait to make sizable gains from your injuries. First and foremost is the insurance industry. With their tentacles wrapped around every inch of our lives, the virtually unregulated insurance companies take twelve cents out of every dollar you earn, whether or not you are ever in an accident. Part of the insurance stranglehold comes in the exorbitant rates charged for car, home, business and health insurance. Then, after a claim, insurers bulldoze over people who stand in the path of their profits by denying as many claims as possible and paying as little as they can get away with on the claims they are forced to honor.

The health industry joins in to increase the financial pain of an injury. Medical care is controlled by a corporate health industry creating wildly expensive medical treatment and contributing greatly to outrageous health insurance costs.

The lack of protection for lost worktime also hikes up individual losses. Employers permit very limited paid time off. Americans average less than 11 paid non-medical days off per year, by far the fewest of all the major industrial nations of the world. The Netherlands, for example, averages 32 days off per year; Germany, 30; and Japan, 24—all with economies healthier than our own. And as anyone who has ever been off work for any length of time knows painfully well, the American government provides precious little back-up for lost days and lost jobs.

Finally, our legal system twists rather than straightens an injured person's road to compensation. The legal system provides few alternatives for obtaining compensation outside of the lawyer-dominated claim and lawsuit system. And when lawyers are involved, they take 33% to 40% of a person's injury compensation—and run up sometimes staggering costs which come out of the injured person's pockets.

A. Why You Can Handle Your Own Claim

Few people realize that after an accident, it is entirely possible to get around this line-up of insurance, legal and medical profiteers. But with basic information about how the accident claims process works, a bit of organization and a little patience, you can handle your own injury insurance claim without a lawyer—and without the insurance company unfairly denying or reducing your compensation. In fact, most often, you can easily and quickly get significantly more compensation for your injury by handling your own claim than you would if you subjected yourself to a lawyer's control and fees. And you can certainly

receive more than if you submitted a claim yourself without knowing how insurance companies and their claims processes work.

1. The Claims Process Is Simple

Despite what the insurance industry and lawyers would like you to think, settling an injury claim with an insurance company is usually quite simple. Most claims involve no more than a few short letters and phone calls with an insurance adjuster who has no legal training and has no more information than you'll find in this book. You don't need to know technical language or complex legal rules. Your right to be compensated usually depends on nothing more than common sense ideas of who was careful and who was careless.

2. You Know Your Claim Best

You know better than anyone else—insurance adjuster or attorney—how an accident happened. You were there, they weren't. And you know best what injuries you suffered and what your physical condition and other circumstances have been since.

3. The Compensation System Is Structured

The amount of fair compensation in any given case does not come out of a crystal ball that only lawyers and insurance companies know how to read. Rather, a number of simple factors—type of accident, injuries, medical costs—go into figuring how much any claim is "worth." The amount an insurance company will be willing to pay actually falls into a fairly narrow range, whether a lawyer handles your claim for you or you handle the claim yourself. An insurance adjuster who learns that you are organized and that you understand the claims process will usually settle the claim with you right away, and for virtually the same amount as if you had a lawyer.

Settling Claims Is Cheaper for Insurers

An insurance company's willingness to settle your claim quickly has nothing to do with fairness and everything to do with the company saving money in the long run. It's simply cheaper for it to pay you than to prolong the fight.

In the first place, insurance companies must spend money to fight. The longer an adjuster works on a claim, the more money the company is spending on that claim. If lawyers get involved, the company's expenses become much steeper. And if the claim actually goes to court, costs skyrocket. Therefore, once an insurance company knows it is likely to have to pay somewhere down the line—because you understand how much your claim is worth and will not drop your claim empty-handed—it makes financial sense for it to pay sooner rather than later.

The cost of fighting claims is so great for an insurance company that it will often pay a claimant at least a small amount—what is called "nuisance value"—even if the odds favor the insured if the claim went to court. In other words, if it costs an insurance company several thousand dollars in legal costs to fight a claim in court, and there is any chance the company might lose, it is statistically much cheaper for it to pay a quarter or a tenth of that as nuisance value compensation to settle the claim early. (See Chapter 5, Section F2.)

4. Save Money on Legal Fees

If you hire a lawyer to handle your claim, the lawyer will take a fee of up to 40% of your recovery—and charge you for "costs" which seem to appear out of thin air and which can quickly run into hundreds of dollars. Yet, except in serious or complicated cases, a lawyer can usually gain for you only an extra 5% to 20%, if anything, above what you can obtain for yourself once you understand the process. Subtract the lawyer's fees and costs from the extra amount of the settlement, and you can actually end up losing more than a third of the money to which you are entitled.

B. When You Might Need a Lawyer

Sometimes, the skills of an experienced personal injury lawyer, or at least the threat to an insurance company that such a lawyer presents, are worth the .

Hiring a Lawyer Later in the Process

If, after you have presented your claim and negotiated with an insurance company as explained in this book, you do not feel the insurer is offering a fair settlement, you can then retain an attorney to finish the process for you. Or you can consult an attorney on an hourly basis to see if he or she can spot a particular legal argument that might help you to move the insurance company toward a more reasonable offer. (See Chapter 9, Section B.)

money you have to pay that lawyer to represent you. You may need a lawyer because of complex legal rules involved in your claim, because your injuries are quite serious so that the potential amount of your compensation might vary greatly, or simply because an insurance company refuses to settle the matter with you in good faith.

There are no hard and fast rules about when you do and do not need to hire a lawyer. Much of the decision has to do with how you feel things are going as you attempt to settle your claim on your own. At some point, you may feel overwhelmed—by too much work, or by some obscure legal rule the insurance company decides to throw at you. Or you may be stonewalled by an insurance adjuster who blusters that the company does not have to honor your claim at all, or who offers you only a piddling amount to settle it. In these situations, you may want to consult an attorney for advice, and perhaps have him or her take over handling the claim.

Before you turn your case over to a lawyer, make sure there is a good reason for doing so and not just the expensive impulse reaction to Get A Lawyer that the legal community has brainwashed us all to have.

A few types of injuries and accidents almost certainly require that you hire a lawyer.

1. Long-Term or Permanently Disabling Injuries

Some accidents result in injuries which for a long time—over six months—or even permanently affect your physical capabilities or appearance. Figuring out how much such a serious injury is "worth" can be a difficult business that may require an experienced lawyer to get the most out of the claim. Even if you decide to handle the matter yourself, an injury with a long period of recovery or a permanent physical effect might signal that you should consult with a lawyer for an hour or two to make sure you have covered all the bases in your claim.

2. Severe Injuries

The amount of your accident compensation is mostly determined by how severe your injuries were. And the severity of your injuries is measured by the amount of your medical bills and your lost income, as well as the length of time you remain in pain or disabled. Once your medical and lost-income figures begin to rise, not only does the amount of compensation rise, but it becomes more difficult to gauge the range of fair compensation an insurance company is willing to pay. And once these figures get high and the range gets broad, it may be worth the fee you would have to pay to have a lawyer handle your claim.

In Chapter 5, we explain how to gauge how much your claim may be worth. In a less serious case, with medical costs and income loss of a few thousand dollars, it is rarely worth your money to hire a lawyer.

Example *Your medical costs and income loss are $2,500. Applying the damages formula (discussed in Chapter 5, Section A), you know that your compensation will be between $5,000 and $10,000—no lower and no higher. Therefore, you can negotiate within that range to get the highest possible amount without worrying that you might instead have received $20,000 or $30,000 if you had hired a lawyer to negotiate for you. Also, you know that even if you got $7,500 on your own and a lawyer could have obtained $10,000, the lawyer's fee and costs would have reduced your actual compensation to less than $7,500, anyway.*

But when the injuries are severe and the medical costs and lost income are high—over $10,000 or so—the range of potential compensation can become very wide—from $20,000 to $100,000. Because the difference between the low end of this range and the high end is so great, it may be a good idea to take advantage of the experience of a knowledgeable personal injury lawyer to ensure that you get the highest possible amount, even taking into account that the lawyer's fee will eat up a large part of your final award.

Example *Your medical bills and lost income are $15,000 and you are able to get a settlement offer of $50,000 by yourself, but a lawyer might be able to get $75,000 to $100,000 for you. Even after the lawyer takes one-third as a fee, you would be left with between $50,000 and $67,000—up to $17,000 more than you obtained on your own. And the lawyer will have done the work.*

No fixed cut-off point in medical bills and lost income determines when you should consider hiring a lawyer. Some people feel more comfortable hiring a lawyer as soon as their bills reach a couple of thousand dollars, regardless of any other factors in the case. Other people would handle a similar claim on their own and avoid the lawyer's fee, even if their medical bills and lost income reached $10,000 and their potential compensation $100,000.

Finding the Right Lawyer

Deciding that you want to consult with or hire a lawyer is one thing, finding the right lawyer is another. Only some lawyers are experienced in personal injury claims. And if your claim were simple enough for an inexperienced lawyer to handle, you would be handling it yourself. It is important to find a lawyer who can handle your particular kind of claim, and also to find one whom you are comfortable having represent you. (See Chapter 9, Section B1.)

The only way to know whether you feel comfortable handling your own claim is to understand how compensation amounts are calculated and apply those criteria to your situation to get a rough idea of what your claim might be worth. (See Chapter 5, Section A.) Then decide—either right away or after negotiating for a while with the insurance company—whether to continue handling the case on your own, to consult with a lawyer on an hourly basis or to hire a lawyer to handle your case. (See Chapter 9, Section B.)

3. Medical Malpractice

If you have suffered an injury or illness due to careless, unprofessional or incompetent treatment at the hands of a doctor, nurse, hospital, clinic, laboratory or other medical provider, the complexities of both the medical questions and of the legal rules involved almost certainly require that you hire a lawyer experienced in medical malpractice matters.

4. Toxic Exposure

In the increasingly chemical world, we sometimes become ill because of exposure to chemicals in the air, soil or water, in products we use or in food we eat. Claims based on such exposure are difficult to prove, however, and often require complex scientific data. Because the chemical and other industries have erected a huge wall to protect themselves from legal exposure while they continue to chemically expose us, the required evidence is very hard to come by. As a result, fighting a claim for toxic exposure requires the services of a lawyer experienced in such cases.

5. When an Insurance Company Refuses To Pay

In some instances, regardless of the nature of your injury or the amount of your medical bills and lost income, you will want to hire a lawyer because an insurance company or government agency simply refuses to make any fair settlement offer at all. If, after repeated efforts, you are unable to obtain an offer of fair and reasonable compensation, you might be forced to see if an attorney can do better for you. In these cases, something—what the lawyer can get minus the fee charged to get it—may be better than nothing.

Such a stonewall refusal to honor your claim can arise in several circumstances.

Denial of liability   It is not unusual for an insurance company initially to deny that its insured was in any way at fault for an accident. Often it does this in the hope that you will either believe it or will quickly become so frustrated that you give up and drop your claim. Usually, though, after you show that you will not immediately fold up your tent at the first refusal to pay, an insurance company will come around and make a reasonable settlement offer.

If, however, an insurance company does not budge from its initial denial of all responsibility, you may need help from a lawyer. You have nothing to lose at that point. If an experienced personal injury lawyer can coax some money out of the insurance company, you will at least have received some compensation. If the lawyer has agreed to handle the case for a contingency fee (see Chapter 9, Section B2) but can get no compensation for you either, you won't have any lawyer's fees to pay and you will at least know you have turned over every stone.

Denial of coverage   An insurance company may not dispute that its insured caused the accident, but will claim that the particular accident is not covered by the insurance policy. Your first step should be to demand a copy of the insurance policy. Read it carefully to see if what the insurance adjuster says is true. (See Chapter 4 for guidance.)

But even if you locate in the policy exactly what the insurance adjuster says is there, that does not end the matter. Most insurance policy provisions can be interpreted several different ways, and courts usually try to interpret them so that injured people are covered. So if an insurance company continues to deny coverage, take your claim to an experienced personal injury lawyer who may well be able to force the insurance company to provide the coverage it has been paid to provide.

Government immunity   The right to sue a government entity—a town, city, county or state, a school, transportation or other local district—for accidents caused by its employees is strictly controlled in each state by a specific set of laws. These laws—known as "sovereign immunity" and the "tort claims act" —establish the situations in which you can and cannot sue the government because of an accident, and the special procedures you have to follow before you can do so. (See Chapter 3, Section C.)

Even after completing these procedures, however, the government's response may be to deny any compensation to you, arguing that it is immune to claims in your particular accident. Like an insurance company's denial of coverage, a government's claim of immunity is sometimes just a knee-jerk response which will disappear after you negotiate for a while. But claims adjusters for public entities do not give up public money easily—and sometimes they will cling to an immunity defense all the way to court. Because of the complexity of the rules involved, if a claims adjuster refuses to make any settlement offer to you because of governmental immunity, you will almost certainly have to consult a personal injury attorney about making a legal attack on that claim.

2

Whose Fault Is It? How Legal Responsibility Is Determined

The beginning of this chapter explains generally how the legal system and the insurance industry decide the questions of who was at fault and therefore who has to pay.

Once you have read this general explanation in Section A, skip to the part of the chapter focusing on the specific type of accident you were involved in:

- Automobile and other vehicle accidents (Section B1)

- Injuries at someone's home, business or public property (Section B2). If you were injured when you slipped or tripped and fell on stairs, read Section B3, also

- Injuries involving children (Section B4)

- Injuries caused by animals (Section B5), or

- Injuries caused by defective or dangerous products (Section B7).

If none of these descriptions fits your accident, see Section B6 for some guidance in how to proceed with your claim.

t he question of who caused an accident, or whose fault it was, forms the basis of any decision about who is legally responsible —or liable—for the damages that result. In other words, deciding who was at fault determines who has to pay for your injuries.

A. Basic Rules of Liability

Although lawyers and insurance companies would like people to think that legal responsibility, or liability, for an accident is a complicated question, the answer usually requires nothing more than common sense. Liability revolves around the simple fact that most accidents happen because someone was careless—or "negligent." And as to this carelessness, the law applies a basic rule: If one person in an accident had been less careful than another, the less careful one must pay for at least a portion of the damages suffered by the more careful one.

Legal liability for almost all accidents is determined by this rule, and by one or more of the following simple propositions.

- If the injured person was where he or she was not supposed to be, or somewhere he or she should have expected the kind of activity which caused the accident, the person who caused the accident might not be liable because that person had no "duty" to be careful toward the injured person. (See Section B2.)

- If a negligent person causes an accident while working for someone else, the employer may also be legally responsible for the accident. (See Chapter 4, Section A2.)

- If an accident is caused on property that is dangerous because it is poorly built or maintained, the owner of the property is liable for being careless in maintaining the property, regardless of whether he or she actually created the dangerous condition. (See Section B2.)

- If an accident is caused by a defective product, the manufacturer and seller of the product are both liable even without the injured person knowing which one was careless in creating or allowing the defect, or knowing exactly how the defect happened. (See Section B7.)

- If the injured person was also careless, his or her compensation may be reduced by the extent such carelessness ("comparative negligence") was also responsible for the accident (See Section A3.)

Liability insurance covers nearly every motor vehicle, home, business and other property. (See Chapter 4.) So in virtually every accident you will only need to deal with an insurance adjuster and not with a lawyer, judge or other technician of legal mumbo-jumbo. And making a successful insurance claim usually requires nothing more complicated than providing a clear explanation to an insurance adjuster, in plain language, of how the insured was careless and how such carelessness caused the accident. (See Chapter 6, Section B.)

If your explanation makes it appear likely that the insured person's or business's carelessness caused the accident, the liability insurance company will pay you for your medical costs, for your lost income and a certain amount for the pain and inconvenience you have suffered. (See Chapter 5.) Once an insurance adjuster knows that you understand how the simple rules of liability apply to your accident, the emphasis in your claim will likely shift quickly from *whether* you can receive compensation to *how much* that compensation will be.

1. You Don't Need To Prove Anything

Most liability claims are settled without anyone ever stepping into a courtroom. So, the process of negotiating with an insurance company does not require that you provide legally perfect "proof" that the insured was negligent and that the negligence caused the accident. To get compensation for your injuries, you need only make a reasonable argument that the insured was negligent, even if there is also a plausible argument that the insured was not.

And in accidents caused by defective products, you don't need to argue at all that the insured was negligent; negligence is automatically presumed under a rule called "strict liability." (See Section B7, below.)

Making a reasonable argument that the insured was negligent shows the insurance company that if

the matter later becomes a lawsuit, there is a good possibility that a court would find its insured to be legally responsible. And once an insurance company believes that—and therefore that it might have to pay not only the injured person but also court costs and lawyers' fees—it will usually prefer to pay a claim settlement rather than run the greater risk.

2. Choosing From Whom To Collect

Automobile accidents often involve the carelessness of several drivers, or of someone not in a car who creates a hazard that a driver carelessly fails to avoid and plows into you. In accidents that happen at a business, both the property owner and the business tenant might be responsible. If you are injured by a defective product, both the maker and the seller are probably legally responsible.

When there is more than one other person responsible for an accident, the law in most states provides that either one is responsible for compensating you fully for your damages. The two of them must decide between themselves as to whether one should reimburse the other. However, the law does not allow you collect the full amount from both.

This rule about collecting from either responsible person provides you with a couple of important advantages. If one liable person is insured and the other is not, you can make your claim against the insured person for the full amount. And even if both are insured, you will only have to settle your claim with one insurance company. Initially, consider everyone you think might be responsible and notify each of them that you may be filing a claim for damages. (See Chapter 3, Section B1.) Then, depending on what you discover about how the accident happened, or on which insurance company takes responsibility, you will pursue a claim against only one. (See Chapter 6, Section B.)

3. How Your Carelessness Affects Your Claim

Even if you were careless and partly caused an accident, in most states you can still recover compensation from anyone else who was also careless and who partly caused the accident. The amount of a person's liability for an accident is determined by comparing his or her carelessness with the carelessness of the person injured. And this percentage of liability determines the percentage of the resulting damages he or she must pay. This rule is referred to as comparative negligence.

Example   *Bob was in a car accident in which he stopped short and was hit from behind. If the other person had been 100% at fault, Bob's medical bills and lost income would entitle him to $1,000. However, the police accident report notes that Bob stopped short because one of a group of children next to a school looked like he was going to dart into the street. The insurance company for the person whose car hit Bob from behind points out that Bob should have been going slowly enough in the school area to be able to stop without having to jam on his brakes.*

In this case, not going slowly enough may have made Bob between 10% to 25% negligent. The person who hit him would not be liable to Bob for the full compensation of $1,000, therefore, but only for $750 to $900 (100% liability minus Bob's 25% to 10% liability = 75% to 90% liability).

Example   *Ted, who was driving the car which hit Bob, also sustained injuries. If another person had been fully responsible for his injuries, Ted's claim would have been worth $2,000. Even though Ted was 75% to 90% liable for the accident, in some states (see below), he could collect an amount from Bob's insurance equal to Bob's negligence. So, since Bob was 10% to 25% negligent, Ted can collect 10% to 25% of his $2,000 damages—between $200 and $500.*

There is no formula for arriving at a precise number for a person's comparative carelessness. During claim negotiations, you and an insurance adjuster discuss the factors which make both you and the insured person seem to have been at fault. Then the question of your comparative negligence will go into the negotiating hopper along with all the other factors which determine how much a claim is worth —such as the seriousness of your injury and the amount of your medical bills. (See Chapter 5.)

Insurancespeak: A Few Definitions

The legal terms below are most likely the only ones you need to know to negotiate with an insurance company. Each term is discussed more fully in Section A of this chapter, but this glossary can serve as a quick reference.

- Duty of care: the legal obligation to be careful in conduct or care of property so that people are not injured by our actions or our failure to act.

- Liability: legal responsibility for an accident; a person who is liable must pay for injuries caused in the accident.

- Negligence: the carelessness that causes, or contributes to, an accident.

- Comparative negligence: the carelessness of an injured person that contributes to an accident; the injured person's right to compensation is reduced by the percentage of his or her comparative negligence.

- Strict liability: legal responsibility for injuries caused by a defective or dangerous product; the injured person is not required to show that the product maker or seller was negligent.

Comparative negligence is applied in three different ways, depending on the state where the accident occurred.

a.   States with no restrictions

Alaska	Mississippi
Arizona	Missouri
California	New Mexico
Florida	New York
Kentucky	Rhode Island
Louisiana	Washington
Michigan	

In these 13 states, the general rule of comparative negligence operates without any restrictions. You are entitled to compensation for your damages in an amount based on the percentage of the other person's fault regardless of how great your own fault was, as in the example, above.

b.   States with some restrictions

Arkansas	Nevada
Colorado	New Hampshire
Connecticut	New Jersey
Delaware	North Dakota
Georgia	Ohio
Hawaii	Oklahoma
Idaho	Oregon
Illinois	Pennsylvania
Indiana	Texas
Iowa	Utah
Kansas	Vermont
Maine	West Virginia
Massachusetts	Wisconsin
Minnesota	Wyoming
Montana	

These 29 states have a more restrictive rule, known as "modified comparative negligence." With this restricted rule, you lose your right to any compensation at all if your own carelessness was 50% or more responsible for the accident. If you were less than 50% at fault, the rule works exactly the same as the general rule of comparative negligence (explained in the examples above). In other words, you have a right to compensation up to the percentage amount of the other person's negligence.

Keep in mind that there is no precise way of figuring the extent of your carelessness. So, in these states, the degree of your comparative negligence—including whether or not it was more than 50%—is a subject about which the insurance company has to negotiate with you.

c.   States with the most restrictions

Alabama	South Carolina
District of Columbia	South Dakota
Maryland	Tennessee
Nebraska	Virginia
North Carolina	

Nine states follow a very restricted and often unfair comparative negligence rule. In these states, you cannot recover any compensation at all if you were even "slightly" at fault for the accident (Nebraska and South Dakota); or your carelessness was anything more than "remotely connected" with causing the accident (Tennessee); or you were at all "contributorily negligent" (Alabama, District of Columbia, Maryland, North Carolina, South Carolina, Virginia), meaning that your carelessness contributed in any way, however slight, to the accident.

In these nine states, it can be difficult to recover damages if the insurance company can point to anything you did that contributed to the accident. However, it is not easy for an insurance company to prove absolutely that you were partly at fault. So, even if you might have been slightly careless, you can still recover some damages from an insurance company as long as your carelessness did not obviously cause the accident.

Example   *Alejandro makes a sudden stop when a dog runs in front of his car. Bernice hits Alejandro from behind. There was no indication that Alejandro's driving was at all careless, but the police accident report notes than one of Alejandro's tail lights was out.*

If the insurance company can show that the tail light was out before the accident, it might claim that Alejandro was comparatively negligent for not having his car working properly. In one of these most restrictive states, the insurance company might say that Alejandro has no right to any compensation because of his comparative, or contributory, negligence. Alejandro would respond, however, that Bernice said nothing to the police officer about Alejandro's tail light being out, so Alejandro's tail light did not contribute in any way to the accident.

Alejandro and the insurance company would then negotiate about this question, along with all the other factors in the case, and because the insurance company cannot prove that the tail light actually contributed to the accident, Alejandro would almost surely receive at least some compensation for his injuries.

4. No Liability for Unexpected Conduct

Even people who might be considered careless in what they do, or in how they maintain their property, may not necessarily be liable to anyone injured by the carelessness. The law says there is no "duty" to be careful toward others who are not where they are supposed to be.

The issue of duty of care does not come up very often. Legally, all of us have a duty of care toward anyone who, while acting reasonably, could be injured by our conduct, regardless of whether they were injured in a "normal" or expected way. About the only time someone does not have a duty of care toward others is after taking active steps to keep others away from the place in which an accident might occur, or warning them of the possibility of an accident.

Example   *The landlord of an old apartment building closes the gate to the roof and posts a sign saying "Danger" and that no one is allowed on the roof. On a hot day, though, Dan and Shelly decide they want to do a little sunbathing. Dan trips on a rotten roof board and breaks his wrist.*

If the rotten board were anywhere else in the building, the landlord would be considered negligent. But because Dan was where he was not supposed to be, the landlord had no duty of care to maintain a safe roof. Dan would probably lose his claim for compensation against the landlord.

Witnesses Can Help Show Fault

If someone saw what happened in your accident and backs up some part of your version of events, you may have a strong tool in showing who was at fault. A witness could be someone else who was involved in the accident—a passenger in your car, for example— or a bystander who just happened to see what went on.

An insurance adjuster might try to convince you that what a witness says is less important if it comes from a friend or relative. But in general, that is not true as long as the friend or relative actually saw the accident; after all, most people traveling in the same car are going to be friends or relatives. If you have a complete stranger as a supporting witness, however, your case might become even stronger. (See Chapter 3, Section A2d, and Chapter 6, Section A1c.)

B. Liability in Specific Types of Accidents

There are no magic formulas or special language you have to master to show why someone was at fault in any particular kind of accident. All you have to bear in mind are the general rules of liability discussed in Section A of this chapter.

You only need to make a reasonable, common sense argument about why a person or business was careless in acting or failing to act, and how that negligence caused the accident which injured you. And in accidents caused by defective products, you need not show any negligence on the part of the product's maker or seller. Instead, you only need to show that you used the product in a normal way and that the defective or dangerous part of the product caused your injuries.

The rest of this chapter discusses how these general rules are applied in specific types of accidents. Remember, though, that an insurance adjuster might claim that you, too, were negligent, or that you were using a product improperly. So, when you think about the facts of your accident, consider how the insurance company will view your actions—and begin to plan your responses.

1. Vehicle Accidents

Anyone who drives or rides in a car long enough is likely to be involved in at least a minor fender-bender. Anyone who rides a bicycle or motorcycle knows the roads are even more dangerous for two-wheelers. And on our crowded streets, pedestrians, too, are often involved in accidents with buses, cars and bikes.

Special Rules for No-Fault Policyholders

Almost half the states have some form of no-fault (also called Personal Injury Protection) auto insurance. No-fault insurance is intended to prevent people with minor auto accident injuries from filing claims for any damages other than their medical bills.

However, every no-fault plan permits claims for damages beyond medical bills in some circumstances. To see if your no-fault policy affects how you can make an auto accident injury claim, see Chapter 4, Section A4.

If you are covered by a no-fault policy that allows you to file a claim for damages against the person who was at fault for your accident, proceed against that person as explained here, exactly the same as if you did not have no-fault coverage.

a. Traffic laws may help determine fault

Figuring out who is at fault in a traffic accident is a matter of deciding who was careless. But for vehicle accidents, there is a set of official written rules telling people how they are supposed to drive and providing guidelines by which liability often can be measured. These rules of the road are the traffic laws everyone must learn to pass the driver's license test. Complete rules are contained in each state's Vehicle Code, and they apply not only to automobiles but also to motorcycles, bicycles and pedestrians.

Sometimes a violation of one of these traffic rules is obvious and was clearly the cause of an accident.

Example *Bob drives through a stop sign and hits Mary's car. Going through a stop sign is an obvious violation which leads directly to a collision with someone coming through an intersection in a cross-direction.*

Example *Juanita does not look carefully and moves over into a lane in which Arlene is riding her bike. Arlene swerves and hits a parked car. Since a bicycle has as much right to the road as does a car, the accident was clearly caused by the traffic violation of an unsafe lane change and is obviously Juanita's fault, even though her car never actually touched Arlene or her bike.*

In other situations, whether or not there was a violation will be less obvious.

Example *Arnie merges onto a freeway. Ed does not give him room to enter, and Arnie's car strikes the side of Ed's car. A little research reveals that the rule in the state where the accident occurred is that the entering driver must give way to the driver who is already in traffic. So, unless Ed was violating some other rule, Arnie was probably at fault.*

And in other situations, there may have been a traffic violation that had no part in causing the accident, and therefore should not affect who is liable.

Example *Beatrice failed to signal when she made a right turn; Chain-Fa ran through a stop sign and plowed into her. Obviously, Chain-Fa's violation led directly to the accident. If he had stopped, he would not have hit Bea. But Bea's violation probably had nothing to do with the accident. Since Chain-Fa would have hit her whether she had gone straight or turned, signaling would not have prevented the accident.*

b.   Accidents with several causes

It is sometimes difficult to say that one particular act caused an accident. This is especially true if what you claim the other driver did is vague or seems minor.

But if you can show that the other driver made several minor driving errors or committed several minor traffic violations, then you can argue that the *combination* of those actions caused the accident.

Example *Lana was riding her bicycle in the right-hand lane when John changed from the left lane to the right and ran into her. In the police report, Lana sees that John says he had already moved into the lane before the collision and that Lana was not paying attention.*

This is the kind of case where it is often difficult to show who was most at fault, and an insurance settlement for Lana might be lower because of what appears to be her comparative negligence. That is, it seems both people were at fault.

But if, through the police report or a witness, Lana can show that John was driving over the speed limit, failed to signal a lane change, changed lanes too abruptly or committed some other driving violation, in combination with Lana's claim that he did not give her the right of way, Lana's argument for liability could be stronger.

c.   Where to find help in showing fault

Your argument to an insurance company that the other driver was at least partially at fault can be strengthened if you can find some official support that the other driver violated one or more rules of the road.

Vehicle Code. One place to look for support for your argument that the other driver was at fault is in the laws that govern driving in your state, usually called the state Vehicle Code. A simplified version of these laws, sometimes called "The Rules of the Road," is often available at your local Department of Motor Vehicles office. The complete Vehicle Code is also available at many local Department of Motor Vehicle offices, most public libraries and all law libraries; there is a law library at or near every courthouse and at all law schools.

In the index at the end of the last volume of the Vehicle Code are references to many rules of the road, one or more of which might apply to your accident. A librarian may be willing to help you with your search, so don't be afraid to ask. If you believe a rule might apply to your accident, copy not only its exact wording but also the Vehicle Code section number so that you can refer to it when you negotiate a settlement of your claim.

Rule violations that always mean liability Many rules of the road are subject to debate with insurance companies: Did the other driver really violate the rule? Did the rule really apply in your case? Did the rule violation actually cause the accident? But there are a few situations in which the other driver is almost always found to be at fault and insurance companies don't even bother to argue about it.

Rear-end collision If someone hits you from behind, it is virtually always his or her fault, regardless of the reason you stopped. A basic rule of the road requires that you be able to stop safely if a vehicle stops ahead of you. If you cannot stop, you are not driving as safely as the person in front of you. The other surefire part of a rear-end accident claim is that the car's damage proves how the accident happened. If the other car's front end and your car's rear end are both damaged, there's no doubt that you were struck from the rear.

In some situations, both you and the car behind you will be stopped when a third car runs into the car behind you and pushes it into the rear of your car. In that case, it is the driver of the third car who is at fault and against whose liability insurance you would file a claim.

Left turn accident A car making a left turn is almost always liable to a car coming straight in the other direction. Exceptions to this near-automatic liability can occur if:

- the car going straight was going too fast, but that is usually difficult to prove
- the car going straight went through a red light, but again, that is very difficult to prove
- the left-turn car began its turn when it was safe but something unexpected happened which made it have to slow down or stop its turn. Nonetheless,

the law says the car making the left turn must wait until it can safely complete the turn before moving in front of oncoming traffic.

Also, as with a rear-end collision, the location of the damage on the cars sometimes makes it difficult for the other driver to argue that accident happened in some way other than during a left turn. So, if you have had an accident in which you ran into someone who was making a left turn in front of you, almost all other considerations of fault go out the window and the other driver is nearly always liable.

Police Reports: Powerful Evidence

If the police responded to the scene of your accident, particularly if they were aware that anyone was injured, they probably made a written accident report.

Sometimes a police report will plainly state that a driver violated a specific Vehicle Code section and that the violation caused the accident. It may even indicate that the officer issued a citation. Other times, negligent driving is merely described or briefly mentioned somewhere in the report.

Regardless of how specific the report is, if you can find any mention in a police report of a Vehicle Code violation or other evidence of careless driving, it can serve as great support in showing that the other driver was at fault. Naturally, the clearer the officer's statement about fault, the easier your job will be. (See Chapter 6, Section A.)

2. Accidents on Dangerous or Defective Property

Injury accidents caused by defective or dangerous property, either inside a building or outside, are called "premises liability" accidents. Premises can be dangerous for all kinds of reasons—faulty design, shoddy construction or building materials, poor maintenance or dangerous clutter. And dangerous premises can lead to all kinds of accidents, including: slipping and falling, tripping or having something hit or fall on you.

These accidents take place:
- on commercial premises—a store, office or other place of business
- at a residence—private home or rental property, or
- on public property—park, street or sidewalk, government building, or public transport such as bus or streetcar.

Regardless of how or where an accident takes place, two basic rules determine who is legally responsible.

a. Owner's duty to keep property safe

The owner or occupier of property has a legal duty to anyone who enters the property—a tenant, a shopper or a personal or business visitor—not to subject that person to an unreasonable risk of injury because of the design, construction or condition of the property. The reason for this rule is simple: The owner and occupier have control over whether the premises are safe, while the visitor has none.

Example   *An apartment building visitor trips and falls on a broken piece of linoleum in the entrance hall. The owner of the building is most likely liable for the injuries caused because the owner has a responsibility to maintain the floor so that broken tiles get replaced and people do not trip over them.*

Other rules protect an employee who is injured on his or her employer's premises. An employee who is injured at work must make a workers' compensation claim instead of a private injury claim. (See Chapter 4, Section C4.) But if the employee is injured on someone's premises other than his or her employer's, the employee has a right to make a claim against the owner of those premises.

b. Your duty to use property normally

The second basic rule of premises liability has to do with your own conduct. There is an "unreasonable risk of injury" if a person using the premises in a normal way has an accident caused by a dangerous or faulty design, construction or condition of the premises, or some combination of these dangerous factors. However, a property owner or occupier is not held responsible for people who get injured while acting in an unexpected, unauthorized or dangerously careless way. You can probably already see where the arguments begin: What does using the premises in a "normal" way mean? And if there was a danger or defect, was an accident caused by that condition or by the carelessness of the person injured?

Example   *People leaving a party one night are rough-housing on the stairs. One of the partygoers swings himself down the stairs on the handrail. The handrail breaks and he is injured. Because a handrail is not a gymnastics apparatus, vaulting on one is not a normal use. The owner cannot be held responsible for the unusual and dangerously careless use of the handrail.*

c. Who is responsible for injuries

The owner of property is often different from the occupier—for example, a store or other business may be operated by one company but the property owned by another, or a residence may be owned by one person and rented by someone else. Both the owner and the occupier may be responsible for injuries caused by the property's dangerous condition. And because both may be legally responsible, it is up to their insurance companies to determine which one will have to respond to your accident claim. Once you file a notice of claim against both, you don't have to worry about deciding which one is more responsible. That's their problem. (See Chapter 3, Section B1.)

The Law Takes You As It Finds You

What happens if you have a bad knee which makes one leg a bit unsteady and it sometimes buckles if you make a sudden turn? Does that mean that the slippery floor you fell on is not legally considered dangerous because someone with two stronger legs might not have fallen?

Absolutely not.

An owner or occupant must permit no unnecessary danger to *any* person who might reasonably be expected to be on the property. That means little kids as well as older people, folks with good eyesight and bad, strong knees and weak knees. The legal rule is that people must be "taken as they're found," meaning that all people, regardless of physical ability, have a right to make their way through the world without unnecessary danger—as long as they have not created that danger by being careless themselves.

Explained below are the ways legal responsibility is sorted out regarding different types of property.

Commercial property   If you file an initial notice of claim (see Chapter 3, Section B) against a store, office or other business at which you were injured, that business's insurance company will either handle your claim itself or pass the matter on to the building owner's insurance company, depending on which one is responsible. The question of whether the owner or occupier is legally responsible is usually determined by where the accident occurred, as stated in the terms of the lease or other business arrangement.

When you file an initial notice of claim against the business, either the business's or the property owner's insurance company will let you know which one will handle your claim.

Private residences   The rules of legal responsibility for private residences are fairly simple.

- *Rented apartment.* If you are injured in an accident on rental property, whether you are a visitor or a tenant, responsibility for the condition of premises can usually be divided into two parts:

1. the movable things inside an apartment, for which the tenant is responsible, and

2. the immovable things inside (floors, walls, fixtures, appliances which came with the apartment) and everything outside (hallways, stairs, entrances), for which the landlord is responsible. An exception to this rule can occur if there is something immovable inside—a floorboard, for example—that the tenant knows is dangerous but he or she has done nothing about. In that case, the tenant as well as the landlord may also be liable for injuries that dangerous condition causes.

If you are injured but are not sure who is legally responsible for the portion of the premises causing the accident, file a notice of claim against both. (See Chapter 3, Section B.)

- *Private home*. If you are injured in an accident caused by a dangerous or defective condition at a private home, the owner of the home is responsible. If the entire home is rented out, the tenant, too, might be responsible.
- Adjoining properties. In an accident which occurs at the edge of premises—for example, at a fence on a neighbor's property line, or on a cracked sidewalk—it may not be immediately clear whether it was one homeowner's or the other's property that caused the accident. Or it may be unclear whether the homeowner or the city was responsible for the particular part of the sidewalk which was defective. In these situations, file an initial notice of claim against both and let them sort out which one will respond to your claim.

d.   Slip or trip and fall accidents

An extremely common kind of accident is slipping on a wet or otherwise slippery floor, stair or ground, or tripping over something on a floor or the ground. It is a normal part of living for things to fall or to drip on a floor or the ground, and some things put in the ground—a drainage grate, for example—serve a useful purpose there. Therefore, the owner or occupant of property cannot always be held responsible for immediately picking up or cleaning every slippery substance on a floor. Nor is the property owner always responsible for someone slipping or tripping on something which an ordinary person should expect to find there or should see and avoid. We all have an obligation to watch where we're going.

There is no precise way to determine when an owner or occupier of property is legally responsible for something on which you slip or trip. Each case turns on whether the owner acted carefully so that slipping or tripping was not *likely* to happen—and whether the person who fell was careless in not seeing or avoiding the thing he or she fell on.

To be legally responsible for the injuries you suffered from slipping or tripping and falling, the owner of the premises or the owner's employee:

- must have caused the spill, worn or torn spot, or other slippery or dangerous surface or item, to be underfoot; or
- must have known the slippery or dangerous material or object was underfoot but did nothing about it; or
- should have known the slippery or dangerous material was on the floors, stair or ground because a "reasonable" person taking care of the property would have discovered and removed or repaired such a thing.

The third situation is the most common, but is also less clear-cut than the first two because of those pesky words "should have known." Liability in these cases is determined by common sense. The law determines whether the owner or occupier of property was careful by deciding if the steps the owner or occupier took to keep the property safe were reasonable.

People who work at, live on and visit property drop and spill things from time to time, and they do not always pick up after themselves. And floors become cracked, torn or worn and slippery and ground can become loose, broken or unusually slippery. A person who is responsible for property must make some regular effort to check the walking safety of the premises and to do some repair and clean-up with safety in mind. On the other hand, the law does not require a premise's owner to stand by round-the-clock to repair or clean up instantly anything that is broken, dropped or spilled.

The law concentrates on the reasonableness of clean-up and repair efforts. Someone who makes regular and thorough efforts to keep property safe and clean is less likely to be found liable than an owner who completely neglects the premises. But usually accident claims arise when the matter of repair or clean-up is not very clear. As a result, you can almost always argue that the owner was not careful enough. The very fact that you tripped or slipped shows that the owner could have been more "reasonable" than he or she was. (Chapter 3, Section A discusses how to preserve evidence of what caused a trip or slip and fall accident. Chapter 6, Section A discusses getting information about property maintenance.)

If you have slipped on or tripped over something and fallen, there are some initial questions you can ask to determine whether the property owner may be liable.

- If you tripped over a torn, broken or bulging area of carpet, floor or ground, or slipped on a wet or loose area, had the dangerous spot been there long enough so that the owner should have known about it?
- If you tripped over or slipped on an object someone had placed or left on the floor or ground, was there a legitimate reason for the object to be there?
- If there once had been a good reason for the object to be there but that reason no longer exists, could the object have been removed or covered or otherwise made safe?
- Was there a safer place the object could have been located, or placed in a safer manner, without much greater inconvenience or expense to the property owner or operator?
- Could a simple barrier have been created or warning given to prevent people from slipping or tripping?
- Did insufficient or broken lighting contribute to the accident?

Example   On a crowded train platform, Clarence slips on a banana peel. The banana peel was dry and black— evidence that it had been dropped a long time before the accident. The train management is likely to be liable for Clarence's fall because the fact that the banana peel had been on the ground for a long time means that management was not doing a reasonable job of regularly cleaning up the platform.

Example   On another train platform, Barbara slips on a yellow, moist banana peel. Since the banana peel had not been there long, nothing indicates that the train management was not sweeping the platform often enough. But at this train platform there is a snack bar which sells bananas, and only one trash container which is over-

flowing. The train management could be held responsible for creating the situation where banana peels need to be disposed of but providing no place for them to be disposed. In other words, the danger of slipping on a banana peel is much greater than it needs to be because of the train management's conduct.

Example   Martina is walking in an unfamiliar neighborhood. She sees some people unloading a truck behind a warehouse, and goes through a gate to ask them directions. As Martina approaches, she slips on an oil spot, falls and hurts herself. A large sign on the gate reads "Authorized Personnel Only."

The owner of the warehouse probably would not be liable for Martina's injuries. Martina was not on the premises as a shopper or regular business visitor, and the warehouse had no reason to expect that she would enter the loading area. It is not "reasonable" to require the owner to do enough clean-up to protect people who are not expected to be there. Also, anyone who enters a truck loading area should be careful where he or she steps; if Martina slipped on oil there, she probably was not careful. And the sign warned her not to enter.

Even though Martina's claim for damages would not be very strong, she might still be able to collect something for her injuries from the warehouse owner's liability insurance company. Although she was not invited into the loading area, the gate was open and it is not totally unexpected that someone should step in there to do something normal like ask directions. The warehouse owner might be considered at least partly at fault for not having protected against danger to a careless but not too unusual person like Martina.

In almost every slip or trip and fall case, your own behavior is part of the issue of who was careful and who was careless. The rules of comparative negligence (discussed in Section A3, above) help measure your own reasonableness in going where you did in the way you did just before the accident occurred. There are some questions you should ask yourself about your own conduct, since an insurance adjuster is probably going to ask them after you file your claim.

Poor Lighting May Make a Bad Scene Worse

In slip or trip and fall accidents, poor lighting is often a contributing cause you should mention in your claim along with the condition of the floor, stair or ground on which you fell. Obviously, if the light is poor, it was more difficult for you to see and avoid the dangerous spot. This is particularly true on stairs, where dim lighting, or alternating bright and dark areas, make it difficult to judge the edge of the step.

If there were lights but the bulbs were burned out, that indicates the owner was not properly maintaining the premises by regularly checking and replacing bulbs. Ask the insurance adjuster for copies of the property owner's maintenance records for the property. Those records might show how often the lighting is checked. And if there is no record of maintenance, you can argue that the lack of records indicates that the owner is not being careful enough in managing property safety. (See Chapter 6, Section A.)

- Did you have a legitimate reason—a reason the owner should have anticipated—for being where the slippery floor or ground was? If the answer is no, you may have a much weaker claim for the property owner's liability.
- Should a careful person have noticed the slippery or dangerous spot and avoided it, or walked carefully enough not to slip or trip? This is not usually a question which can be answered simply, but if it can be—for example, slipperiness which should be obvious, such as around a swimming pool—your claim may be significantly reduced by your own comparative negligence.
- Were there any warnings that the spot might be dangerous? If so, and the signs were easily visible, the liability of the property owner is probably lessened by your comparative negligence in not heeding the warning.
- Were you doing anything which distracted you from paying attention to where you were going, or were you running, jumping or fooling around in a way that made falling more likely? If so, the owner's liability is probably reduced by your comparative carelessness.

Remember that you do not have to "prove" that you were careful. But think about what you were doing, and pay careful attention to how you will describe it so that it is clear to the insurance adjuster that you were not being careless.

3. Special Concerns About Stairs

Stairs present a number of special dangers, some obvious, some hidden, which cause thousands of people to trip or slip and fall every year. With the more obvious defects—a torn or loose carpet, a step or handrail which breaks—the liability of the property owner is usually clear. With things which have been spilled or dropped or left on stairs, the responsibility of the owner is the same as described above in any slip or trip accident.

But in addition to normal considerations of things spilled or left on stairs, there may have been additional dangers with stairs which made your fall more likely. Some defects in stairs may remain hidden even after your accident. As for these, you may have to make an effort to figure out what happened and how the stairs should have been constructed or maintained differently.

a. Slippery surfaces

A common hidden stair danger is worn-down carpet or wood which makes the "run" part of a stair—the part your foot lands on—dangerous, both going up and coming down. Even a slightly worn stair or carpet, particularly on the edge of a step, can be perilous because a person is not likely to notice slight wear and may be even more likely to slip than on obviously worn stairs.

Some stairs may have a tile or highly polished wood surface which is more slippery than stone, painted wood or carpeted stairs. If so, the owner may have sacrificed safety for beauty, and may now be liable because of that choice.

b. Wet or icy outdoor stairs

Many people slip and fall when rain, snow or ice collects on outdoor stairs. The first response of an insurance adjuster is often to say that the property owner is not responsible for the weather, and that everyone must be extra careful when it has been cold, raining or snowing. While this is partly true, it does not end the question of the owner's negligence.

Outdoor stairs must be built and maintained so that water or ice does not unnecessarily build up on the stairs. If there was an extra buildup of rain, snow or ice on which you slipped, the step was dangerous and the owner should be liable. Further, an outdoor step must have a surface which does not become extra slippery when wet or icy. If an outdoor step does not have an anti-slip surface, the owner has not taken reasonable safety precautions and may be liable if you slip and fall.

c. Building code violations

Almost every city or county has a building code which must be followed by builders and owners when constructing any building, including the stairs. Your city or county building department, and perhaps your local library, will have a copy of the local building code. Check the stair requirements of the code to see if the stairs on which you fell fail to meet any specifications. If your fall occurred on, or was made worse by, the part of the stairs which fails to meet the code, the code becomes very strong support for your argument that the stairs were dangerous.

A building code stair violation might be measured in no more than quarter inches. But even a very small violation can make a set of stairs dangerous.

You need not use technical or legal language in citing a building code violation as support in an injury claim. The code simply provides you with an official declaration of what the city or county believes is the minimum of safety for a set of stairs. If the stairs you fell on did not meet the standard set by the building code, you have a very strong argument that the stairs were not reasonably safe, regardless of how, or even whether, the building code actually applies. (See Chapter 6, Section A1d.)

Handrails Most building codes require one or more handrails on stairs of a certain width or a certain height; some building codes also have different requirements for commercial premises, multiple-unit apartments and private homes.

Building codes also require that handrails be installed properly—that is, firmly attached—and at a certain height. Reaching for a handrail which is at the wrong height can actually cause you to fall when nothing else is wrong with the stairs.

Improper stair height or depth The vertical and horizontal part of each step are called the "riser" and the "run." Building codes prescribe a maximum and minimum riser height for each step, and a maximum and minimum depth for the part on which you put your foot, the run.

If you have slipped or taken a sudden and unexplained fall on a stair, measure the stair's risers and runs and compare the measurements with the minimums and maximums in the building code. If either the riser or the run violates the code, the stairs were defective.

The question then becomes whether the defect caused your fall. But once you have established that the stairs were defective in a basic way—the wrong height or depth—you have gone a long way toward showing that the stairs were dangerous. Unless the building owner's insurance company can show clearly that you fell because of your own carelessness, the improper stair alone will normally be enough to gain a settlement for you.

Uneven stair height or depth   Building codes not only set maximum and minimum stair heights and widths, they also set a maximum variance from one step to another—that is, the differences permitted in the heights and depths of any one step from another.

The variance standard is important because when we go up or down stairs, our brains remember how far the last steps were and automatically tell our legs to move the same distance the next time. If the leg moves the same distance but the step isn't in the same place—even slightly—we may lose balance and fall. So, even if each riser and run is within the code limits, variance from one step to another may violate another section of the code and create a dangerous set of stairs.

4. Accidents Involving Children

The law assumes that children do not have the same well-formed judgement as adults do, and has fashioned special rules for compensation and liability in accidents involving children.

a.   Injuries to children

Although the procedures for collecting compensation for a minor—in most states, a person under age 18—vary somewhat from state to state, in general a child has a right to compensation for pain and suffering, permanent injury or disability in the same manner and for the same amounts as an adult. (See Chapter 5.) Also, a parent has a separate right to be compensated for medical bills paid on behalf of a child.

A child obviously cannot negotiate a claim for itself, so a parent is permitted to negotiate on behalf of the child. In some states, the parent must get the approval of a judge before the child's claim can be finally settled. This process is usually short and straightforward and involves nothing more than filling out a simple form and filing it with the court for approval. An insurance company with which you reach a settlement can help by providing you with the proper form and giving you instructions on where to file it. It is in its interest as well as yours to see that the settlement is properly approved so that a lawyer for the child doesn't go to court months or years later and claim more money for the child. The form will also be available from the court clerk's office.

b.   Accidents caused by children

Legal liability for accidents caused by minors is based on the same notion of care and carelessness as accidents caused by adults. But the same standards of care that are expected of an adult cannot be applied to minors: carefulness implies understanding risks, and minors—particularly young children—do not understand risks the way adults do.

The law applies different standards to different age groups when deciding if a minor is liable for injuries he or she caused. Very young children (seven years old or under) are generally not held liable for accidental injuries they cause; they are too young to understand that they have been careless. This does not mean, however, that parents or legal guardians might not be liable for their negligence in failing to control a child. (See below.)

Once a child is old enough to know right from wrong, the child can be held responsible for *intentional* injuries he or she causes. Thus, if a child intentionally injures another child, for example, or intentionally throws a rock at a car which causes an accident, the child who commits the intentional act, and its parents, may be held liable.

Older children are generally held liable for negligent conduct if they did not behave as carefully as other children of the same age would understand is reasonably careful. And once children become middle teenagers, they are held to pretty much the same standard as adults. When driving a car, a minor is held to exactly the same standards as adults.

Children don't normally have much money of their own, but if a minor can be held legally responsible, there are several ways for a person injured by the minor to collect compensation. First, the actions of minors are very often covered by insurance. If a minor is driving a car, either his or her own automobile insurance or the insurance of the car owner (parent or employer), will cover the accident.

If the accident does not involve a vehicle, a homeowner's or renter's insurance policy may cover the conduct of a minor who lives in the home, so the injured person may be able to deal directly with the parent's insurance company. (See Chapter 4, Section B3.)

If you are seriously injured in an accident caused by a minor, but there is no insurance covering the minor's conduct, it may be worth pursuing a lawsuit against the minor. If you obtain a legal judgment from a court stating how much the minor owes, the minor will have to pay it when he or she comes of age—21 years old in most states—and begins to earn money. Because this process can be long and cumbersome and is usually worth pursuing only in cases of serious injury, however, it probably requires the assistance of an attorney. (See Chapter 9, Section B.)

5. Injuries Caused by Animals

Pets, and most commonly dogs, cause injuries in a variety of ways: biting; clawing; jumping and knocking people down; running and barking at people and making them lose their balance; running into the street and causing vehicle accidents. A few states have laws making dog owners liable for any injuries their dogs cause away from the dog owner's property, regardless of the circumstances in which they occurred. But in most states, a dog owner is only liable for injuries caused by the dog if the owner knew or should have known that the dog was likely to cause the type of injury which occurred.

A dog owner is usually covered by his or her homeowner's or renter's insurance for injuries caused by the dog. And a business owner is covered by his or her business liability insurance for any injury caused by an animal kept on the premises by the owner or any employee.

What you and an insurance company will be discussing, in a claim for injuries caused by a dog, is whether a dog owner knew or should have known of a danger presented by the dog. The answer usually lies with the dog's past behavior. If the injury is a bite, and you can find any evidence that without provocation the dog had bitten, snapped or lunged at anyone before, then you have gone a long way toward establishing a good claim. If the dog is of a "fighting breed," you may be able to recover compensation even though you cannot prove any prior incidents of actual biting or snapping at humans.

If your injury was caused by a dog jumping up and knocking you over, evidence that the dog frequently jumps up is enough, whether or not anyone has been knocked down before. If the dog is large, that too should make the owner aware of the danger, especially to small or unsteady people. And if an accident was caused by an animal running into the street, the fact that it has run out into the street before but the owner still lets the animal loose is good evidence of liability by the owner.[1]

6. General Rules for Other Accidents

There is no limit to the kinds of accidents—some pretty strange and many beyond one's capacity to invent—which cause people injuries. The categories of human behavior which most frequently lead to injury-producing accidents—such as driving, going

---

[1]For more information on the laws and liabilities that affect dog owners, see *Dog Law* by Mary Randolph (Nolo Press).

up and down stairs—have been discussed above, and it is impossible to list all the other possibilities here.

Regardless of the particular facts of an accident, in deciding who is legally responsible, the law looks basically at one common sense question: Did the person involved in the accident act with reasonable care, or was he or she careless in a way that contributed to the happening of the accident?

In some situations, the question of whether someone is legally liable for injuries may turn on whether there is a "duty of care" to protect against injuries for someone who is not expected to be in the place where the accident happens.

Example   *Sameer wanted to ask a question of the produce manager at his local supermarket. He knocked on the door of the produce back room, but no one answered. Although the door was marked "Employees Only," Sameer went in. While he was looking around for someone, he leaned against a stack of crates. The crates collapsed onto Sameer, injuring him.*

Sameer would not have a good liability claim because the store had no duty to protect customers who ignore Employees Only signs and wander around where they are not supposed to be.

In the basic negligence rule that everyone must take "reasonable care" in what they do to avoid injury to others, reasonable care can vary with time and place, and with the relationship between people, so that the same conduct might be considered negligent in one instance but not in another.

Example   *Players are on a softball field. A foul ball accidentally strikes someone who was watching at the edge of the field. Since the players were acting reasonably in playing on a field, and since hitting a foul ball is a normal part of the game, they were probably not negligent. If anyone was careless it may be the person who sat too close to the field where a ball was flying around.*

Example   *One of the players in a softball game gets angry and throws his bat, accidentally hitting someone who was sitting at the edge of the field watching. Since*

throwing a bat in anger is not a "reasonable" part of softball, and since the person watching had a right to be there, throwing the bat is a negligent act and the bat-thrower would be liable for the injuries caused.

Example   *People are playing softball in a parking lot and accidentally hit the ball onto the sidewalk where it strikes someone walking by. The softball player who hit the ball would be considered negligent and held responsible. When the law balances the carefulness of people lawfully using the sidewalk against the carefulness of someone hitting a ball in an area where other people are walking, the person hitting the ball is obviously more careless than the person walking by.*

Regardless of how your accident happened, obtaining fair compensation for your injuries almost certainly involves no more than an application—with simple language in a common sense way—of the few basic principles discussed throughout this chapter:

- If you show that you were careful and the other person was careless, the careless, or negligent, person must pay for your damages.
- If a negligent person causes an accident while working for someone else, the employer is also legally responsible.
- If an accident is caused on dangerous property or by a defective product, the owner of the property or maker or seller of the product is liable regardless of whether he or she actually created the danger or defect.
- If you were also careless, your right to be compensated is reduced by the extent your carelessness was responsible for the accident—or your comparative negligence.

You do not need to "prove" anything, only to make a reasonable argument that the other person was negligent, even if there is a plausible argument that the other person was careful. If you apply these basic rules to your accident, you will be able to negotiate a fair settlement of your claim regardless of the specific facts or peculiar situations in your accident.

7. Dangerous or Defective Products

A lot of people have heard tell of exploding soda bottles, and while most product defects do not make their appearance quite so dramatically, defective or dangerous consumer products are the cause of many thousands of injuries every year. "Product liability"— the legal rules concerning who is responsible for defective or dangerous products—is slightly different from ordinary injury liability law, and this set of rules sometimes makes it easier for an injured person to recover damages.

Ordinarily, to hold someone liable for your injuries, you must show that they were careless—that is, negligent—and that their carelessness led to the accident. With products sold to the general public, though, it would be extremely difficult and prohibitively expensive for one individual to have to show how and when a manufacturer was careless in making a particular product. Neither can the consumer be expected to prove whether the seller or renter of the product had a proper system for checking for manufacturer's defects, or whether the seller was the cause of the defect after receiving the product from the maker. Nor, finally, can a consumer be expected to check each product before using it to see if it is defective or dangerous, except for obviously dangerous products—a chain saw, for example, or a drain cleaner with a warning on it.

a. Strict liability defined

The law has developed a set of special rules known as strict liability that allows a person injured by a defective or unexpectedly dangerous product to win compensation from the maker or seller of the product —whether or not the manufacturer or seller was actually negligent.

States With A Slightly Different Rule

To win a claim for damages in **Delaware**, **Massachusetts**, **Michigan**, **North Carolina** or **Virginia**, you are theoretically required to show that the manufacturer or seller was negligent in making or selling a defective or dangerous product.

However, these states have an additional rule which has the same practical effect as strict liability and makes the injury claim process move in virtually the same way.

This rule is called by the Latin name *res ipsa loquitur*, which means "the thing speaks for itself." This rule holds that if a product is sold or rented and has a dangerous defect, the defect speaks for itself that someone in the manufacturing, selling or renting process *must* have been negligent—or else the defect would not be there.

In dealing with an insurance company for a manufacturer or seller in one of these states, just as in a strict liability state, the existence of an obvious defect is enough by itself to entitle you to receive compensation, without having to prove specifically how and where the manufacturer, seller or renter was negligent. Of course, as with strict liability, in these states, you must still show that the defect caused the accident.

Here's how strict liability works. If you have been injured by a consumer product, you are entitled to compensation from the manufacturer or from the business which sold or rented the product, or the business which rented it out, whether or not they sold or rented it directly to you. Strict liability operates against a non-manufacturer who sold or rented a product only if it is in the business of regularly selling or renting those particular kinds of products. In other words, if you bought something at a flea market stall, garage sale or thrift store which sellws all kinds of things but not any one type of item on a regular basis, strict liability might not apply.

b.   Filing a claim against the seller

It is not always easy to tell who manufactured a certain product—and some products have different parts made by different companies. But since both the product manufacturer and the store where the product was sold or rented can be held responsible, you can file an initial notice of claim against the store where the item was purchased or rented. (See Chapter 3, Section B.) Then the store will contact the manufacturer and the two of them and their insurance companies can figure out which one will settle your claim.

c.   Filing a claim against the manufacturer

If you know who manufactured the product but are not certain where it was purchased, file a claim directly against the manufacturer. If the product was purchased at a flea market or from a private party, you cannot file a strict liability claim against the person who sold it or against the flea market proprietors—unless the seller is a business which also sells its regular products at flea markets—so in that case, too, file a claim directly against the manufacturer.

Watch the Time

Most states have laws limiting how long after a product has been sold to the public the manufacturer or seller can be held liable under strict liability rules. The limits are usually from 6 to 12 years after the product has been initially sold by the manufacturer. So, in a strict liability claim, you might need to determine how old the product is that injured you.

d.   Rules of strict liability

Regardless of what steps a manufacturer or seller says it takes in making and handling a consumer product, you can make a strict liability claim—without showing any carelessness on the part of the manufacturer or seller—if all three of the following conditions exist.

1. The product had an "unreasonably dangerous" defect which injured you as a user or consumer of the product. The dangerous defect can come into existence either:
   * in the design of the product, making it dangerous even if it is perfectly manufactured, known as a "design defect,"
   * during manufacture of the product, causing a dangerous flaw in the specific unit you wind up using, or
   * during handling or shipment after the product has been manufactured.

Example *Aretha bought a toaster oven, and a month after she bought it she was moving it to a different spot in the kitchen when a handle snapped off and the toaster oven fell. Not only did the oven break but so did Aretha's foot.*

Handles are supposed to help you to hold things, so a handle which breaks after only a month is obviously defective. And the defect was "unreasonably dangerous" because a handle snapping off entirely is likely to cause injury with a heavy, sharp-edged metal object like a toaster oven.

Example *Mack buys a refrigerator. While unloading it from his pick-up truck, he grabs the fridge under one side and his wrist is badly cut by a sharp piece of metal along the bottom edge. It turns out the piece of metal was not a mistake but was a designed part of the fridge's exhaust system.*

In his claim for damages, Mack demands to know: why the piece of metal had to be close to the edge where someone was likely to be cut if they grabbed the edge; why the piece was not rounded off or otherwise protected; and why there was no warning of the danger given to the consumer. If the manufacturer has no convincing answers for all these questions, it would be held liable for Mack's injuries.

2. The defect caused an injury while the product was being used in a way it was intended to be used.

Example *Leticia is working on her house and takes a break to have a cold drink. She can't find the bottle opener, so she uses the claw end of a hammer to pry off a bottle top. The bottle breaks and badly gashes her hand.*

Because the hammer was not designed to open bottles and the bottle was not designed to be opened by a hammer, Leticia has no claim against the manufacturer of either one.

Example *Leticia couldn't find the bottle opener because Randy has taken it into another room to pry apart two pieces of metal. The opener has a defective crack in it which breaks and injures Randy's arm.*

Even though the bottle opener had a defect, Randy cannot claim that the defect was unreasonably dangerous since it did not break during a bottle opener's "normal" use. If it had broken during normal use it probably would not have injured him.

If You Were Not the Purchaser

If you were given a gift, or bought something second-hand, your rights under strict liability laws are the same as if you had bought it yourself. Similarly, if you are injured while using a product that belongs to someone else, or by a product while someone else is using it, you have the same rights as the owner to be compensated by the manufacturer or seller—as long as you or the other person were using the product in a normal way.

---

3. The product had not been substantially changed from the condition in which it was originally sold. "Substantially" means in a way that affects how the product performs.

Example *Alphonso bought one of those overpriced food processors with more attachments than a centipede. Alphonso tried to use the processor to mix pizza dough. The processor jammed and a rubber washer burned out. At the hardware store Alphonso got another washer but it didn't quite fit.*

When Alphonso tried to use the processor again, he noticed that the new washer made it difficult to get the blades onto the rotating stem. He finally managed to get a blade on, but when he turned on the processor, the blade flew off and cut his hand.

Alphonso does not have a very good strict liability claim against the manufacturer because the food processor had been substantially changed from the condition in which it was sold—the wrong washer had been put on, making the blade fit incorrectly on the stem.

e.   Awareness of the defect

Manufacturer and sellers have a defense to claims of strict liability which may be particularly important if you have owned the product for a while. That is, you may not be able to claim strict liability if you knew about the defect but continued to use the product. If it appears—either from the condition of the product (which the manufacturer's or seller's insurance company will have a right to examine) or from your description of your use of the product—that you were aware of the defect before the accident but used the product anyway, you may have given up your right to claim injury damages.

Example   *Manjusha bought an electric coffee grinder and when she got it home, she noticed that the cord at the back was loose. Instead of taking it back to the store, she reconnected it and put some electrical tape over the connection. In a couple of weeks, she turned on the grinder and got a bad electrical shock.*

Even though the manufacturer or seller caused the defect in the product, Manjusha's claim for damages would be weaker, because she knew the connection was defective but used the grinder anyway.

Checking With Consumer Reports

For many years, one of the consumer's best friends has been the national magazine *Consumer Reports*, which regularly tests and reports on the safety and performance of many consumer products. If you have been injured by a defective or dangerous product and want to see whether others have also found the product dangerous, you can check the magazine's cumulative index. Under the type of product involved, you will be referred to all the magazine's articles in which that product has been reported on.

If you find a report which criticizes your specific brand of product as dangerous or often defective—particularly if the magazine reports accidents or injuries similar to yours—you have found strong support for your argument that the product was defective and "unreasonably dangerous." If you find such a report, make a copy of it and, when you make your written demand for settlement of your case (see Chapter 6, Section B) you may want to quote the article directly to the insurance company for the manufacturer or seller. The manufacturer's insurer will undoubtedly already know about the article, but when it knows you also know, your negotiating hand may be a bit stronger.

Consumer Reports can be found in any local library.

CHAPTER

3

Initial Steps in Settling Your Claim

how well you settle your accident claim often depends on how well you start it. The sooner you get organized and begin documenting the facts of the accident, the better your chances of clearly showing an insurance company your side of the incident and receiving all the compensation to which you are entitled.

A. The First 72 Hours: Protecting Your Rights

Immediately after being injured in an accident, you are probably angry, in pain and maybe a little depressed. That is not the best frame of mind in which to get organized for an insurance claim. But taking some of the following simple steps in the first few days after your accident can help make the entire claim process easier on you—and increase your chances of receiving all the compensation to which you are entitled.

1. Write Everything Down

Jot down things about the accident as soon as possible after it happens, including details of your injuries and their effect on your daily life. These notes can be very useful two or six or ten months later, when you put together all the important facts into a final demand for compensation. Having notes to remind you of all the details of what happened, and what you went through, is far easier and far more accurate than relying on your memory.

Get into the habit of taking notes on anything you think might possibly affect your claim and carry it through the entire claims process. Anytime you remember something you had not thought of before —while you're in the shower, just before you fall asleep, as you're biting into a pastry—write it down and put it with your other notes.

There are several kinds of notes you should keep.

a. Accident notes

As soon as your head is clear enough, jot down everything you can remember about how the accident happened, beginning with what you were doing and where you were going, the people you were with, the time and weather. Include every detail of what you saw and heard and felt—twists, blows and shocks to your body immediately before, during and right after the accident. Also include anything you remember hearing anyone—a person involved in the accident or a witness—say about the accident.

b. Injury notes

In the first days following your accident, make daily notes of all pains and discomfort your injuries cause. You may suffer pain, discomfort, anxiety, loss of sleep or other problems which are not as visible or serious as another injury but for which you should demand additional compensation. If you don't make specific note of them immediately, you may not remember exactly what to include in your demand for settlement weeks or months later. Also, taking notes will make it easier for you later to describe to an insurance company how much and what kind of pain and discomfort you were in.

And writing down your different injuries will help you remember to report them to a doctor or other medical provider when you receive treatment. A relatively small bump on the head or snap of the neck, for example, may not seem worth mentioning, but it might help both the doctor and the insurance company understand why a bad back pain developed two or three days, or several weeks, after the accident. Also, by telling the doctor or other medical provider about all of your injuries, those injuries become part of your medical records that will provide evidence later that such injuries were caused by the accident. (See Chapter 6, Section A2a.)

Reporting To the DMV

Many states have laws requiring that those involved in a vehicle accident causing any physical injury or property damage over a certain amount must report that accident in writing to the state's department of motor vehicles. Check with your insurance agent or your local department of motor vehicles to find out the time limits for filing this report; you often have only a few days. And ask whether you'll need any specific form for the report.

If you must file a report, and the report asks for a statement about how the accident occurred, give a very brief statement only—and admit no responsibility for the accident. Similarly, if the official form asks what your injuries are, list every injury and not merely the most serious or obvious. An insurance company could later have access to the report, and if you have admitted some fault in it, or failed to mention an injury, you might have to explain it later.

---

c. Notes of economic or other losses

You may be entitled to compensation for economic loss and for family, social, educational or other losses, as well as for pain and suffering. (See Chapter 5.) But you will need good documentation. Begin making notes immediately after the accident about anything you have lost because of the accident and your injuries: work hours, job opportunities, meetings, classes, events, family or social gatherings, vacation or anything else which would have benefited you or which you would have enjoyed but were unable to do because of the accident.

d. Notes of conversations

Make written notes of the date, time, people involved and contents of every conversation you have about your accident or your claim. In-person or telephone conversations worth noting may include those with any witness, adjuster or other insurance representative, or with medical personnel.

e. Confirming letters

In the course of your claim, you may be told or promised something or given some information that you want to make sure is not later denied or changed. Immediately after the conversation, send a letter confirming what the person told you. The letter does not have to be elaborate, just a brief restatement of what was said. Make a copy for your own files before you send it.

SAMPLE CONFIRMING LETTER

Paula Thompson
23 Broadway
Anytown, Anystate 00000

January 2, 199X

Mr. Clarence Smolten
Claims Adjuster
Do Right Insurance Company
Thiscity, Thisstate 00000

Re: Claimant: Paula Thompson
      Insured: Rocky Polletto
      Claim No. 3244949K100
      Date of Loss: September 9, 199X

Dear Mr. Smolten:

This letter is to confirm our telephone discussion of January 1, 199X in which you informed me that you would be making me an offer of settlement on behalf of the Do Right Insurance Company no later than January 15, 199X.

Thank you for your attention to this matter.

Sincerely yours,

Paula Thompson

Organization Is the Key

As you move along in the claims process, you will probably gather more and more pieces of paper—notes, letters, medical records, photos. Keeping them organized can be important not only so you can find things easily, but also so you can keep track of what records and documents you have and what you still need to get.

Keep categories of documents together. For example, all your notes, witness statements and photographs belong in one place. All correspondence with insurance companies should be clipped together in chronological order. And all documents concerning medical treatment, diagnosis and billing and financial losses belong together.

There are no special rules or tricks to organizing the file. Do it however you like, but separate things by category. Then keep all papers in each category in a separate file, folder or large envelope, marked on the outside so you can easily tell one from another, and keep all of them in the same, safe place.

Use the Accident Claim Worksheet at the back of the book to help get organized and keep track of the information you accumulate.

2. Preserve Evidence of Fault and Damages

The first few days immediately following an accident are often the most important for finding and preserving evidence of what happened—and documenting your injuries.

a. Physical evidence

Who was at fault for an accident is sometimes shown by a piece of "physical" evidence—something you can see or touch, as opposed to a description of what happened. Examples include a worn or broken stair which caused a fall; the dent in a car showing where it was hit; an overhanging branch that blocked visibility on a bike path. Also, physical evidence can help prove the extent of an injury: damage to the car can demonstrate how hard a collision was; and torn or bloodied clothing can show your physical injuries very dramatically.

Moreover, physical evidence that is not preserved or photographed in the first few days following an accident can get lost, modified by time or weather, destroyed or repaired. So, any physical evidence you have—your damaged car or bike, your damaged clothing, a defective product—should be preserved exactly as it was at the accident. You can later show it to an insurance company as proof of what happened.

b. Photographs

If you do not have a piece of physical evidence, or for any reason cannot preserve it, the next best option is to photograph it. Regular photos are better than Polaroids. Not only do they usually show greater detail and more accurate light conditions, but you will be able to give an insurance company prints while holding onto the negatives. Take a number of photos from different angles so that you can later pick out the ones that show most clearly whatever it is you want to highlight to the insurance company.

Take the photos as soon as possible so that they will accurately represent the condition of the evidence immediately after the accident. To establish the date the photos were taken, ask a friend to both watch you take the pictures and to write a short note stating that he or she observed you taking the pictures on that date. Also, get the film developed immediately and make sure the photo shop indicates the date on the back of the prints, or at least on your receipt.

A Picture Is Worth . . . A Lot

A camera can be one of your best tools in helping you get a fair settlement of your accident claim—for a number of reasons.

Photos preserve scenes, evidence and injuries which change over time.

Photos often show things better than you can describe them.

Photos sometimes reveal details you do not notice at first with the naked eye.

Photos are dramatic. They highlight whatever they are focused on, without the distractions of surrounding sights and sounds.

Photos are difficult to contradict. An insurance company may say you are wrong when you describe how an accident happened or how badly you were injured, but it is much more difficult for it to deny what is in a photograph.

Photos help you focus your claim. You select which photos to show to an insurance company.

Photos impress insurance companies. They show that you have been organized and thoughtful in preparing your claim.

c. Returning to the scene

If an accident occurred somewhere other than in your home, return to the scene as soon as possible to locate any evidence and photograph any conditions you believe may have caused or contributed to the accident. You may be amazed to find something you were not aware of when the accident occurred but which may help explain what happened: a worn or torn spot on which you fell, a traffic light that isn't working. And while looking around, you may also find someone who saw what happened, or who knows of other accidents which have happened in the same spot. (See Section d, below.)

Take photographs of the accident scene from a number of different angles—particularly your view of things right before the accident—to keep a good picture of it in your mind and to give to the insurance company later on to indicate how well prepared you are to get the settlement you deserve. Photograph the scene at the same time of day as your accident occurred, and for vehicle accidents, the same day of the week, to show the appropriate amount of traffic.

d. Witnesses

A witness to an accident can be immensely valuable to you in making your case to an insurance company. Witnesses may be able to describe things in an accident that confirm what you believe happened, backing up your story. And they may provide you with information you were not aware of but which shows how the other person was at fault. Even a witness who did not actually see the accident may have seen you soon after you were injured and can confirm that you were in pain or discomfort. Or, a witness may have heard a statement made by another person involved in the accident indicating that someone other than you was at fault.

However, time is of the essence. If witnesses are not contacted and their information confirmed fairly soon after the accident, what they have to say may be lost. People's memories fade quickly, and soon their recollections may become so fuzzy that they are no longer useful. Also, a witness might no longer be around if you wait too long; people move frequently.

Dealing with witness-strangers People whom you don't know but who saw your accident may be helpful to your claim. They may have seen the accident or can tell you something else useful, such as the fact that a dangerous condition has caused previous accidents on the same spot.

Look for such witnesses by returning to the scene and talking with people who live or work within sight of the accident spot. With traffic accidents, another place to look for witnesses is in the police report. If the police responded to the scene of your accident, they will probably have made a police report, also called an accident report or collision report. Listed in that report may be the names, addresses and phone numbers of witnesses. (See Chapter 6, Section A1.)

If you find people who witnessed your accident, and what they saw indicates that someone else was at fault, act promptly.

- Write down witnesses' names, addresses, home and work phone numbers or as much of that information as they are willing to give. If they will give an address but not a phone, or a work phone but not home, don't push. You need them to be on your side, so don't scare them away or irritate them.

- Talk with witnesses about what they saw and ask exactly where they were when they saw it.

- If witnesses seem cooperative, ask if it would be all right if you type up what they told you and send it to them to check for accuracy. Explain that you may need a written statement to back up your facts when you make your claim to the insurance company. If the witnesses consent, write down what they told you as soon as possible —on the spot, if they are willing to be that patient. Then send a typed copy to them, politely asking them to review it, sign it and send it back to you in a return envelope you provide.

- If witnesses seem uncomfortable about getting involved even though they support your side of what happened, jot down quickly what they have told you and ask them on the spot to read it to make sure it's accurate. Ask them to sign the description to show that it's accurate. Be sure to get an address or telephone number so that you can later prove to an insurance company that this statement was from a real person. Once you have the handwritten statement, you can also contact the witness to get him or her to sign a typed version if the handwritten statement is difficult to read.

Witnesses you know Many witnesses to accidents are people we know. If a friend or relative or acquaintance witnessed your accident, or your pain and suffering following the accident, your job is essentially the same as with a stranger, only easier. You don't have to go looking for the witnesses, and you usually don't have to worry that they will quickly disappear. But go over the facts of the accident with them while their memory is fresh—and make notes of what they tell you so that, if necessary, you can later type up a statement and have them sign it. (See Chapter 6, Section A1 and Chapter 7, Section A.)

Sometimes an insurance adjuster will independently track down witnesses—from information in a police accident report or otherwise—and will get in touch with them. Because it may be important for you to contact the witnesses first, to learn what they saw or heard and to prevent the insurance adjuster from putting false or distorted recollections into their heads, speak with your witnesses as soon as possible and discuss the possibility that an insurance adjuster might call. Witnesses do not have to discuss the accident with the insurance company if they do not want to. And they certainly have a right to limit their involvement to the statement—written or not—that they have already given you. While you can tell witnesses that they have the right not to talk to the insurance company, do not tell them not to talk. That would be interfering with the other side's right to obtain information and could jeopardize your claim. The decision about whether or not to talk to the insurance company should be left up to each witness so that he or she can remain as independent, and therefore as believable, as possible.

e.   Documenting your injuries

The best ways to preserve evidence of your injuries are by promptly reporting all of them to a doctor or other medical provider, and by photographing any visible marks, cuts, bruises or swelling, including any casts, splints, bandages or other devices. Without an early medical record of all your injuries, and photos if possible, it will be more difficult later to convince an insurance company that you were injured in the ways and to the degree you claim you were. Visible injuries heal and will not look as serious later, and failing to seek immediate treatment can lead an insurance company to believe that your injuries were not so serious, or even that you invented or exaggerated them after the accident.

Get immediate medical attention   Where to go for treatment is first and foremost a medical decision. But the kind of treatment you get, and the type of medical provider from whom you receive it, can affect how much your claim is worth. (See Chapter 5, Section B2.)

Telling you to get prompt medical care, and to let the medical people know about *all* your injuries, pains and discomforts, sounds obvious. But too often, people try to do without medical care, or only report to a doctor what seems to be their worst injury. They have no medical records of their injuries, or have records only of one injury but not of something that first seemed to be minor but which turns out to be very painful and persistent.

Of course, the high cost of medical care often makes people reluctant to begin medical treatment unless absolutely necessary. But in the case of an accident where someone else was at fault, that person or business, through its insurance, will be obligated to repay you for all reasonable medical expenses as well as the pain and suffering caused by your injuries.

(See Chapter 5, Sections B and C.) And getting medical treatment is the best way to support your claim that you have gone through pain and suffering. So, even if you have to pay for medical treatment now, it will benefit you both because you receive prompt attention for your injuries and also because it demonstrates what those injuries really are.

B. Getting a Claim Started

Starting the claim process is simple. You don't have to know who was at fault for the accident; you only have to think about who *might* have been at fault. And in the beginning, you don't have to give the people involved, or their insurance companies, any detailed information about the accident or your injuries. All you have to do is notify them that there was an accident at a certain time and place, that you were injured and that you *intend* to file a claim. Even filing a formal claim against the government is simple, as long as you do so within the legal time limit. (See Section C2, below.)

The important thing about getting a claim started is simply not to wait. Except for claims against government entities, you need not give notice that you intend to file a claim within any specific number of days following an accident. However, it is best to start early, preferably within the first few days, and certainly within the first couple of weeks, after the accident. The sooner you get started, the sooner you may be able to settle your claim. And if you wait too long to notify those responsible or their insurance companies, you may have to explain why you waited.

Rather than get into that hassle, notify those responsible as soon as possible that you intend to file a claim for your injuries. After you give this initial notice, you can move at your own pace in processing and negotiating your claim with the insurance company or government agency that winds up taking responsibility.

Filing a notice of an injury accident with people or agencies does not obligate you to file a claim against them later. But if you do file a claim later, they will not be able to say that the claim has unfairly surprised them.

1. Determine Who Might Be Responsible

Before you can notify those responsible for an accident, or their insurance companies, of your intention to file a claim, you have to decide whom to notify. At this point you don't have to try to decide who is actually responsible; notify all those who *might* be responsible.

In general, those who are most likely to be responsible depend on the type of accident in which you were involved.

a. If you're in a vehicle accident

- the drivers of all vehicles involved—including the vehicle in which you were riding if you were a passenger—whether or not they actually hit you or your car
- the owners of all vehicles if the owners are different from the drivers
- the employer of a driver of any vehicle if the employee might have been on company business at the time of the accident; if it is a government employer, see Section C, below
- the parent of a minor who was driving, or who owned a vehicle involved in the accident, or of a minor who otherwise contributed to the accident
- anyone not in a vehicle who contributed to the accident, such as someone jaywalking or a property owner who allowed something to obstruct or interfere with the roadway
- your own vehicle's insurance company, if you need to make a claim under your own uninsured motorist, medical payments, collision or no-fault coverage

b. If you slip or trip and fall, or are struck by an object

- the person who caused you to fall or caused an object to strike you
- the owner of the property on which you fell or from which the object came
- the renter of the property on which you fell or from which the object came
- the owner of the business at which you fell or from which the object came
- the parent of a minor who caused you to fall or who caused you to be struck with an object
- the employer of a person who, apparently during worktime, caused you to fall or to be struck with an object

c. If you are injured by a dangerous or defective product

- the business where you, or someone else, purchased or rented the product
- the business where you were supplied with the product to use on the business's premises
- the manufacturer of the product

2. Write Notification Letters

Once you have determined those who might be responsible for your accident, your next step is to notify each of them that the accident happened and that you were injured. This may mean you will need to send more than one letter—for example, one letter each to both the business and to the person who owned the property where you fell. If it was a vehicle accident, also notify your own insurance company if you believe you might file a claim under your own medical payments or uninsured motorist coverage. If you have no-fault (Personal Injury Protection) automobile coverage, you *must* file an immediate notice with your own insurance company.

Write a letter of notification even if the others involved have assured you they will notify their insurance companies. Your notification should be a simple typed letter giving only basic information and asking for a written response. It should not discuss fault or responsibility, or the extent of your injuries; you will discuss those things later on. The first letter of notification needs to include only basic information.

- Your name and address. You do not have to include your phone number if you do not wish. Once you begin dealing with an insurance adjuster, though, you will probably want to be able to communicate over the phone as well as by letter. You are free to put whatever restrictions you want on such calls: only at home but not at work, or vice versa; only in the evening but not during the day, or vice versa.

- The date, approximate time of day and general location of the accident. The details of the location, if they become important, can be discussed later. In this letter, you only need to give a description identifying what accident you are talking about, for example: "at the intersection of Main and Howard Streets," or "at your store in the Broadway Shopping Center."

- If your letter is to an individual or business rather than to an insurance company, ask those involved to refer the matter at once to the appropriate insurance carrier—and request that they inform you by return letter what insurance carrier it is. If a non-auto accident occurred away from the other person's home, you may remind him or her to refer the matter to the company issuing a homeowner's policy.

- If your letter is directly to an insurance company, ask that it confirm by return letter whom it represents and whether it is aware of anyone else who might be responsible for the accident.

- If you are writing to your own automobile insurance company after a vehicle accident, include not only information about the accident but also the basic information you have about the other driver and vehicle—name, address, telephone number, license number, insurance policy.

Double Check Before Mailing

Include the date on every letter—and make a copy for your own files before sending it.

3. Sample Notification Letters

Here are examples of letters giving first notification that you have been in an accident.

SAMPLE LETTER TO AN INDIVIDUAL WITH WHOM MARIA JONES HAD AN AUTO ACCIDENT

Maria Jones
123 Pine Street
San Dimas, TX 00000

February 12, 199X

Henry Parks
45 Webster Avenue
Hollowtown, TX 00000

Dear Mr. Parks:

You and I were involved in an automobile accident on February 9, 199X at the intersection of 4th Street and Appian Way in San Dimas, Texas. Please provide me with the name and address of your insurance carrier and forward this letter to it regarding coverage of the accident.

Very truly yours,

Maria Jones

SAMPLE LETTER TO MARIA'S OWN AUTOMOBILE INSURANCE COMPANY IF SHE HAD AN INSURANCE POLICY WITHOUT NO-FAULT COVERAGE

Maria Jones
123 Pine Street
San Dimas, TX 00000

February 12, 199X

Claims Department
Safety Plus Insurance Company
888 Pesky Boulevard
Dallas, TX 00000

Re: Insured, Maria Jones
     Policy No. 9HQ-678-B
     Date of Accident: February 9, 199X

To Whom It Concerns:

I was involved in an automobile accident in which I received personal injuries and damage to my vehicle on February 9, 199X at the intersection of 4th Street and Appian Way in San Dimas, Texas.

The other person involved in the accident was Henry Parks, 45 Webster Avenue, Hollowtown, Texas 12346. He was driving a red 1989 Chevrolet pick-up with Texas license plate number B899 324.

At this time, I intend to proceed against Mr. Parks rather than file a claim under my own medical payments or collision coverages. However, I reserve the right to file a claim under either or both of those coverages.

Very truly yours,

Maria Jones

SAMPLE LETTER TO MARIA'S OWN AUTOMOBILE INSURANCE COMPANY IF SHE CARRIED A NO-FAULT POLICY

Maria Jones
123 Pine Street
San Dimas, TX 00000

February 12, 199X

Claims Department
Safety Plus Insurance Company
888 Pesky Boulevard
Dallas, TX 00000

Re: Insured: Maria Jones
     Policy No. 9HQ-678-B
     Date of Accident: February 9, 199X

To Whom It Concerns:

I was involved in an automobile accident in which I received personal injuries and damage to my vehicle on February 9, 199X at the intersection of 4th Street and Appian Way in San Dimas, Texas. The other person involved in the accident was Henry Parks, 45 Webster Avenue, Hollowtown, Texas 12346. He was driving a red 1989 Chevrolet pick-up truck with Texas license plate number B899 324.

At this time the extent of my injuries is not clear, and I reserve my rights under my policy to proceed under my Personal Injury Protection coverage as well as to proceed against the others responsible for the accident.

Please confirm in writing that you have received this notice. Thank you for your attention to this matter.

Very truly yours,

Maria Jones

**SAMPLE LETTER TO A BUSINESS WHERE
ROBIN SMITH HAD A SLIP AND FALL**

Robin Smith
6922 Main Way
Sintex, NH 00000

February 12, 199X

Snack-n-Chat Restaurant
666 Alamo Circle
Grinel, NH 00000

To Whom It Concerns:

At approximately 8:00 p.m. on February 9, 199X,
I was a customer in your restaurant when I slipped
on an unknown substance just outside the entrance
to the restaurant and fell, injuring myself.

Please refer this matter to your insurance carrier.
Please also inform me by letter at the above address
of the name and address of your insurance carrier.

Thank you for your prompt attention.

Sincerely,

Robin Smith

**SAMPLE LETTER TO AN INSURANCE COMPANY
WHICH INSURES THE PREMISES WHERE
ROBIN SMITH HAD A SLIP AND FALL**

Robin Smith
6922 Main Way
Sintex, NH 00000
(111) 443-4433

February 12, 199X

Claims Department
All Risk Insurance Company
6000 Breakneck Boulevard
Houston, TX 12355

Re: Your Insured: Snack-n-Chat Restaurant
     Claimant: Robin Smith
     Date of Accident: February 9, 199X

To Whom It Concerns:

Please be advised that I received injuries in an
accident on February 9, 1993 on the premises of
your insured the Snack-n-Chat Restaurant. Please
confirm in writing to the above address your liability
coverage of the Snack-n-Chat Restaurant.

Please also advise whether Snack-n-Chat
Restaurant contends that anyone other than the
Snack-n-Chat Restaurant may be in whole or in part
legally responsible for accidents on or near the
premises.

As requested, please respond in writing. If necessary,
I may be reached by telephone at the above number
between the hours of 7:30-8:30 a.m. or 6:30-9:00 p.m.
Monday through Friday.

Thank you for your prompt attention to this matter.

Yours truly,

Robin Smith

**SAMPLE LETTER TO THE PARENTS OF
A CHILD WHO CAUSED WALTER PASHEHA
TO FALL IN AN ACCIDENT**

Walter Pasheha
37 9th Avenue North
South Fork, IN 00000

February 12, 199X

Norbert and Rosetta Stone
3757 East Bowden Lane
South Fork, IN 00000

Dear Mr. and Mrs. Stone:

On February 9, 199X, I was injured in a fall in front of your residence caused by wooden blocks left on the sidewalk by your child or children. Please refer this matter to the insurance carrier of your homeowner's liability insurance policy and have them contact me directly at the above address.

Thank you for your cooperation.

Very truly yours,

Walter Pasheha

---

4. First Contact With Another's Insurance Company

By the time you get home from an accident, your phone may already be ringing—and it may well be an insurance adjuster or other representative of the other person involved on the line. Or perhaps you will hear from someone as soon as your notification letter has been received.

Very often, insurance adjusters will try to get you to say or write an immediate statement about what happened, or about your injuries or lack of injuries, so that they can pin you down before you know what really happened or how badly you are injured. Or they will make a quick offer of a small amount of money, in the hope that you will jump at it instead of developing a full claim for compensation. Do not rush to give detailed information or to take any money.

Follow the guidelines below for what you should and should not be saying and doing during your first contacts after an accident with the other person or his or her insurance adjuster or representative.

a. Phone conversations

Your first conversations after an injury may be difficult. You may be agitated and in pain. But common sense and a few guiding principles will help keep you from saying anything that will adversely affect your claim.

Remain calm and polite Although you may well be angry about the accident and your injuries, taking out your anger on the insurance adjuster does not help you get compensated. Insurance adjusters are used to dealing with angry claimants, but they are human and do not respond kindly to abuse. So, while you may not know exactly how or when an insurance adjuster's good will toward you may pay off—in promptly handling your claim, or in believing you about something it is difficult for you to prove—it is a good idea to avoid losing your temper with or heaping abuse on the agent during your negotiation process.

Identify the person with whom you speak Before you discuss anything, get the name, address and telephone number of the person you are speaking with, the insurance company he or she is with and the person or business the company represents.

Give only limited personal information You need only tell the insurance adjuster your full name, address and telephone number. You can also tell what type of work you do and where you are employed, but at this point you need not explain or discuss any more than that about your work, your schedule or your income. You do not have to give detailed family or other personal information.

Give no details of the accident   Insurance adjusters or other representatives may try to get you to "give a statement" about how the accident happened. Or, they may simply engage you in conversation during which they will try more subtly to get you to tell them about the accident. Politely refuse any discussion of the facts of the accident except the most basic: where, when, the type of accident and the vehicles involved if it was a traffic accident. Say that your investigation of the accident is still continuing and that you will discuss the facts further "at the appropriate time." Later, you will be making a written demand for compensation in which you will describe the accident in detail. (See Chapter 6, Section B.)

If they ask about witnesses and you know of some, respond that there "may be" witnesses and that you will let the insurance company know "at the appropriate time." Do not commit yourself to identifying witnesses or to providing witness statements. Also, if they ask you about witnesses, ask them if they know of any.

If adjusters or representatives ask about potential responsible parties other than you and their insured, give any basic identifying information you may have and a general description of how this other person was involved, but do not discuss the accident in detail. Also, ask whether the adjuster is aware of anyone else who might be responsible for the accident.

Give no details of your injuries   Naturally enough, an insurance adjuster is going to want to know about your injuries. Do not give any detailed description yet, in case you leave something out, or discover an injury later, or your injury turns out to be worse than you originally thought.

Later, when you know the true extent of your injuries and treatment, your written demand for compensation will include a complete medical description of your injuries. (See Chapter 6, Section B.) Until then, give only a very general description of injuries ("I've hurt my knee and back," or "My wrist is broken and I have neck and back pain") and tell the adjuster you do not yet know how severe your

injuries are. Also tell the adjuster that you will be seeking or continuing medical treatment. You do not have to say what doctors or other medical providers you are seeing, and you should not yet give the adjuster their names and addresses.

Take notes   As soon as your conversation is over, write down all the information you received over the phone, as well as whatever information you gave to, or requests you made of, the person with whom you spoke. Get in the habit of this note-taking for all conversations with anyone from the insurance company.

Resist the push to settle immediately   Insurance adjusters sometimes try to offer a settlement during the very first one or two phone calls. Quick settlements like that save the insurance company work, and more importantly, it gets you to settle for a small amount before you know fully what your injuries are and how much your claim is really worth. Don't do it. Agreeing may seem like a simple way to get compensation without having to go through the

---

Never Give Access to Your Records

Never agree to give another person's insurance company access to your medical, employment or any other personal records. Later in the claims process, you will be presenting the adjuster with the appropriate records. And do *not* agree to be examined by a doctor who is affiliated with or recommended by the insurance company. You have a right to see only the doctors or other medical people you want—and the insurance company has no right to have you examined unless your claim actually becomes a formal lawsuit and goes to court.

claims process, and a quick settlement is often tempting, but it will almost certainly cost you money, perhaps quite a bit of money.

Set limits on conversations In your first contact with an insurance adjuster, make it clear that you will not be discussing much on the phone. Not only should you give very limited information in this first phone call, as discussed above, but you should also set clear limits on any further phone contact.

Let the adjuster know that until you have finished investigating the accident, have completed medical treatment and have fully recovered from your injuries, you do not want to discuss any further either how the accident happened, what your injuries are or what a settlement amount should be. Ask that the adjuster communicate with you in writing until you present your written demand for compensation (see Chapter 6, Section B) and actual settlement negotiations begin (see Chapter 7).

In some situations, however, it may not be practical to stop all phone conversations. For example, if you have been in an auto accident, you may need to discuss repairs to your car. If you do need to speak to the adjuster again in person, set whatever limits you want on the place and times—home or work, morning, evening, weekends—for telephone contact.

There are good reasons to limit your phone conversations with insurance adjusters. Some will call frequently in an attempt to get you to settle quickly, and they can become a real nuisance. It's good to nip this in the bud.

More importantly, until you have had a full opportunity to investigate and think about the accident, and to determine the extent of and to recover from your injuries, you will not have accurate information to give. And if you give incomplete or inaccurate information on the phone, the insurance company may try to make you stick to it later on. Some insurance adjusters are good at getting you to say something which could be considered an admission of some fault on your part, or which limits the seriousness of your injuries. It is therefore much better to have no discussions at all until you have made your compensation demand in writing and you

are fully prepared to discuss a settlement. (See Chapter 6, Section B.)

b. Written communications

Do not sign anything Among the first things you might receive in the mail from an insurance company handling an accident claim are various forms an adjuster describes to you as "just routine" or "normal procedure." However, these forms may give the insurance company direct access to your medical, personal or work records—or even be a disguised release from any liability for the accident. No matter what an adjuster says about any forms, do not sign anything sent to you by another person's insurance company.

You are not required to give the insurance company permission to get any records or information about you. Later in the claims process, you will send it certain medical and income loss information, but in your own time and on your own terms. (See Chapter 6, Section B.) If you are pressured to sign any forms, politely refuse and emphasize that you will relay all necessary information at the appropriate time. If you continue to receive pressure you believe is inappropriate, you may need to take other steps to get the adjuster to back off. (See Chapter 7, Section C.)

Often an insurance company's first contact with you will be a simple letter informing you that it represents so-and-so regarding an accident on such-and-such date, and that you should get in touch concerning any claim you may have. But insurance companies also sometimes ask for information from you—about the accident, your injuries, your doctors, your work. Until you are ready to make a formal demand for settlement, you are not obligated to give any more information than the things described above concerning your first notification letter. Insurance companies are supposed to do their own investigation of an accident, and you are not required to do their work for them.

5. First Contact With Your Own Insurance Company

Your relationship with your own insurance company is established by your policy; it operates as a contract between you and your insurer. You may be obligated by the rules of the policy to provide your company with more information than you would to someone else's insurance company.

Some of the common differences are discussed here.

a. Notification through your agent

If you give notice of the accident to your insurance agent rather than to the company's claims office, ask the agent for a letter stating the date you notified him or her and confirming that the information has been passed along to the company's claims department. You should also get some kind of confirming letter from the claims department. If you do not, contact it directly with the information.

b. Release of medical and work records

Virtually all insurance policies state that the company has a right to examine directly the policyholder's medical and work records. Even though it has this right, your insurance company might not bother obtaining and going through your records; that means extra work. Instead, it may wait for you to submit your medical records and income loss information along with your settlement demand. However, very often, your insurer will send you a form entitled Authorization for Release of Medical Records, or something similar. If your own insurance company does send you such a form, you will have to complete the authorization if you want it to process your claim.

c. Right of subrogation

Your own insurance company may also send you a form entitled Right of Subrogation. This form means that if the insurance company pays you, you give the company the right to recover the money, or be subrogated, from whoever else might be liable for the accident—for example, an uninsured driver who has money the insurance company wants to go after. This right of subrogation does not affect your right to collect compensation from your own company, but if you file a claim under your own policy, you must agree to give subrogation to your insurer.

d. Cooperation

Most policies say that to collect on a claim under your own policy, you must cooperate with the insurance company in its investigation of the accident. That means that, if asked, you must give it the names of witnesses, the medical providers you are seeing and a statement about how the accident happened.

However, you only need to cooperate in a reasonable way. For example, the insurance company is entitled to a statement about how the accident happened, but you don't have to write an essay or undergo an interrogation. You don't have to repeat information you have already given. And you don't have to go places or do things on the company's schedule. Be reasonable but make sure the insurance company is reasonable in return.

C. Special Rules for Accidents Involving the Government

As mentioned several times, there are special rules to follow if your accident might have been *even partially* caused by a government entity or its employee—the city, county, state, federal government, or any public agency or division. This would include, for example, an accident with a municipal bus or a car driven by a local, state or federal employee during worktime; an injury suffered because of the dangerous condition of a building or other property owned or operated by a government agency; or any accident caused by an employee of a government agency during the course of his or her work.

In general, local, state and federal governments get to set their own rules for who can sue them, for what and how. To pursue a claim against the government, you must carefully follow your state's specific rules for such claims. In particular, you must file a formal written claim against the government entity responsible for your injury within a relatively short time after your accident—usually 30 to 180 days. If you fail to file a claim within the time limit, or fail to include required information, you may forever lose your right to collect compensation.

1. Filing a Claim

If you believe that a government entity was in any way at fault for your injuries, file a claim against it. So, for example, if you are in a three-vehicle accident involving you, another car and a city bus, file a claim against the city even if you believe the other car was primarily at fault. It may turn out that the other driver was uninsured. Or the bus was more at fault than you first realized, and the driver of the other car will only be responsible to compensate you partially. In either case, you would have to look to the city for compensation—and if you have not filed a formal claim in time, you will not be allowed to seek damages against it.

2. Time Limits for Filing a Claim

Each state has its own time limits within which you have to file a formal claim against a government entity. The limits are as short as 30 days after the

accident, although most are six months. If you have been in an accident which may have involved government liability, check your state's time limit so that you file your claim on time. (See Section C7, below, for a state by state listing of all time limits.)

No matter what time limit you are up against, do not wait until the last minute to file your claim. You might have forgotten to include something, or you might have picked the wrong government entity—and you may have trouble correcting the error before the time runs out.

3. Contents of the Claim

The claims that state laws require you to file are usually very simple lists of basic information in plain language. Some cities, counties and states have specific claim forms which you can pick up at the office of your local city or county attorney, but most require only a plain signed piece of paper with the information clearly written or typed.

Although there may be slight variations in the information each state requires, all claims should include the following:

- Name and address of claimant. "Claimant" means the person injured; if you are filing a claim on behalf of a minor, list the minor's name and the name of the parent or guardian, as follows: "Claimant Robert Logan, a minor, by Andrea Logan, parent."
- Address to which notices are to be sent. You may want official notices sent to your work or to some address other than your home.
- Date, place and circumstances of the accident. Do not go into any detail here. Just generally describe what happened, such as: "On January 13, 199X, I was driving north along 4th Street approaching the intersection of Broadway when a municipal bus pulled into my lane and struck my car."
- Nature of your injury and other loss. Do not go into detail. Describe your injuries very generally— neck and back injuries, wrist injury. Mention lost

income, without stating how much, and any other losses you incurred—damage to car, clothes, other property.

If a form asks you to list your medical expenses, list what you have incurred so far, but also state: "Medical treatment is continuing." This will protect you in case you have to receive more treatment after you have filed your claim.

- Public employees who caused the injury. If you know the name of the driver of the bus or car, for example, put it down. If you don't know who directly caused the accident, do not bother trying to figure out which government employee was legally responsible for the accident. Simply say: "Not known."

- Amount of compensation claimed. Pick a figure considerably higher than you think your case is worth. (See Chapter 5, Section A.) So, for example, if you think your case is worth $3,500 to $5,000, make a claim for $25,000. A high number is useful because you may have to file your claim before you have completely recovered from your injuries and therefore before you know how much your claim will be worth. Also, the figure in the claim is just an "opening bid." Once you actually start negotiating for a settlement, you will narrow the figure down. (See Chapter 6, Section B, and Chapter 7.)

- The date and your signature.

4. Sample Claim Against the Government

The sample claim below is for an accident Martin Johnson had when he tripped in a hole in the public parking lot of the county medical building where he was going for a medical appointment. He sprained his left wrist and right knee in the fall, and also jammed his back. His medical bills, at the time of filing the claim, were $680. He missed two weeks of work for which his pay was $1,450.

SAMPLE CLAIM AGAINST THE GOVERNMENT

CLAIM OF MARTIN JOHNSON
AGAINST WABASH COUNTY

The claimant's name is Martin Johnson, 323 Cannonball Lane, Wabash, Missouri 00000.

All notices regarding this claim should be sent to 323 Cannonball Lane, Wabash, MO 00000.

This claim arises from injuries I suffered on January 13, 199X when I tripped in a hole in the county parking lot next to the county medical building on East Pine Street, Wabash, Wabash County, Missouri. I was in the parking lot after having parked my car there on my way to an appointment in the county medical building.

As a result of the fall, I suffered injuries to my left wrist, my right knee and my back and neck. I also missed two weeks of work as a result of my injuries.

I do not know the name of any public employee who may have caused this accident.

I claim compensation in the amount of $20,000.

Dated: February 10, 199X

_____

[signed]

Martin Johnson

---

5. Where To File a Claim

The clerk's office of the government agency or entity you believe was responsible for your accident is the first place to contact about filing your claim. For example, if you have a claim to file against the county, check with the County Clerk's office. It might accept claims directly, or direct you to another agency, such as the County Attorney or Controller's office. If your claim is against the state, call the state Board of Claims, Board of Control or state Attorney General's office to find out where to file.

If you are not sure whether your claim is against the city, the county or some state agency, file a separate claim against each of them. In most states, it does not cost anything to file a claim against the government, and filing in each place will protect you against failing to file against the correct entity before the time limit runs out. If it turns out later that one or another government entity was not responsible, you can simply ignore or drop your claim against it.

Double Check the Date

Make sure the office where you file your claim marks the date received on a copy you keep for your own records. If you mail in your claim, include at least one extra copy and a return envelope with a request that they send you back a copy stamped with the date it was filed. If you have not received a dated copy near the end of the time limit, go to the office in person to file your claim, making sure your copy is marked "received" or "filed," and that it includes the date.

6. What Happens After You File a Claim

While there may be some variety in the way different claims against the government are handled, there are some common procedures you can expect to be followed.

a. Contact by government claims adjuster

Soon after you file your claim, you will be contacted by a claims adjuster. This person might work directly for the government entity involved in the accident, or the city, county or state attorney's office, or might be a private claims adjuster for the government entity's insurance company. In any case, deal with this person as you would an insurance adjuster representing a private business or individual. That is, until you are ready to make a formal demand for settlement and begin actual negotiations, give only the basic information discussed earlier in this chapter. (See Section B4, above.) Your formal demand for settlement and the negotiation process will come later and will operate the same as with a private insurance company. (See Chapter 6, Section B and Chapter 7.)

b. Notice of insufficiency

The first thing that may happen after you file your claim is that you receive a letter from the government telling you that your claim is insufficient because it failed to include some required information such as a date or location. Getting a notice of insufficiency does not mean that your claim has been denied. It simply means that, before your state's time limit is up, you must provide the government entity with the missing information, in writing.

c. Negotiating a settlement

In some states, government entities will negotiate with you about a settlement only after your formal claim has been denied in writing (see Section d, below) or after the time period has elapsed within which the government has a right to grant or deny your claim (see Section e, below). In other states, since the written claim and its denial is usually nothing more than a formality, the government entity will begin to negotiate with you as soon as you file your claim. Regardless of when it begins, the negotiating process is exactly the same as for the insurance company with a private business or individual. (See Chapter 6, Section B and Chapter 7.)

d.   If your claim is denied

The formal claim process is intended to give the government a chance to investigate your claim before you are allowed to take the government to court, but the process is usually just a formality and almost all formal claims are denied. However, official denial of your claim does not mean the government will refuse to compensate you for your injuries. A denial merely ends the formal claims process and legally permits you to file a lawsuit against the government, if necessary. Once the formal claim is denied, the government entity will negotiate with you about settling your claim just as if it were a private business.

In most states, the government only has a limited time—30 to 180 days—after you file your formal claim by which to grant or deny it. Within that time, you should receive a written notice from the government officially denying your claim. The significance of the formal written denial is that it permits you to file a lawsuit against the government agency if you do not agree to settle the case. And in some states, the government entity will not begin to negotiate with you until the formal claim is officially denied.

e.   If your claim is neither granted nor denied

Often a government entity receives your formal claim and you never hear anything more about it. Instead of officially granting or denying the formal claim, it simply ignores it. If so, the claim will be considered denied after the government's time period for granting or denying it has run out. You are then legally permitted to pursue your claim against it, by lawsuit if necessary, just as if you had received an

official written denial. Note, however, that the government's silent denial of your formal claim also starts the clock running on the time within which you can legally file a lawsuit, just as if it had denied your claim in writing. (See Section d, above.)

Check the Time

In many states, the official written denial of your claim not only permits you to file a lawsuit against the government entity, but also begins the running of a time period within which you are allowed to file a lawsuit. Check Section C7 for the time period in your state within which you can file a lawsuit after your claim is denied.

f.   If you miss the filing deadline

For some time after an accident, you may not realize that a government entity was to blame. And by the time you do realize it, the time period within which to file a formal claim may have passed. If so, it does not necessarily end your chances of collecting compensation from the government, although it does make the task much harder. Most states permit you to file a late claim if you can show good reason for the delay.

What is legally required to establish a good reason, however, can vary greatly from state to state. In some states, it means that you were not aware the government entity was responsible; in others, you must show that you actually investigated who was responsible but you received incorrect information or otherwise made an excusable error.

No matter what your reason, if you missed the deadline, file your claim along with an explanation of why it is late. The government entity may still grant you permission to file the claim. If it does not, in most states you can then go to court to ask permission to file a late claim. For that process, though, it is best that you seek the assistance of a personal injury lawyer. (See Chapter 9, Section B.)

7. State Summaries of Time Limits for Filing

This section lists, for each state, the time within which you must file a formal claim against a government entity responsible for an accident.

In parenthesis following each state's time limit is the state statute establishing this time limit.

Also noted are additional rules concerning a formal claim or a lawsuit against a government entity, along with references to the statutes establishing those rules.

In some states, there is no requirement that a formal claim be filed. Instead, there are special rules about when a lawsuit must be filed against a government entity.

ALABAMA

180 days to file formal claim against a municipality. (Ala. Code §11-47-23)

ALASKA

2 years to file formal claim. (Alaska Stat. §§09.65.070 and 09.10.070)

ARIZONA

180 days to file formal claim. (Ariz. Rev. Stat. Ann. §12-821)

Double Check the Laws

Because laws change frequently, always double check the time limit listed here. There are at least two ways to double check. The first is to call your city or county attorney's office, and ask. Although they may be the ones defending against your claim once you file it, they are under a legal obligation to give you correct filing information. As with all communications concerning your accident, write down and keep the name and position of the person who gives you the information.

Another way to double check the time limit is to go to your local city, county or law school law library and ask the librarian to help you find the current law. This listing gives the title and number of the law for each state, so it will be easy for the law librarian to help you find the information you need.

ARKANSAS

Government immunity does not normally permit any claim against the state of Arkansas for injuries suffered in an accident. (Ark. Stat. Ann. §19-10-305 and 21-9-301)

If you have been injured in an accident caused by a city, county or state government entity or employee, see an attorney for possibilities of getting around the government immunity laws.

CALIFORNIA

180 days to file formal claim. (Cal. Gov't Code §911.2) Government entity must accept or reject claim within 45 days after receipt, or else it is deemed denied. (Cal. Gov't Code §912.4)

After denial or date claim is deemed denied, have six months to file a lawsuit against the government entity. (Cal. Gov't Code §§913 and 945.6)

COLORADO

180 days to file formal claim. (Colo. Rev. Stat. §24-10-109)

Lawsuit must be filed against a government entity within 2 years of the accident. (Colo. Rev. Stat. §13-80-102)

Special rule requires that a lawsuit against a law enforcement or firefighting agency must be filed within 1 year of the accident. (Colo. Rev. Stat. §13-80-103)

CONNECTICUT

Written notice of intention to commence lawsuit against a municipality or public agency within 180 days; file lawsuit within 2 years. (Conn. Gen. Stat. Ann. §7-101(a))

Claims against the state are made to state claims Commissioner within 1 year of accident. (Conn. Gen. Stat. Ann. §4-147 and 4-148)

If accident caused by the condition of state property, also must give notice within a "reasonable time" to the agency in control of that property. (Conn. Gen. Stat. Ann. §4-146)

Lawsuit against the state within 1 year of denial of claim (called "authorization" of lawsuit) by claims Commissioner. (Conn. Gen. Stat. Ann. §4-160)

DELAWARE

1 year to file formal claim by written notice. (Del. Code Ann. vol. 10, §4013(c), and vol. 10, §8124)

DISTRICT OF COLUMBIA

180 days to file formal claim. (D.C. Code Ann. §12-309)

FLORIDA

3 years to file formal claim both to the Department of Insurance and to the specific entity or agency responsible for the accident. (Fla. Stat. Ann. §768.26)

4 years to file lawsuit. (Fla. Stat. §11.065)

GEORGIA

180 days to file formal claim. (Ga. Code Ann. §69-308)

HAWAII

2 years to file formal claim. (Hawaii Rev. Stat. §§661-5 and 662-4)

IDAHO

180 days to file formal claim. (Idaho Code §6-905)
2 years to file lawsuit. (Idaho Code §6-911)

ILLINOIS

Claim against the state filed in Court of Claims within 2 years. (Ill. Ann. Stat. §439.8(d) and §439.22)

INDIANA

180 days to file formal claim. (Ind. Code Ann. §§34-4-16.5, 34-4-16.6, 34-4-16.7)

IOWA

2 years to file formal claim against the state. (Iowa Code Ann. §25A.13)

KANSAS

No special claim or notice; lawsuit within same time limit as if private party. (Kan. Stat. Ann. §75-6103(b))

KENTUCKY

1 year to file formal claim against state. (Ky. Rev. Stat. §44.110)

LOUISIANA

No formal claim required. In general, same rules regarding time to file a lawsuit as if against a private party, but some special limits regarding service of a lawsuit. (La. Rev. Stat. Ann. §§13:5101-13:5111)

MAINE

180 days to file formal claim. (Me. Rev. Stat. Ann. vol. 14, §8107)

2 years to file lawsuit. (Me. Rev. Stat. Ann. vol. 14, §8110)

MARYLAND

180 days to file formal claim, 3 years to file lawsuit. (Md. Ann. Code §12-106)

MASSACHUSETTS

2 years to file formal claim. (Mass. Gen. Laws Ann. Art. 258, §4)

3 years to file lawsuit. (Mass. Gen. Laws. Ann. §4)

MICHIGAN

180 days to file formal claim against the state. (Mich. Comp. Laws §600.6431)

2 years to file lawsuit. (Mich. Comp. Laws §691.1411)

Special rule, only 120 days to file formal claim regarding defective highway or public building. (Mich. Comp. Laws §§691.1404 and 691.1406)

MINNESOTA

180 days to file formal claim against the state. (Minn. Stat. Ann. §3.736(5))

MISSISSIPPI

Formal claim must be filed at least 90 days before you can file a lawsuit, and lawsuit must be filed within 2 years of accident. (Miss. Code Ann. §11-46-11)

MISSOURI

90 days to file formal claim against city government. (Mo. Ann. Stat. §77.600)

No formal claim needed against state or county. (Mo. Ann. Stat. §79.480 and 82.210)

MONTANA

Must file a claim within same period as given to file lawsuit against private person. Government entity has 120 days after claim to grant or deny it. During the 120 days, time suspended toward the statute of limitations. (Mont. Code Ann. §2-9-301)

NEBRASKA

1 year to file formal claim against city or county; 2 years to file lawsuit against city or county. (Neb. Rev. Stat. §13-919)

2 years to file formal claim against state. (Neb. Rev. Stat. §81-8227)

No lawsuit until claim denied or 6 months with no decision on claim. (Neb. Rev. Stat. §81-8213)

2 years to file lawsuit against state (Neb. Rev. Stat. §25-218), but this 2 year statute of limitations period is suspended while claim is pending, up to 6 months. (Neb. Rev. Stat. §81-8227)

NEVADA

2 years to file formal claim. (Nev. Rev. Stat. Ann. §41.036)

NEW HAMPSHIRE

60 days to file formal claim against all government entities other than the state; 3 years to file lawsuit against all entities other than the state. (N.H. Rev. Stat. Ann. §507-B:7)

180 days to file formal claim against the state; 6 years to file lawsuit against the state. (N.H. Rev. Stat. Ann. §541-B:14)

NEW JERSEY

90 days to file formal claim; may file lawsuit 6 months after claim is filed and within 2 years from date of accident. (N.J. Stat. Ann. §59:8-8)

NEW MEXICO

90 days to file formal claim. (N.M. Stat. Ann. §41-4-16)

2 years to file lawsuit. (N.M. Stat. Ann. §41-4-15)

NEW YORK

90 days to file formal claim against city; 1 year to file lawsuit. (N.Y. Gen. Mun. Laws §50-e)

90 days to file formal claim against county; 1 year to file lawsuit. (N.Y. County Law §52)

90 days to file claim (or notice of intent to file claim if no final damage figure within the 90 days) against the state. (Court of Claims Act §10)

NORTH CAROLINA

3 years to file formal claim against the state. (N.C. Gen. Stat. §143-299)

NORTH DAKOTA

3 years to file lawsuit against state (N.D. Cent. Code §28-01-22.1) or against other government entity. (N.D. Cent. Code §32-12.1-10)

OHIO

2 years to file lawsuit in the Court of Claims. (Ohio Rev. Code Ann. §2743.16(A))

OKLAHOMA

90 days to file formal claim. Claim is also permitted after 90 days and before 1 year, but amount of recovery under claim is reduced by 10% if claim filed after 90 days. (Okla. Stat. Ann. Ch. 51, §156(B))

OREGON

180 days to file formal claim. (Or. Rev. Stat. §30.275)

PENNSYLVANIA

180 days to file notice of intent to sue. (42 Pa. Con. Stat. Ann. §5522)

RHODE ISLAND

3 years to file lawsuit. (R.I. Gen. Laws §9-1-25)

SOUTH CAROLINA

No requirement to file formal claim, but if claim is filed, must wait to file lawsuit until claim is denied or 6 months passes with no decision on claim. 2 years to file lawsuit if no formal claim is filed; 3 years to file lawsuit if claim is filed. (S.C. Code Ann. §§15-78-90 and 15-78-110)

SOUTH DAKOTA

180 days to file formal claim. (S.D. Comp. Laws Ann. §3-21-2)

TENNESSEE

File claim against state with State Board of Claims. (Tenn. Code Ann. §9-801)

Claim mandatory against city or county; no time limit to file claim except that no suit can be filed until 60 days after claim filed and have only a total of 1 year to file suit. (Tenn. Code Ann. §§29-20-304 & 29-20-305)

TEXAS

180 days to file formal claim. (Tex. Civ. Prac. & Rem. Code §101.101)

UTAH

1 year to file formal claim. (Utah Code Ann. §§60-30-12 to 60-30-15)

Lawsuit must be filed within 1 year after denial of claim. (Utah Code Ann. §78-12-30)

VERMONT

No notice requirement other than lawsuit must be filed within statute of limitations.

VIRGINIA

180 days to file formal claim against city or town. (Va. Code §8.01-222)

1 year to file formal claim against state. (Va. Code §8.01-195.6)

WASHINGTON

Formal claim against state within statute of limitations; no suit until 60 days after claim filed. (Wash. Rev. Code Ann. §§4.92.100 & 4.92.110) Formal claim against town, city or county within statute of limitations. (Wash. Rev. Code Ann. §4.96.010)

120 days to file formal claim against government entities other than town, city, county or state. (Wash. Rev. Code Ann. §4.96.020)

WEST VIRGINIA

No formal claim time requirement; 2 years to file suit. (W. Va. Code §29-12A-6(a))

WISCONSIN

120 days to file formal claim against local government entity (Wis. Stat. Ann. §893.80) or against state. (Wis. Stat. Ann. §893.82)

WYOMING

2 years to file formal claim; suit within 1 year after claim filed. (Wyo. Stat. Ann. §§1-39-113 and 1-39-114)

UNITED STATES

2 years to file formal claim against any agency of the federal government; suit within 180 days after denial of claim. (28 U.S.C. §2401)

CHAPTER

4

Understanding Insurance Coverage

This chapter helps you understand what each type of insurance will cover and the consequences for you: when it will pay, how much it will pay and how it affects payments received under other coverage.

YOU CAN SKIP THIS ENTIRE CHAPTER IF:

- It is already clear who was responsible for your accident, and

- You have contacted that person's liability insurance company.

In such a case, that insurance company will likely be the only one with which you need be concerned.

READ THIS CHAPTER IF:

- You have any doubt about whether certain insurance will cover your accident, or

- You have questions about which of several insurance coverages is best for you to pursue.

Proceed directly to the section that covers the type of accident in which you've been involved.

Read Section A for motor vehicle accidents, and check Section D to see whether your state has no-fault insurance that will affect your claim.

Section B covers business liability, homeowner, renter and personal liability insurance for non-vehicle accidents.

Section C explains when to use and when not to use your health coverage to pay for your accident injuries.

t here is at least one good thing about insurance companies having their hooks in everyone's lives. If you have an accident, there's a good chance there will be an insurance company around from which you can collect compensation for your injuries. And finding the insurance coverage is usually a simple matter. With most accidents, it will be obvious who was at fault, or liable—and that person or business usually will have some kind of liability insurance. You merely have to contact that insurance company and let it know that it is finally its turn to do the paying.

But there are some situations when you might not be certain which insurance policy covers your accident. Or there may be some confusion because more than one insurance coverage—yours as well as the person's who is liable for the accident—is available to you, under different terms and for different amounts.

A. Motor Vehicle Insurance

The first and usually the only place a person injured in a vehicle accident need turn for compensation is to the other driver's liability insurance company. Almost all states require that every registered vehicle or licensed driver have some vehicle liability insurance. And even where it is not required by law, most drivers have some liability coverage.

Considering the cost of today's medical care, the minimum amount of coverage legally required in some states is quite low—$5,000 or $10,000 total per accident victim, $10,000 to $20,000 total for all injured people per accident. But in most states, the required minimum is higher and many people carry coverage well above the legal requirement. The result of minimum insurance requirements plus voluntary insurance protection is that except in very serious accidents, the person at fault is likely to have sufficient liability insurance to pay for all your damages. (See Section A1c.)

If the other driver or owner has no insurance, or has insufficient coverage to pay you fully for your injuries, you may be able to get additional compensation through the uninsured or underinsured motorist coverages of your own policy. (See Section A3.) Your own policy may also provide medical payments coverage for immediate payment of some medical bills. However, medical payments coverage should be used with caution. You may save money by using your general health insurance or other health coverage, instead. (See Section C.)

1. The Other Driver's Liability Insurance

Most of the time, the question of coverage will not even come up. The driver of the other car in your accident will be covered by liability insurance and that's all you'll need to know. But disputes over liability coverage do develop. Most of them revolve around whether the driver or vehicle in the accident fits into any of the specific categories included or excluded from a liability policy. Below is a quick guide to common inclusions and exclusions.

a. What drivers are covered?

Named insured The named insured is the person or people named in the policy. Liability policies cover named insureds no matter what car they are driving.

Spouse Even if a husband or wife of the named insured is not named on a policy, liability insurance almost always covers him or her as well, while driving any car. If a husband and wife no longer live together, however, the policy will not cover accidents caused by the spouse not named on the policy unless that spouse was driving the vehicle named in the policy with the permission of the named spouse. (See Section b, below.)

Other relative Anyone living in the household with the named insured who is related to the insured by blood, marriage or adoption, usually including a legal ward or foster child, is covered regardless of what car he or she is driving.

Anyone driving the insured vehicle Any person who is using, with permission, a vehicle specifically named in the policy is covered. So, someone who steals the car is not covered because he or she was not using it with permission. The permission question also comes up if, for example, a teenager lets another teen drive a car without the parent owner's permission. In that case, an insurer might argue that the parent's policy does not cover the unrelated teenager who was driving.

Understand Overlapping Medical Coverages for Auto Accidents

If you have been in a motor vehicle accident, two sources may be immediately available to pay your medical bills long before you settle your claim against the other driver: the medical payments coverage of your own auto insurance policy, and your own health insurance. It is a good idea to understand how these insurance policies interact before reaching out for any of the coverages.

Your own automobile medical payments coverage may require you to repay your own insurance company if you also collect damages from another person's liability insurance, whereas your health insurance policy might not. Claiming coverage under one or the other could easily mean hundreds of dollars difference in the total amount of compensation you wind up with. If you have both medical payments auto coverage and health insurance, read Section A2 carefully.

Some auto policies also exclude coverage for an employee using an employer's personal car for business. In that case, though, a person injured in an accident could file a claim for compensation under the business's liability insurance.

b.   What vehicles are covered?

Named vehicles   Any vehicle named in the liability coverage declaration is covered. An accident in a non-named vehicle is only covered if a named insured (see above) was driving.

Added vehicles   Any car, utility vehicle (see below) or other vehicle with which the named insured replaces the original named vehicle, and any additional vehicle the named insured owns during the policy period, is also covered. Some policies, however, cover replacement or additional vehicles only if the insured person notifies the company of the new or different vehicle within 30 days after it is acquired.

Temporary vehicles   Coverage extends to any car not owned by the named insured, or by another resident of the household, used as a temporary replacement—including rental cars—for any insured vehicle that is out of use because it needs repair or service, or has been destroyed.

Utility vehicles   Most policies cover an insured person driving a few types of vehicles somewhat larger than a normal passenger car, but only up to a limit. This usually means coverage is limited to a pick-up, flat-bed, delivery or panel truck to a certain rated load capacity stated in the policy. Larger vehicles might be covered if they are specifically listed in the owner's individual policy. The same holds true for a motorcycle: to be covered, it must be specifically named in the policy. Most policies, however, do not cover utility vehicles while used for business.

States With No-Fault Auto Insurance Coverage

The following states have some form of no-fault automobile insurance law. If you live in one of these states, read Section A4 of this chapter to see how no-fault rules affect which insurance will pay your claim.

Arkansas	Michigan
Colorado	Minnesota
Connecticut	New Jersey
Delaware	New York
District of Columbia	North Dakota
Florida	Oregon
Georgia	Pennsylvania
Hawaii	South Carolina
Kansas	South Dakota
Kentucky	Texas
Maryland	Utah
Massachusetts	Virginia

Even if you have no-fault auto insurance coverage, in many circumstances, you can also file a claim against the other person's liability insurance company. No-fault plans always permit such additional claims when the nature or extent of your injuries moves beyond the limits of the no-fault policy.

c.   What damages are covered?

Medical costs for diagnosis and treatment of injuries, property damage, loss of use of damaged property, expenses incurred and lost income are all covered by liability insurance. In addition, an injured person is entitled to a certain amount of "general damages," also referred to as pain and suffering. (See Chapter 5, Section C.)

2. Liability Coverage by More Than One Policy

More than one person's liability policy may cover your damages. When that happens, one insurance policy will provide what is called "primary" coverage, while the other will provide "secondary" or "excess" coverage. The primary coverage will pay your damages, and the secondary policy will kick in only if the total amount of coverage available under the primary policy was not enough to cover all your damages. In those cases, the secondary coverage will pay to the extent necessary to make up the difference between the limits of the primary policy and your total damages.

Example   *You are injured in a car accident and you are entitled to $20,000 in damages. The driver of the other car, however, has only $15,000 worth of liability insurance coverage. You could collect the $15,000 under the driver's primary insurance coverage. If there was any secondary coverage under the policy of another person partly responsible for the accident, you would collect the remaining $5,000 of your total damages from the insurance company issuing that secondary coverage.*

You will not have to worry about figuring out which policy is primary and which is secondary. When more than one liability policy is available to you, file a notice of claim with the insurance companies for both people. (See Chapter 3, Section B.) The insurance companies will then notify you which one will be primary and which one secondary. The primary insurance company is the one with which you will initially negotiate your claim.

The availability and sources of double coverage depend on facts such as who owns the vehicles involved in your accident and how much insurance they have.

a. When you are a passenger

If you are a passenger in a vehicle involved in an accident, you may file an injury claim under both (1) the liability insurance coverage of the driver or owner of the car you were in and (2) the coverage of the driver or owner of any other vehicle involved. You cannot collect from both drivers or owners any more than your total claim is worth, but if one driver or owner does not have insurance to cover your total damages, you can make up the rest against another. And you can collect against either the other driver or owner even if he or she was not greatly at fault because as a passenger you weren't at all at fault.

Example   *You are a passenger in car X which has an accident with car Y in which car Y seemed to be most at fault. Your total damages are $20,000, but the driver of car Y has only $15,000 insurance coverage. After you collect that $15,000 from car Y driver's insurance, you can collect the remaining $5,000 from car X's insurance.*

If either driver did not own the car he or she was driving, you will collect compensation from the insurance company of the owner of the car before you would collect from the insurance of the person driving.

You may not, however, file a liability claim against the driver of the car you are riding in if the driver is a relative with whom you live. In that case, you are considered an "insured person" under liability insurance—and an insured person cannot file a liability claim against his or her own liability coverage.

In the immediate aftermath of your accident, you may also file a claim under the medical payments coverage of your driver's or owner's auto policy. Medical payments coverage is not based on liability and therefore, does not require any discussion with insurance companies about who was at fault. But medical payments coverage does not include compensation for pain and suffering, lost income or anything other than actual medical bills—and those only up to the limits of the coverage. If you do collect under medical payments coverage and then later also receive liability compensation from that same insurance company, the amount you collected under medical payments will be deducted from your liability settlement.

Example   *You are injured in an auto accident and have $2,500 in medical bills in the first two weeks. You can immediately collect that amount under the medical payments provision of the insurance policy of the driver of the car you were riding in.*

It turns out that the driver of the other car was uninsured, and so you file a liability claim against the driver of the car you were riding in. You settle that claim for a total of $10,000. The settlement amount you actually receive from the insurance company, however, will only be $7,500— your $10,000 settlement minus the $2,500 medical payments you received earlier from the same company.

b.   When the other driver is not the owner

If you have a car accident and the other driver doesn't own the vehicle he or she was driving, the liability insurance of the vehicle's owner is the primary coverage—that is, the source which will take the first and main responsibility for your compensation. Only if the owner's policy limits are not high enough to cover all your damages does the driver's liability insurance kick in the difference as secondary coverage.

If either the driver or the owner is uninsured, the liability policy of the one who is insured will compensate you. If neither one is insured, you will have to turn to your own uninsured motorist coverage. (See Section A3a, below.)

c.   Employer's liability for employees

If the driver of a car or other vehicle is using the vehicle on the job, then the driver's employer is liable for any injuries caused in accidents for which the employee was at fault. This is true whether the employer is a private individual, a business or a public agency. This rule of employer liability applies whether you were the driver of another vehicle, a pedestrian, a passenger in the employee's personal car being used on the job or in the employer's car being driven by the employee. (See Section B1.)

Whether someone is on the job while driving is not always a simple question. In general, anytime someone is performing any duties related to work, he or she can be considered on the job even though also doing personal business and driving a personal car. For example, running errands in a personal car during lunch is not considered work-related, but if the employee is also picking up or dropping off something for work, the lunchtime driving becomes "on the job" time. Likewise, commuting to and from work generally is not considered on the job driving, even in a company car. But if the driver has to make work-related stops on the way, or has to drive to and from a job site other than the usual place of business, the driving might legally considered to be on the job.

The question of whether someone was on the job when they had an accident is not usually something you will need to sort out. Most drivers have personal automobile liability insurance, so if you believe the driver might have been on the job, send a notice of the accident to both the employer's business insurance company and to the driver's personal insurance company. Then the two insurers will have to sort out which one will provide the primary coverage.

Only if the driver is personally uninsured, or has insurance coverage so low that it does not provide full compensation for your injuries, will you have to concern yourself with the question of whether the employee was on the job when the accident happened. If there is no simple answer, then the issue becomes another factor thrown into the general hopper of negotiations—along with whose fault the accident was and how much your injuries are worth.

d. Parents' liability for minors

Usually, a minor teenager who is driving a car or motorcycle will be included in and covered by either his or her own insurance or a parent's insurance policy. If the minor is not named on a parent's insurance policy, or if the car the minor is driving is owned by a parent, liability can be imposed on the parent and collected from the parent's insurance company because of vehicle owner liability. (See Section b, above.)

Even if the minor is the registered owner of the car or motorcycle but has no insurance, most states make the parent responsible for damages—usually limited to between $5,000 and $25,000—caused in an accident when the minor is at fault. So, if you are involved in an accident with a minor who has little or no insurance coverage, you may be able to file a claim against a parent and collect from one or both policies up to the limit of your damages.

e. When you are driving another's car

If you were driving someone else's car when you were in an accident caused by another, you may make a claim for all your damages against that other driver. But you may also make a claim for immediate payment of your medical bills only, up to the coverage limit, under the medical payments coverage of the owner of the car you were driving. For damages to the car, however, the owner of the car must file his or her own claim against the other driver.

Occasionally, the condition of the vehicle you are driving contributes to an accident. Brakes may fail, lights go out, tires might be bald. If someone lends you a car, the owner is legally responsible to the extent the car's unsafe condition contributes to an accident. Therefore, if a borrowed vehicle's unsafe condition contributed to your accident, file a claim for damages not only against the driver of the other vehicle but also against the owner of the vehicle you were driving. If it is determined that the unsafe condition of the vehicle you were driving was the sole cause of the accident, a claim against the owner would be your only source of compensation.

If you are driving someone else's car and have an accident with an uninsured driver, the uninsured motorist coverage of the owner of the car you were driving is usually the primary coverage and your own uninsured motorist coverage is secondary. Notify both your own insurance company and the company that insures the car you were driving, but expect to negotiate a settlement only with the company insuring the car you were driving. (See Section A3.)

f. When several others are responsible

It is not uncommon for more than one other person to contribute to a car accident. It may have been the drivers of two other vehicles, or another vehicle plus a hazard in the roadway. Whatever the combination, if more than one person contributed to the accident, file a claim under the liability insurance of each.

You cannot collect more than the full amount of your damages from all of them together, but you can collect up to the entire amount of your damages from any one of them, depending upon their percentage of fault and your comparative fault. If the coverage of one person at fault is not sufficient to cover all your damages, you can collect the remainder of what your claim is worth from the other person who was at fault.

Example *You are involved in a three-car collision with cars driven by Anice and Jim. You file a claim against both of them. Since Anice was most at fault, her insurance company pays you up to the limits of her liability coverage of $15,000. But your total damage claim was worth $20,000. You can collect the remaining $5,000 value of your damages from Jim's insurance company.*

It is not your responsibility to figure out which one of the other drivers should pay you first or most as primary coverage. When you notify the insurance companies for both of the people responsible for the accident, the companies will decide between themselves which will be the primary coverage and which will serve as secondary coverage. Then you can negotiate a settlement with the insurance company which identifies itself as the primary coverage, and settle with the secondary company only if the primary coverage is not enough.

3. Your Own Vehicle's Coverage

Usually, the liability insurance of the person who was at fault for an accident pays for all of your damages. But you might also need to file a claim under your own policy—in addition to or instead of a claim against another person—if:

- You have an accident in which both driver and owner are uninsured, or an accident with a hit-and-run driver. You will have to file a claim under your own uninsured motorist coverage. (See Section 3a.)
- You have an accident in which the insurance coverage of the person at fault is insufficient to fully cover your damages—a situation which sometimes arises when several other people are injured. You will have to file a claim under your own underinsurance coverage, if you have it. (See Section 3b.)
- You want an immediate payment to cover your medical expenses. Your own medical payments coverage may provide immediate coverage, but you must decide beforehand whether it is better to use your health insurance instead. (See Section 3c.)

a. Uninsured motorist coverage

There are an unfortunately large number of cars and drivers on the road today without liability insurance. And we all know that the hit-and-run driver is an all-too-common beast. If you have an accident with an uninsured vehicle or hit-and-run driver, the place to turn for compensation for your injuries is the uninsured motorist (UM) coverage of your own vehicle insurance policy.

Normally uninsured motorist coverage does not include property damage to your own vehicle. Damage to your vehicle caused by an uninsured motorist would be covered by the collision coverage of your own policy.

But most UM coverage will pay up to your policy's UM limits for injuries caused to:

- you or a relative who lives with you, while a driver or passenger in the vehicle named in your UM insurance policy or in any other vehicle you do not own, or while a pedestrian
- anyone else driving your insured vehicle with your permission, and
- anyone else riding in the vehicle named in your insurance policy, or in any other vehicle you are driving but which you do not own.

UM coverage usually has rules limiting your ability to collect compensation and the amount you receive.

- If your accident is with a hit-and-run driver, you must notify the police within 24 hours of the accident.
- If your accident is with a hit-and-run driver, most policies require that you or your vehicle was actually hit by the other car; being forced off the road by a driver who disappears is not sufficient.
- If you are injured while on the job, your UM payments will be reduced by any workers' compensation or other disability payments you receive.
- If you receive payments for medical bills from your own insurance company under medical payments coverage, the amount you are entitled to recover under UM coverage will be reduced by the amount of those medical payments. (See Section 3c, below.)
- If you or a relative are injured by an uninsured motorist while you are in another's car, the UM coverage of that other car's owner is the primary coverage and your own UM coverage is secondary. You can collect from your own UM coverage only to the extent your damages are not covered by that car owner's UM policy.

If you file a claim under your UM coverage, an insurance adjuster from your insurance company will handle your claim just as if it were a regular liability claim. You will negotiate with the adjuster about the other person's liability, the extent of your own comparative negligence and the extent of your injuries and other damages. (Liability is discussed in Chapter 2, Section B; how much your claim is worth in Chapter 5; how to prepare your claim in Chapter 6; how to negotiate a settlement in Chapter 7.)

b. Underinsured motorist coverage

Some drivers carry enough insurance to meet the state's minimum liability insurance coverage requirement but not enough to cover all your damages. Since the other driver has some insurance, your uninsured motorist coverage does not apply. However, if you have what is called "underinsurance coverage" in your own vehicle policy, you may be able to collect compensation beyond what the other driver's insurance will pay.

Once you have settled a claim with the other driver's insurance company, negotiate with your own underinsurance coverage company about how much more than this amount your case is worth. Up to the extent of your underinsurance policy limits, you can collect this extra amount from your own company. However, any medical payments coverage you have collected from your own insurance company will be deducted from the amount you collect from it in underinsurance coverage.

Example *To pay medical bills right after an accident, you collected $2,000 from your own insurance company under the medical payments coverage of your automobile policy. Several months later, you settle your accident claim against the other driver for $15,000, which was the limit of the other driver's liability coverage.*

Your own underinsurance coverage has $50,000 policy limits. You convince your own insurance company that your claim is worth a total of $25,000. (See Chapter

5.) Under your underinsurance coverage, you can collect an additional $8,000—the $25,000 total value of your claim minus the $15,000 you collected from the other person's liability insurance, and also minus the $2,000 medical payments.

To collect under your underinsured motorist coverage, you must first show your insurance company that the other driver was underinsured for your damages. Obtain from the other driver's insurance company a letter that includes: the policy limits for that person's liability coverage and a statement that you have settled your claim with that company for an amount equal to the policy limits.

You probably will not even have to make a special request for such a letter. When you negotiate your case with the other driver's insurance company, the documents you exchange in finally settling the claim may already include the information you need.

c. Medical payments coverage

Most vehicle insurance coverage will pay up to certain limits for medical bills arising out of an accident—*regardless of who was at fault.*

The following people are usually covered by medical payments provisions:

- you or any relative who lives with you, when driving or riding in your insured vehicle or in anyone else's
- anyone else who is driving with your permission, or riding in your insured vehicle
- anyone riding in someone else's vehicle while you or a covered relative is driving.

However, medical payments provisions usually do *not* cover accidents occurring:

- on a motorcycle or other two-wheeled vehicle, unless that vehicle is specifically listed in the policy
- while anyone was a passenger in a car owned or used by you or a relative if that car was not listed in your insurance policy

- in a vehicle other than a regular passenger car if used in business
- during the course of the injured person's employment, if those injuries are also covered by workers' compensation laws
- while you were driving another person's car, unless you have already claimed and collected the maximum of that car owner's medical payments coverage

Your insurance company's right to recover from you
Under medical payments coverage, the insurance company has a right to recover the amount of its medical payments to you if you also collect damages from a third source—such as the liability insurance company for the other driver. When you receive a settlement from another source, you will have to repay out of your settlement the amounts you received under your medical payments coverage.

Example *Shortly after an accident you collect $1,000 in medical payments coverage from your own insurance company to pay for immediate hospital bills. Several months later, you collect $7,500 in damages from the driver of the other car involved in the accident. You are now required to repay your own insurance company the $1,000 medical payments it made to you, reducing the amount you have in pocket to $6,500.*

Use health insurance instead It may be possible, however, to have your medical bills paid immediately and also avoid any repayment by using your non-automobile health insurance or other health plan instead of the medical payments provision of your auto policy. Review the rules on repayment under health insurance or health plan coverage discussed in this chapter. (See Section C.) Then carefully inspect your own health policy or plan to decide if using it would be better for you than a claim under the medical payments provision of your own automobile policy.

d. Collision coverage for property damage

If your own policy includes coverage for property damage, also called "collision," and you are in an accident with another vehicle whose driver was at least partly at fault, you can apply for property damage compensation under either policy.

The main advantage of filing a claim for damages to your car under the collision coverage of your own policy is that your own coverage sometimes pays you more quickly. The other driver's insurance company might not pay to fix your car until it decides if its insured was at fault in the accident. Your own collision coverage insurance company, however, cannot make you wait for the other insurance company to make this decision. Your company must reimburse you immediately after you have complied with its rules on inspection and estimates. Then it can go after the other insurance company to be reimbursed for those property damage payments. And you are still free to go after the other driver's insurance company for any property damage your own coverage did not pay for—such as your deductible and uncovered equipment or property.

Disadvantages of your own collision coverage
However, if you collect a claim under your own collision coverage, you will have to come up with cash to meet your collision coverage deductible. Also, there may be restrictions on the amount you can collect, including a total dollar limit as well as specific limits on clothing, luggage, non-permanently installed sound equipment, rental car replacement and other items. And your own policy may require that you permit the insurance company to inspect the car and obtain two or more competitive estimates before getting approval for repairs.

By contrast, because your right to repairs from the other driver's insurance arises from the other driver's liability and not from any agreement between you and the insurance company, the other driver's insurance company has no right to impose these restrictions. You will still have to negotiate about how much the property damage is worth, however. (See Chapter 5, Section E.)

If you are driving someone else's car when in an accident and that car was not covered by collision insurance, your own policy's collision coverage can pay for the damage. The car owner's collision coverage pays first, however, and your collision coverage only kicks in if the owner's coverage does not fully pay for the damages.

e. Claims against you

When there has been an accident in which you were a driver, there may be damage claims against you even though you were only slightly at fault. Regardless of how much or little the other person's damages are, your claim and the other person's claim have no effect on one another. You pursue your damage claim against those you believe were at fault—and the amount you receive is reduced by the degree you were comparatively negligent, regardless of how much or how little negligence the other driver accepts responsibility for in the claim against your insurance company. (See Chapter 2, Section A3.)

Any person involved in the accident who believes you were partly responsible for his or her injuries or other damages may file a claim against you through your liability insurance company. Regardless of the degree of your fault, your liability insurance company must defend you in any claim or lawsuit—and must provide a lawyer to represent you in court if necessary. And it must settle and pay any claim against you up to the limits of your liability coverage. The success or failure of anyone else's claim against you has no bearing on your claim against others.

4. No-Fault Automobile Insurance

The following states have some form of no-fault automobile insurance law—often referred to in policies as Personal Injury Protection (PIP).

No-fault auto insurance is a little like cod liver oil. Everyone's heard of it, most everyone's been convinced it must be good for you, a lot of people have been forced to take some, but nobody seems to know if it does any good. One group, however, has clearly benefited from no-fault: the insurance industry. Although lower insurance rates was one of the basic promises on which no-fault was sold to legislators, it has failed to deliver lower costs to the consumer.

States with No-Fault Insurance

Arkansas	Michigan
Colorado	Minnesota
Connecticut	New Jersey
Delaware	New York
District of Columbia	North Dakota
Florida	Oregon
Georgia	Pennsylvania
Hawaii	South Carolina
Kansas	South Dakota
Kentucky	Texas
Maryland	Utah
Massachusetts	Virginia

Despite its failings, about half the states have some form of no-fault law. In general, no-fault coverage eliminates injury liability claims and lawsuits in smaller accidents in exchange for direct payment by the injured person's own insurance company of medical bills and lost wages—up to certain dollar amounts—regardless of who was at fault for the accident. No-fault often does not apply at all to vehicle damage; those claims are still handled by filing a liability claim against the one who is responsible for the accident, or by looking to your own collision insurance.

After you file your PIP claim, you may also be able to file a liability claim against the person at fault. The circumstances under which you can file a liability claim vary from no-fault state to no-fault state, and are explained in the following sections.

Prompt payment of medical bills and lost wages without any arguments about who caused the accident is the simple part of no-fault. But most no-fault insurance provide extremely limited coverage to the injured person.

- It pays benefits for medical bills and lost income only. It provides no compensation for pain, suffering, emotional distress, inconvenience or lost opportunities.

No-Fault? You Can Tell By Looking

Whether you have no-fault coverage and the amount of PIP benefits you carry—that is, the amount of medical bills and lost income your own company will pay regardless of fault in the accident—depends on your individual insurance policy. To make certain whether you have PIP coverage, and to determine what your PIP benefits are, read your policy carefully. If your policy includes PIP protection, file your first claim for injury compensation—medical costs and lost income only, up to the dollar limit of your coverage—with your *own* insurance company, following the procedures set out in the PIP section of your policy.

- No-fault coverage does not pay for medical bills and lost income higher than the PIP benefit limits of each person's policy. PIP benefits often fail to reimburse fully for medical bills and lost income.

a.   Liability claims are also allowed

To make up for what PIP benefits do not cover, all no-fault laws also permit an injured driver to file a liability claim, and lawsuit if necessary, against another driver who was at fault in an accident. The liability claim permits an injured driver to obtain compensation for medical and income losses above what the PIP benefits have paid, as well as for pain and suffering and other general damages, the same as a liability claim in a state with a no-fault law.

Whether and when you can file a liability claim for further damages against the person at fault in your accident depends on the specifics of the no-fault law in your state. (Section D contains a summary of your state's no-fault law.)

Some states have what are called "add-on" no-fault laws that put no restrictions on your right to file a liability claim in addition to your PIP claim. In these states, you can always file a liability claim against the person at fault for all damages in excess of your PIP benefits.

Other no-fault states have different types of thresholds that an injured person must reach before being permitted to file a claim for full compensation against those at fault for an accident. Some states have a monetary threshold only and some a serious injury threshold only, and some have both. States with both requirements permit a liability claim if an injured person meets *either one*.

b.   States with add-on coverage

In the states listed below, you always have a right to file a liability claim against the other driver or owner in addition to your PIP claim—and for any kind and any amount of damages above what you have been paid by your own PIP insurance. Since this kind of PIP coverage is merely "added on" to an injured person's rights under traditional liability law, it has gained the shorthand name of "add-on" coverage.

Arkansas   South Carolina
Delaware   South Dakota
Maryland   Texas
Oregon   Virginia
Pennsylvania

In these states, a liability claim is handled exactly the same as a claim in a state without no-fault, and you can follow all the information and directions in this book on filing and settling a liability claim.

c.   States with monetary thresholds

The no-fault laws in the states listed below permit a liability claim and lawsuit against the person at fault whenever the injured person has medical expenses over a certain limit. The threshold limit is listed next to each state. Once you have reached that medical expense threshold, you are free to file a regular liability claim against those who are at fault for your accident by following the directions in this book. All of these states also permit a liability claim or lawsuit if a certain "injury threshold" is met instead of the medical expense threshold. (See Section d, below.)

COLORADO	$2,500
CONNECTICUT	$ 400
D.C.	your policy's PIP benefit amount
GEORGIA	$ 500
HAWAII	your policy's PIP benefit amount
KANSAS	$ 500
KENTUCKY	$1,000
MASSACHUSETTS	$ 500
MINNESOTA	$4,000
NORTH DAKOTA	$2,500
UTAH	$1,000

Medical expenses that count toward reaching this threshold include not only the obvious things most medical insurance covers—costs of an ambulance, hospital, clinic, doctor, nursing, laboratory—but also other professional health services, including dental work to repair or replace injured teeth, physical therapy and chiropracty. To find out what is counted toward the threshold limit in your state, look at the definition of medical expense in your own no-fault (PIP) insurance policy.

Collecting Benefits: Once Is All You Get

Under some PIP policies, if you file a liability claim and recover damages after you also collected PIP benefits, your own PIP insurance company has a right to be reimbursed by you for the amount it paid you. Under these policies, no-fault coverage works just like an auto policy's medical payments coverage—except that it also pays for some amount of income loss. (See Section A3c, above.) In other words, the amount of liability compensation you finally get to keep is reduced by whatever your PIP coverage already paid you.

Under other no-fault policies, your PIP insurance company does not have a right to reimbursement from you but it does have a right of "subrogation"—which means it can recover your PIP benefits directly from the liable person's insurance company. Under those subrogation policies, the damages you can collect from the other person's insurance will not include any amounts your PIP coverage paid you—otherwise you would be receiving those benefits twice.

Carefully read the terms of your own PIP benefits coverage to see whether your PIP insurance carrier has a right of reimbursement or subrogation.

The monetary threshold can be reached only by counting covered medical expenses which are "necessary." Occasionally, the insurance company for the person at fault might argue that you have not reached the threshold because a particular medical treatment or service you received was either not really related to the accident or was not necessary to treat your injuries. Then, after subtracting or reducing that supposedly unnecessary medical expense, the insurance company could claim that your medical expense total does not reach the no-fault threshold and, therefore, you are not permitted to file a liability claim. (How to avoid this problem, and how to deal with an insurance adjuster who tries this tactic, are discussed in Chapter 6, Section A2 and Chapter 7, Sections B and C.)

Keep Track of Medical Expenses

As you receive treatment for your injuries, keep track of how close you are to reaching your state's no-fault threshold level. There are times when we all have difficulty choosing whether to undergo one more examination or one more treatment toward the end of a course of a treatment for a particular injury. If you are close to reaching the threshold level for being allowed to file a liability claim for damages but are not certain you will reach it, the need to go over the threshold might be another thing to consider when deciding whether to undergo that final treatment or to have that final examination.

And the fact that you could choose not to undergo a particular examination or treatment does not make having that treatment medically unnecessary. A treatment or examination is medically necessary if it serves a reasonable diagnostic or therapeutic purpose.

Example *Your state has a medical expenses threshold of $1,000. You have medical expenses of $1,250, including $650 for physical therapy.*

The insurance adjuster for the person at fault in your accident claims that there was no evidence that most of the physical therapy did any good, and was therefore unnecessary. The adjuster claims that half the physical therapy expenses were unnecessary, reducing the necessary physical therapy expenses by $325. When that $325 is subtracted from your total medical expenses, the total shrinks to $925, less than your state's threshold and therefore not enough to allow you to file a liability claim in addition to your PIP benefits.

d. States with serious injury thresholds

The states listed below permit an injured person to file a liability claim against those at fault in an accident if the insured had a "serious" injury, regardless of how much was spent on medical treatment. Florida, Michigan, New Jersey and New York also have a monetary threshold. (See Section c, above.) Injuries that qualify as serious are defined by each state's law, as indicated. If you meet your state's injury threshold, follow all the other information and directions in this book on filing and settling a liability claim.

COLORADO permanent disability or permanent disfigurement

CONNECTICUT permanent injury, permanent significant disfigurement or fracture of any bone

DISTRICT OF COLUMBIA substantial permanent scarring or disfigurement, substantial permanent impairment, or substantially total impairment lasting 180 days

FLORIDA permanent injury or significant and permanent scarring or disfigurement

GEORGIA over 10 days total disability, any fracture, permanent disfigurement, loss of a bodily function, or partial loss of hearing or sight

HAWAII significant permanent loss of use body part or function, or permanent and serious disfigurement resulting in mental or emotional distress

KANSAS   permanent disfigurement, fracture of weightbearing bone or compound, comminuted, compressed or displaced fracture of any bone, permanent injury or permanent loss of a body function

KENTUCKY   permanent disfigurement, fracture of weightbearing bone or compound, comminuted, compressed or displaced fracture of any bone, permanent injury or permanent loss of a body function

MASSACHUSETTS   permanent and serious disfigurement, fractured bone, substantial loss of hearing or sight

MICHIGAN   serious impairment of a body function or permanent and serious disfigurement

MINNESOTA   60 days disability, permanent injury or permanent disfigurement

NEW JERSEY   some permanent disability or full disability of over 180 days, significant disfigurement or permanent loss of a bodily function

NEW YORK   significant disfigurement, bone fracture, permanent limitation of use of body organ or member, significant limitation of body function or system, or substantially full disability for 90 days

NORTH DAKOTA   serious and permanent disfigurement or disability of more than 60 days

UTAH   bone fracture, permanent disability or permanent disfigurement

The categories of injuries legally considered "serious" by the various state no-fault laws are explained below.

Bone fracture   The probable fracture of any bone, as shown by X-rays and a doctor's statement, which was the result of the accident—that is, was not an old fracture. Some PIP laws require that the fracture be of a "weight-bearing bone"—large bones of arm or leg, or a vertebrae. Some also define serious injury as the compound, crushed, displaced or compressed fracture of any bone. And other state laws merely mention "fracture," which would include chipped or cracked bones or vertebrae as well as full breaks.

Permanent injury   In some states, a "permanent" injury (if the term "disabling" is not included) can permit a liability claim even if the injury is not a severe one. For example, a broken bone that will remain crooked can be a permanent injury even though it is a small bone like a finger or toe and its crookedness does not affect the use of hand or foot. Similarly, a joint that suffers ligament, cartilage or other damage may be permanently injured if the joint is not as strong or as flexible after healing as it was before the injury. Neck and back injuries are common in automobile accidents, and any injury to the spine that cannot be corrected without surgery might be considered a permanent injury, even though it may not prevent you from working or performing other normal daily life functions.

The Threshold Is a Subject for Negotiation

Because of the sometimes vague definitions of the threshold injury categories under PIP laws—and the subjective nature of many medical evaluations—it may not be clear whether your injuries qualify under your state's no-fault threshold. But you don't have to have a sure-fire qualified injury to pursue a liability claim. The issue of whether your injury qualifies is something to negotiate with an insurance company for the person at fault.

File your liability claim against the person at fault and include the no-fault threshold question among the other issues you will be negotiating with the insurance company. (For explanation of how to prepare and negotiate a claim for serious, permanent or disabling injury, see Chapter 6, Section B, and Chapter 7, Section A.)

Laws using the word "significant" to describe a threshold permanent injury require that the injury be more serious than states that do not use that term.

Disabling injury   Some state no-fault laws speak in terms of "disabling" injuries rather than "permanent" ones. In these states, your medical records must show that you have suffered some loss, though not necessarily all, of the function of a part of your body. For example, if you cannot straighten your arm all the way out because of an elbow injury, or you can no longer bend and pick up heavy things because of a back injury, your injury may be disabling even though you still have most of the use of your arm or back.

In some states, the loss of function has to be "significant" while in others it does not. Under some rules, the injury has to be "permanent" as well as disabling, while other rules require that the disability only last more than 60 days.

In general, an injury is "disabling" if, despite medical treatment and the passage of time, the injured part will not heal to function as well as it did before your accident, and that loss of function interferes in some way with your ability to perform normal functions of daily life, including your particular kind of work. Differences of opinion between you and an insurance company about whether an injury is disabling, or whether the disability is significant or permanent, become part of the normal negotiation process which takes place when you file a claim.

Permanent disfigurement   Disfigurement refers to what can be seen. Scarring is the most obvious example. A scar of any sort on the face is disfiguring if it can be seen by normal observation. Scarring on other parts of the body are considered disfiguring if large or severe enough. Other examples of disfigurement might be a broken nose which heals crooked, the loss of the tip of a finger or toe or any other change in the shape or coloration of the body which is visible to others. If scarring is only visible when you wear shorts or a bathing suit, for example, it may be worth less in damages than a facial scar, but that

doesn't necessarily mean it is not "disfiguring." (See Chapter 5, Section C.)

B. Non-Vehicle Liability Insurance

Although everyone is aware that insurance covers most automobile accidents, coverage also pays compensation to those injured in most other kinds of accidents as well. From business insurance to property owners' coverage, if you have been injured almost anywhere, it is likely there is some insurance to cover your damages.

1. Business and Landlord Liability Coverage

Virtually every commercial property owner and business carries liability insurance covering injuries for which the business or property owner could be held legally liable—usually in amounts high enough to compensate for almost any injuries. The people and accidents usually covered range broadly, including:

- any customer or business visitor accidently injured from a dangerous physical condition of the business premises
- any customer or business visitor accidently injured by an employee of the business
- any person other than a co-worker accidently injured by an employee of a business if the employee was engaging—on or off the business premises—in any work-related conduct at the time of the accident
- any person injured by the dangerous or defective condition of a product made, sold or rented by a business
- any person accidently injured by the dangerous or defective condition of rental property (See Chapter 2, Section B2.)

If you have been injured on business property, file your claim against the business owner. If the owner of the business claims the accident was the legal responsibility of the property owner from whom the business owner leases or rents, it is up to the insurance companies for the business owner and the property owner to decide between themselves which one will compensate you for your damages. You do not have to get involved in that decision. File your notice of claim with the business owner, and if the property owner's insurance company determines that it will cover your damages instead, it will notify you.

2. Workers' Compensation

Every state has workers' compensation laws to compensate people who are injured on the job. In general, anytime you have been injured while working for an employer, whether at your place of work or while doing business away from your normal job site, workers' compensation will cover your medical bills and lost wages.

But the law also says that in work-related accidents, a workers' compensation claim is the only claim you are allowed to file against your employer. In other words, if you are injured at work, you cannot file a liability claim against your employer even though a customer or visitor injured in the same way could file such a claim.

However, if anyone other than your employer or a co-worker was even partly responsible for the accident, you are free to file your own liability insurance claim against that person or business. In the "regular" liability claim, you can collect damages beyond the mere payment of medical bills and lost wages.

Example *While driving your car on company business, you are rear-ended by another car. You have $650 worth of medical bills and lose three days of work. You can file a workers' compensation claim for the $650 medical bills and for your lost wages. You can also file a regular liability insurance claim against the other driver in the accident. In that liability claim, you can seek compensation for your pain and suffering caused by the accident.*

Example *You are injured at work when the copy machine repair person drops a part on your foot. You can file a workers' compensation claim to recover your medical bills and any lost income for missed work, and you can also file a liability claim against the copy machine repair company for compensation for the pain and suffering accompanying your foot injury.*

If you file both a workers' compensation claim and a private liability insurance claim for the same accident, the workers' compensation system automatically has a lien against any compensation you recover from the liable person or business—known as the third party. A lien means that if you recover any damages from the third party, you have a legal obligation to repay to workers' compensation any money it paid you for medical bills or lost wages. Notice of this lien is usually included in any papers you receive from workers' compensation, but the law says the lien exists whether or not you receive any such notice.

3. Property Owner and Renter Policies

Anytime you have an accident caused by a defective or dangerous condition in someone's home, on their property or in the common areas of an apartment or condominium building—such as hallways, stairs, parking areas—the property owner or renter, or both, is probably liable to you for your injuries. (See Chapter 2.) And in almost all such cases, the property owner and sometimes the renter will have liability insurance to cover your injuries.

Landlords of residential income property (residences they own but others live in) have business liability insurance similar to the liability insurance carried by any other business. It operates the same way as business liability insurance. (See Section B1.)

Homeowners' and business liability policies also frequently cover injuries caused by the insured business person, homeowner or family member even if the accident occurs away from the business or home, except for a vehicle accident. This all-inclusive coverage is known as "personal liability," "all perils" or "comprehensive family liability" coverage or other similar name, and can cover your injuries in many situations in which you might not think there would be any insurance coverage at all.

A look at whom and what typical personal liability coverage would include can give you the best idea of the wide variety of accident situations in which it could apply.

Example   *Jack goes to the park and hits a softball that injures Candy, who is sunbathing in the picnic area nearby. If Jack had personal liability coverage as part of a business, homeowner's or renter's policy described above, Candy could file a claim even though the accident took place away from Jack's business or home. The definition of "covered liability" in the personal liability coverage includes "all amounts the insured shall become legally obligated to pay" because of "any occurrence." Since neither the activity of softball nor the location of the park is specifically mentioned in the exclusions, the accident would be covered.*

Example   *An 11 year-old named Johnny and his 10 year-old cousin Madonna, visiting from out of state, are up in a tree throwing rotten fruit at passing cars. A tomato splats on Roger's windshield, causing him to swerve his car and crash into Vera's jeep parked in her driveway. Roger's injuries are probably covered by Johnny's parents' homeowner's policy. Johnny is covered because he is a "relative" living with the named insured— one or both of his parents.*

And if it was Madonna who threw the tomato, the insurance would still cover the accident because she was a minor "in the care of" the insured when the accident happened, even though she does not live with Johnny's parents. Even though the kids were not at home when they caused the accident, the personal liability coverage of the homeowner's policy covers injuries caused by "any occurrence," without being limited to accidents on the property.

Although an automobile accident is involved, it would be covered by the homeowner's policy despite the exclusion for vehicle accidents. Since the exclusion only refers to vehicle accidents caused by an insured who is driving a vehicle, the fact that the accident involved a car does not matter.

Finally, Vera can file a claim under Johnny's parents' coverage rather than against Roger, since the kids caused the "occurrence" which resulted in damage to her jeep, and since personal liability coverage includes property damage.

Business, Homeowner or Renter's Personal Liability Coverage

PEOPLE INSURED

- the named insured (person named in the policy)
- any relative living with the named insured
- any minor living with or in the care of the named insured

COVERED LIABILITY

The company agrees to pay on behalf of the insured all amounts, up to the coverage limits herein, which the insured shall become legally obligated to pay as damages because of bodily injury or property damage caused by any occurrence.

EXCLUSIONS

Not covered are accidents caused while the insured is operating a motor vehicle or watercraft, accidents on other premises owned, rented or controlled by the insured, or in the course and scope of any business operated by the insured.

Personal liability insurance may also cover injuries caused by:

- animals (the animal's owner would be liable, and therefore covered by a personal liability policy), and
- a condition of the insured's property which causes an accident off the property (an overgrown bush which blocks a driver's view of an intersection, contributing to a car accident; or a tree root which has grown under the sidewalk causing it to buckle and someone to fall over it).

In fact, any kind of conduct—not involving the insured driving a vehicle—which causes an accident, may be covered by personal liability coverage contained in a business, homeowner or renter insurance policy. So, if there is any reason why someone (other than the driver of another car) is legally liable to you for an injury accident, including a car accident, it is worth pursuing a claim if he or she has personal liability coverage.

C. Your Own Health Coverage and Accident Claims

Normally, when you are ill or injured, you look to your own health coverage—whether through health insurance, a health maintenance organization (HMO) or your work's self-insurance program—to take care of your bills. When you have been injured in an accident, however, one of the major bases for receiving damages from the liable person's insurance company is the very medical bills your health coverage has already paid.

This section discusses when it may be to your advantage to submit your accident-related medical bills under your personal health insurance and when it may be better not to use your own health coverage, if you can avoid it.

In many cases, your own health plan will pay no attention to whether you have received a damage award for the same injuries the health plan covered.

Under some coverages, however, your health plan may have a right to be reimbursed by you, out of the damage award you receive, for medical expenses which that health plan already paid. The health plan's right to reimbursement depends on your agreement with the health plan provider and varies with the type of health coverage you have.

1. Health Coverage With an Insurance Company

Whether you must reimburse your private health insurance company depends on the terms of your health insurance policy and on the state you live in. Some states have made it unlawful for a health insurance company to seek reimbursement from an insured person who has also received a damage award for that accident. In those states, the insurance company will not seek reimbursement even if the policy says it has that right. Since most health insurance policies are written to cover all states, they may include reimbursement provisions even though the provision cannot be enforced in your state.

Most states, however, do not have such protection, so health insurance companies can seek reimbursement from you if you have collected liability damages related to the accident. The first place to look to see if your insurance company has a right to reimbursement is your health insurance policy. Read carefully the part which discusses "Right to Reimbursement." If your policy states that the company has a right to reimbursement, you may have to pay back medical bills it has covered if you receive a notice or other demand from the company seeking such reimbursement.

If you have any doubt whether such reimbursement is lawful in your state, or you do not understand exactly what the provisions of your policy mean, call your state's Department of Insurance. You can find the number in the Government Pages at the beginning of the white pages of the telephone directory.

Even if a health insurance company has a right under the policy to seek reimbursement from you, whether it actually does so depends on whether it knows you have filed an accident claim. When you file your health insurance claim, it may ask whether the injuries were the result of an accident. It may also ask whether or not you have filed a claim for damages against the liable party. But if your claim form does not pose such questions, the insurance company may have no idea that you have filed and settled a claim for damages. Even if the company does file a request for reimbursement, you don't necessarily have to repay the full amount it claims. (How liens work and how to negotiate a smaller reimbursement is discussed in Chapter 8, Section D.)

2.   Health Coverage With an HMO

Health maintenance organizations (HMOs) are group health plans which provide not only coverage for illness and injury but which actually provide or arrange for the treatment. Most HMO membership agreements require you to reimburse them for medical expenses they have expended for accident injuries if you also receive compensation from the person at fault for the accident. When processing your claim for compensation (see Chapter 6, Section A2) you will have to request copies of your medical billing from the HMO, which will probably alert the HMO that you are also filing a liability insurance claim.

Since it's an HMO, you will not have actually received a traditional bill for your treatment. When the HMO sends you copies of what it decides the cost of your treatment would have been, it will probably also send you a notice of the right to be reimbursed, called a lien. As with health insurance right to reimbursement, you may not have to repay the full amount the HMO claims. (See Chapter 8, Section D, for tips on negotiating a smaller reimbursement.)

3.   Employer's Self-Insured Health Plan

If you work for a large company or organization, it may provide you with its own self-insured health care plan instead of health insurance through an outside insurance company. If so, the law permits the employer to require that you reimburse it out of your damage award for any medical expenses the health plan pays for you. Whether such a right to reimbursement is included depends on the terms of your specific plan. Check with your union, benefits, personnel or human resources office to see if your plan has a reimbursement clause. If it does, you should still try to negotiate for a smaller reimbursement. (See Chapter 8, Section D.)

4.   Workers' Compensation

If you receive workers' compensation benefits for a job-related accidental injury and also receive a damage award from a person other than your employer, the workers' compensation system has a right to be reimbursed by you for any amounts it paid for medical care. And be aware that workers' compensation operates slowly. Even if it has been many months since you collected both your workers' compensation claim and your liability damages, don't spend all your liability damages too quickly. A workers' compensation representative might still come knocking on your door one day asking for repayment of the money.

5.   Medicare and Medicaid

Medicare and Medicaid (called Medi-Cal in California) are federal government programs which provide some medical coverage for over-65 (Medicare) and low-income (Medicaid) people. Both Medicare and Medicaid have a legal right to reimbursement from you if you collect a damages award from a person liable for your injuries.

However, Medicaid and Medicare administrators often don't have any idea that you have filed a claim for damages against a third person, and as huge bureaucracies, they usually don't bother to check. Therefore, if you have had some of your accident injury medical bills paid by Medicare or Medicaid, and you have also collected damages from those liable for the accident, Medicare or Medicaid is entitled to reimbursement but it is very possible that it will simply never request it.

D. No-Fault Laws: State Summaries

This section lists each state which has some form of no-fault automobile insurance law. Under each state is a description of the rules controlling when a person injured in a vehicle accident is permitted to file a liability claim or lawsuit against the person who was at fault for the accident. Also listed are miscellaneous other rules of which you should be aware.

How To Use These Listings

The information here concerning no-fault rules is divided into a number of categories, explained below.

Statute No-fault rules are contained in the official laws of the state, called statutes. Statutes are identified by individual number, and in some states by an article or title number—referring to the actual volume in which the law can be found—as well. For example, the Connecticut no-fault law is found in the Connecticut General Statutes, title 14, section 38-319.

In this listing, common legal abbreviations are used when referring to the statutes. They include:

Stat. statutes
§ section, referring to the specific numbered statute

et seq. latin for "and following." It appears after the number of a statute and means that the sections which immediately follow also apply to the same subject.
Rev. revised, signifying that these are the updated statutes.
Gen. general
Ann. annotated, meaning the volumes also include lists of cases which interpret the laws
Art. article; the laws denoted this way have been divided into large separately numbered chunks, each chunk called an article, and within each article are numbered sections

PIP Personal Injury Protection, the official name for no-fault coverage. The PIP insurance carrier is your own insurance company with which you have no-fault coverage.

Add-on An add-on type no-fault policy means that you can file a liability claim against the person at fault for the accident in addition to (added on to) making a claim under your no-fault coverage. In add-on states, you do not have to meet any injury threshold before being allowed to file a liability claim. (See Section A4b, above.)

Monetary threshold In some no-fault states you are permitted to file a liability claim in addition to your PIP claim if your medical expenses have reached a certain level, called the monetary threshold. (See Section A4c, above.)

Injury threshold In some no-fault states you are permitted to file a liability claim in addition to your PIP claim if your injuries are of a certain level of seriousness, usually defined by either the type of injury or its permanent effects. (See Section A4d, above.)

Right to reimbursement In some states, if you collect both PIP benefits and liability compensation from the party at fault, your PIP insurance carrier has a right to be repaid by you for the PIP benefits it paid you.

Make Sure The Law Is Current

Laws frequently change. If you become involved in a dispute with an insurance company over the application of your state's no-fault rules, it's best to double check the exact language in its latest version. You can find the statute, as the laws are called, at your nearest law library. The listing below gives the name and section number of the state statute in which the no-fault law is found.

ARKANSAS

Statute: Ark. Stat. Ann. §4014 et seq.
Add-on version
Monetary threshold: minimum benefits of $5,000 medical, $140/week loss of income up to one year
Right to reimbursement

COLORADO

Statute: Colo. Rev. Stat. §10-4-701 et seq.
Monetary threshold: $2,500
Injury threshold: permanent disability or permanent disfigurement

CONNECTICUT

Statute: Conn. Gen. Stat. Ann., title 14, §38-319 et seq.
Monetary threshold: $400
Injury threshold: permanent injury, permanent significant disfigurement, or fracture of any bone
Right to reimbursement

DELAWARE

Statute: Del. Code Ann. §2118 et seq.
Add-on version
• Includes property damage
• Expenses paid under PIP may not also be recovered in liability claim against party at fault

DISTRICT OF COLUMBIA

Statute: D.C. Code Ann. §35-2101 et seq.
Monetary threshold: medical expenses or lost work income greater than PIP benefits actually available
Injury threshold: substantial permanent scarring or disfigurement, substantial permanent impairment which significantly affects the ability to perform professional activities or usual daily activities, or substantially total disability for 180 days
Right to reimbursement

FLORIDA

Statute: Fla. Stat. §627.730 et seq.
Injury threshold: permanent injury or significant and permanent scarring or disfigurement
Right to reimbursement

GEORGIA

Statute: Ga. Code Ann. §33-34-1 et seq.
Monetary threshold: $500 in "reasonable" medical expenses
Injury threshold: more than ten days disability, any fracture, permanent disfigurement, permanent loss of a bodily function, or permanent partial or total loss of hearing or sight

HAWAII

Statute: Haw. Rev. Stat., title 17, §294-1 et seq.
Monetary threshold: medical expenses or damages in excess of benefits provided by no-fault policy
Injury threshold: significant permanent loss of use of part or function of body, or permanent and serious disfigurement resulting in mental or emotional distress

KANSAS

Statute: Kans. Stat. Ann., art. 31, §40-3101 et seq.
Monetary threshold: $500 medical expenses
Injury threshold: permanent disfigurement, any fracture of weightbearing bone or compound, comminuted, compressed or displaced fracture of any bone, permanent injury or permanent loss of a body function

KENTUCKY

Statute: Ky. Rev. Stat. Ann. §304.39-010 et seq.
Monetary threshold: $1,000 medical expenses
Injury threshold: permanent disfigurement, any fracture of weightbearing bone or compound, comminuted, compressed or displaced fracture of any bone, permanent injury or permanent loss of a body function

MARYLAND

Statute: Md. Code Ann., art. 48A, §538 et seq.
Add-on version
No right to reimbursement

MASSACHUSETTS

Statute: Mass. Gen. Laws Ann., ch. 90, §34(A) et seq.
Monetary threshold: $500 reasonable medical expenses
Injury threshold: permanent and serious disfigurement, fractured bone, or substantial loss of hearing or sight

MICHIGAN

Statute: Mich. Comp. Laws §500.3101 et seq.
Injury threshold: serious impairment of a body function or permanent and serious disfigurement
Note: Michigan's threshold for a liability claim is the toughest in the country, but Michigan's PIP benefits are the highest, with no limit on medical expenses paid and the highest and longest income loss benefits.
Right to reimbursement

MINNESOTA

Statute: Minn. Stat. §65B.41 et seq.
Monetary threshold: $4,000 in medical expenses
Injury threshold: 60 days disability, permanent injury or permanent disfigurement
• Claim against liable party allowed only for amounts not paid by PIP coverage

NEW JERSEY

Statute: N.J. Stat. Ann. §39:6A-1 et seq.
Injury threshold: some permanent disability or full disability of over 180 days, significant disfigurement or permanent loss of a bodily function

NEW YORK

Statute: N.Y. Ins. Laws §5101 et seq.
Injury threshold: "serious," which includes significant disfigurement, bone fracture, permanent limitation of use of body organ or member, significant limitation of use of body function or system, or substantially full disability for 90 days

NORTH DAKOTA

Statute: N.D. Cent. Code §26.1-41 et seq.
Monetary threshold: medical expenses over $2,500
Injury threshold: "serious," which includes serious and permanent disfigurement, disability of more than 60 days

OREGON

Statute: Or. Rev. Stat. §743.800 et seq.
Add-on version

PENNSYLVANIA

Statute: 25 Pa. Cons. Stat. §1701 et seq.
Add-on version
• Cannot recover medical expenses or income loss from liable party which were already paid under PIP benefits

SOUTH CAROLINA

Statute: S.C. Code Ann. §56-11-110 et seq.
Add-on version

SOUTH DAKOTA

Statute: S.D. Comp. Laws Ann. §58-23-6 et seq.
Add-on version

TEXAS

Statute: Tex. Ins. Code Ann. §5.06-3 et seq.
Add-on version

UTAH

Statute: Utah Code Ann. §31A-22-301 et seq.
Monetary threshold: medical expenses over $1,000
Injury threshold: bone fracture, permanent disability or permanent disfigurement

VIRGINIA

Statute: Virg. Code §38.2-2201 et seq.
Add-on version

How Much Is
Your Claim Worth?

This chapter explains the formula insurance companies use to arrive at a fair amount of compensation for accident injuries.

- If you have been injured, read Sections A, B, C and F to understand the damages formula and how factors in your accident increase or decrease the compensation you may get. Section G contains a number of examples of specific injuries—and explanations of how damages would be calculated for each.

- If your injuries caused you to lose time from work or miss out on a social or business opportunity, read Section D.

- If your property—a car or its contents, your clothing or other personal belongings—was damaged or destroyed in the accident, read Section E.

You may have heard that insurance companies use a secret mathematical formula to figure out how much compensation should be paid to someone for accident injuries. The formula part is true, but it certainly isn't secret. And the formula doesn't actually determine how much compensation someone receives. It is just a device insurance adjusters use to *begin* the process of figuring out how much a claim is worth. A final determination about compensation is not made until several other facts are considered.

This chapter explains how insurance adjusters use the compensation formula and how they combine it with other facts to arrive at a figure they are willing to pay for a personal injury claim. Once you understand how the compensation formula works, you will be able to negotiate confidently for a final settlement figure within the same range as an attorney would have gotten for you. And you will have saved the cost of paying the attorney.

In general, a person liable for an accident—and therefore his or her liability insurance company—must pay an injured person for:

- medical care and related expenses
- missed work time
- pain and other physical suffering
- permanent physical disability or disfigurement
- loss of family, social and educational experiences, and
- emotional damages resulting from any of the above.

While it is usually simple to add up the money spent and money lost, there is no precise way to put a dollar figure on pain and suffering, and on missed experiences and lost opportunities. That's where the damages formula comes in.

A. The Damages Formula

At the beginning of negotiations on a claim, an insurance adjuster will add up the total medical expenses related to the injury. These expenses are referred to as "the medical special damages" or simply "specials." As a way to begin figuring out how much to compensate the injured person for pain and suffering, permanent disability and emotional damages —together called "general damages"—the insurance adjuster will multiply the amount of special damages by about one-and-a-half times when the injuries are relatively minor, and up to five times when the injuries are particularly painful, serious or long-lasting. After that amount is arrived at, the adjuster will then add on any income you have lost as a result of your injuries.

That total—medical specials multiplied by 1.5 to 5, then added to lost income—becomes the starting number from which negotiations begin to arrive at the final amount of compensation paid on the claim.

Example *Mary was injured in an auto accident. Her medical specials—the cost of her medical treatment—amounted to $600. There were no permanent effects from her injuries. Applying the damages formula to her claim, an insurance adjuster would begin with a figure of between $900 and $3,000 (1.5 to 5 x $600). This is added to Mary's lost income of $400 to get the figure from which negotiations will begin as compensation for Mary's injuries.*

Once this figure is arrived at, the adjuster would then factor in all the other variables discussed in this chapter (see Section F) to determine how much total compensation the insurance company was willing to pay Mary for her injuries.

1. Insurance Adjusters Don't Reveal Their Formula

During negotiations on an insurance claim, adjusters usually will not tell you what formula they use to arrive at how much they believe a claim is worth, or even that they are using any formula at all. They are following a basic rule of negotiations: Do not let the other side know how or what you are thinking. Since the insurance adjusters won't let you know what formula they are using, it's probably a good idea not to let them know your thinking, either.

2. The Deciding Factor: Which End Is Up?

There are two important points to remember about a damages formula. One is that the figure arrived at by multiplying special damages is only the starting point for reaching a final settlement amount. After this starting point is reached, other facts about the accident and your injuries come into play. (See Section F.) The second point is that since the starting

formula could be anywhere between one-and-a-half to five times specials, it can produce considerably different numbers depending on which end of this multiplier spectrum is applied to your claim.

Several things determine which end of the damages formula to apply to the special damages in your claim.
- The more painful the type of injury you suffered, the higher the end of the formula you use.
- The more invasive and longer-lasting your medical treatment, the higher the formula.
- The more obvious the medical evidence of your injury, the higher the formula.
- The longer the recovery period from your injuries, the higher the formula.
- The more serious and visible any permanent effect of your injury, the higher the formula.

The rest of this chapter explains how these considerations raise or lower the numbers you plug into a damages formula, as well as the things which can increase or decrease your compensation once the formula has been arrived at. At the end of the chapter are a number of examples of accident injury situations with descriptions of the accidents, injuries, treatments and expenses, plus explanations of how damages in those cases would be calculated.

B. How Injuries Affect Compensation

As mentioned above, the amount you have spent on medical bills while having your injuries diagnosed and treated is referred to by insurance adjusters as medical special damages, or simply medical specials. Medical specials are part of the damages formula used to figure out total damages. The amount that the specials are multiplied by—from one-and-a-half to five—depends on: the injuries you have suffered, the type of medical treatment you receive and the kind of medical provider from whom you receive treatment.

1. Types of Injuries

The difficult part of figuring out compensation for someone injured in an accident is how to put a dollar value on pain and suffering. Since that is a large part of what the damages formula attempts to do, it stands to reason that the more painful the injury, the higher the multiplying number which gets plugged into the formula. And the way insurance companies begin looking at pain and suffering is by connecting types of injuries with levels of pain.

Of course, this is not very scientific. A sprained ankle can sometimes be more painful and persistent than a cracked ankle bone. Still, insurance adjusters use the type of injury as a starting place in deciding what numbers to plug into the damages formula. If your injury fits into one of the more serious injury categories described below, this typecasting can work to your advantage. If your injury is normally typecast as less serious, however, then you have to show through other means that your injury did indeed cause significant pain and suffering. (See Section C.)

The accident insurance adjusting business divides injuries into two main categories:

1. soft tissue injury, of which the major evidence is the description of discomfort by the patient, and
2. "hard" injury, which is an injury that can be specifically observed through medical examination.

a. Soft injuries

Injuries such as a sprained or strained back, neck, knee or ankle are referred to as soft tissue injuries because they involve only muscles and other soft connective tissue. Insurance companies regard them as less serious than hard injuries and assign to them a damages formula multiplier of only one-and-a-half to three times specials. Insurers reason that soft tissue injuries are usually not permanent or dangerous regardless of how painful they may be. And insurance companies also know that, should a claim ever get to court, it would be difficult for an injured person to prove clearly what the soft tissue injuries were.

b. Hard injuries

Hard injuries are considered more serious and are awarded higher damages—four or five times specials—than soft tissue injuries. So if you can point to anything in your medical records identifying an injury actually observed by the doctor, by X-ray or by other test, or describing the injury as something other than a strain or sprain (a compressed or pinched nerve, for example, or a joint separation), the value of your claim for damages goes up. Likewise, an injury requiring any physical repair or intrusive examination by a doctor, from stitching a wound to setting a bone to arthroscopic examination of a joint, increases the value of your case regardless of all other considerations.

Categories of hard injuries include:

Broken bones   If X-rays show that any bone has suffered even a minor break, including a chip or crack, the numbers in your case will immediately move higher. Of course, insurance adjusters are not robots who simply see "broken bone" and then automatically raise the damage formula. They do distinguish between less and more serious breaks. If the break is a fine crack in a tiny bone, for example, and does not require any treatment or affect the way you go about your daily life, the broken bone will not raise the damages formula as much as a more substantial, life-disrupting break which may have permanent consequences. As with all other injuries, the more serious you can show the break to be, the higher you move up the compensation ladder.

Example 1 *Werner tripped and fell over a hose. At the emergency room, doctors found a small crack in his wrist. The bone required no cast, Werner required no treatment and he lost no time from work.*

Because they found a break, the multiplier in Werner's damages formula would go up from one-and-a-

half times medical specials to perhaps three times, but because it involved no treatment, no substantial recovery time and no permanent effects, it probably would not go any higher than that.

Example 2 *Alicia tripped an fell on a broken stair. Her wrist was fractured badly enough to require a cast for six weeks, another four weeks of physical therapy and eight more weeks of only light use before it returned to normal.*

Because the break required a cast and the time of recovery was relatively long, the damages formula applied to Alicia's injury would probably be about five times medical specials.

Head injuries Anytime someone suffers a head injury, there is the possibility that the effects of the injury will be much longer-lasting than is obvious at first. What seems like a simple concussion from which you quickly recover can later turn into months or years of recurring headaches and dizziness. And this kind of recurring long-term head injury often does not appear in the original diagnosis because its causes can only be detected by very sophisticated and expensive testing.

Insurance adjusters know that head injuries can last a long time and can reoccur after recovery seems to be complete. A head injury not only increases how much the claim is worth, often it also speeds up the negotiation process because an adjuster wants to settle the claim before greater head injury-related medical bills are incurred.

If you suffered any kind of head injury, check your medical records for any notation of the injury: concussion, a period of unconsciousness—however brief—dizziness, disorientation, nausea. Make specific mention of it in your claim even if other injuries seem more serious. And if you have any long-term effects such as continuing headaches or dizziness, report them to your doctor and emphasize in your claim that you are still suffering from the effects of your head injury.

Some Injuries Deserve Special Mention

Anytime you suffer an injury to a joint, there is the possibility of future arthritic problems in the joint. When a joint is injured, blood usually collects there and eventually calcifies, creating a hard and rough surface in the joint which can later—often not until years later—cause pain and difficulty in movement. In your medical records, however, doctors do not normally mention such potential arthritic changes because it is not usually possible to predict whether such changes will later prove troublesome.

If you suffer a joint injury, ask your doctor whether future arthritic change is a possibility. If the doctor makes a note of the possibility in your medical records, it will give you more ammunition in your claim for damages.

Whether or not the possibility of arthritic change appears in your medical records, make sure specifically to mention this possibility in your claim for damages to the insurance company. Such a reminder helps make the insurance adjuster take your injury more seriously, and may also help by showing the adjuster that you are organized and have done your medical homework.

Separations, dislocations and ligament or cartilage tears
Whenever a doctor describes your injury with a name other than a sprain, strain or bruise, the injury is considered more serious—that is, given a higher multiplier in the damages formula. Joint dislocation or separation gives the impression of great pain and delicate recovery whether or not it was actually more serious than something called a sprain. The same

thing is true for the word "torn" for a ligament or cartilage. A tear is considered more serious than a stretch or strain or sprain, even though the treatment and healing time may be exactly the same.

Wounds If your injuries include any gash, tear or cut serious enough to require treatment, it may slightly increase the value of your claim. If the treatment included stitching the wound, the value of your claim goes up slightly more. And if the wound leaves a scar which may be permanent, the value of the case may go up significantly. (See Section C.)

Spinal disc or vertebrae injury Movement or displacement of a spinal disc or of the space between vertebrae sounds more serious than strained neck or back—and insurance adjusters often respond with higher compensation to such specific descriptions of back or neck injuries than to a general "strained back" description, even if it is exactly the same injury. Emergency rooms and orthopedists usually take X-rays of the area of the spine—lumbar or lumbosacral (lower), thoracic (middle) or cervical (upper)—in which an injured person complains of pain. Those S-rays may reveal some slight abnormality either in a disc or in the space between vertebrae which will be described by reference to the number of the vertebrae in question, such as "slight narrowing in L4-L5 spacing" or "narrowing of L5-S1."

If you find any mention in your medical records of such abnormality in a numbered vertebra, repeat that diagnosis word-for-word in your negotiations with the insurance company as a way of demonstrating the seriousness of your injury, regardless of how much or how little treatment you received.

2. Nature and Extent of Medical Expenses

According to insurance adjusters, not all medical services were created equal. Both the nature and the duration of a medical service can affect how it is viewed by insurance companies, as can the type of medical person or facility providing the service.

Some of the variables are discussed here.

Treatment versus diagnosis Before you can be treated for an injury, medical personnel have to diagnose itIn many cases, the diagnostic process is relatively quick, and the charge for it amounts to a small part of your medical bills, as compared with the cost of treatment. In such cases, insurance companies do not usually bother to make any distinction between diagnosis and treatment. They lump all your medical bills together into one medical specials amount.

Sometimes, though, doctors will put a person through many tests and examinations simply trying to diagnose what is wrong, running up large medical bills in the process. If most of the medical bills are for diagnosis only, and the injury winds up requiring little treatment, an insurance adjuster might not view the total medical specials as accurately reflecting the injured person's pain and suffering. Consequently, the adjuster might use a lower multiplier for those medical bills in arriving at the appropriate range of damages.

M.D.s and hospitals versus non-M.D.s   One of the insurance industry's strong prejudices is in favor of mainstream Western treatment by physicians, hospitals and medical clinics—and against physical therapy, chiropracty, acupuncture and other non-mainstream medicine. Any medical bill you have incurred at the hands or machines of a medical doctor, hospital or medical clinic, no matter how outrageously expensive, will be considered legitimate by almost any insurance adjuster and will usually be given a high multiplier in the damages formula. The often much less costly but equally effective treatments of non-physician medical providers, on the other hand, are often multiplied by lower numbers.

For example, in accidental injury claims, physical therapy is a common treatment, yet it is generally considered to be lower in the pecking order than other kinds of medical treatment. If you receive a few weeks of physical therapy prescribed and administered by your doctor's office, an insurance adjuster may lump it in with other medical specials. But if you have physical therapy for months and the therapy accounts for the largest part of your medical bills by far, the insurance adjuster is likely to use a lower multiplier when fitting your medical specials into the damages formula.

Also, where you receive physical therapy may affect how the insurance company views it. If your doctor prescribes physical therapy but you receive the actual treatment outside the doctor's office and beyond the doctor's control, the insurance adjuster

might discount the physical therapy bills because insurance companies know that when left to their own devices, physical therapists tend to treat patients endlessly. And if you seek physical therapy independently, without it having been recommended or prescribed by your physician, an insurance adjuster is likely to discount it even more.

Treatments by chiropractors, acupuncturists, acupressurists, herbalists, massage therapists and other non-physician healers   Unless bestowed with the rare blessing of a doctor's prescription, other non-traditional treatments are given even less weight than physical therapy. This does not mean that you cannot be reimbursed at all by the liable person's insurance company for these treatments. But it does mean that the insurance adjuster handling your claim will not count these expenses very highly when deciding how to multiply medical specials within the damages formula. Of course, your primary concern should be to obtain the kind of medical care with which you are most comfortable. But you should be aware that if you choose non-doctor services, an insurance company is likely to compensate you at a lower rate.

Duration of treatment   Logic says that a long period of medical treatment means injuries requiring a long period to heal, and that translates to a high degree of pain and suffering. So, if you undergo a long period of treatment, you can argue to an insurance adjuster that the long treatment was evidence of the seriousness of the injury. (See Chapter 6, Section B, and Chapter 7.)

However, insurance adjusters are suspicious of physical therapists and chiropractors, believing that they often give treatment longer than necessary to keep their money rolling in. So, if you have had a long period of physical therapy or chiropractic treatments, an insurance adjuster is not nearly as likely to consider that as good evidence of the seriousness of your injury than if you had received a long period of treatment from a physician or medical clinic.

C. Demonstrating Pain and Suffering

The type of injury you suffer and the nature and duration of your treatment are the two basic indicators to an insurance company of the degree of pain and suffering you have endured. This section discusses some additional things you can point out to raise an insurance adjuster's awareness of your pain and suffering caused by the accident.

1. Medication

The fact that you have been prescribed medication to relieve pain, inflammation or any other injury symptoms may influence an insurance adjuster that your injuries were serious. The stronger the medication and the longer it is prescribed, the greater its influence on your settlement. This is not a very precise measure, of course. Some doctors prescribe medication much more readily than others. And some patients request medication at a certain level of pain while others don't want it or need it. But insurance adjusters are always looking for something concrete indicating that a doctor thought an injury was painful—and a medication prescription serves that purpose.

2. Length of Recovery

To an insurance company, the longer recovery period, the greater an injured person's pain and suffering. The most effective way to let an insurance adjuster know how long your recovery takes is to have that fact indicated in your medical records. Sometimes that task is easy because your doctor has made a notation in your medical chart that recovery is expected to take a certain number of weeks or months, or that you should not engage in certain activities for a certain amount of time.

In many cases, however, the only way your actual recovery time makes it into your medical records is if you report your progress, or lack of it, to the doctor. Many of us get tired of going to the doctor when we know all the doctor will do is nod, write something down, tell us to come back if things don't get better . . . and then send a bill.

But going to your doctor to report on your recovery can be very important to your claim for two reasons. First, the mere fact that your records show a doctor visit four, six or twelve weeks after an accident indicates that your injury required ongoing attention. And second, when you visit your doctor and report continuing pain, discomfort, stiffness or immobility, that specific continuing problem will be noted in the medical records you will later send to the insurance company as part of your claim. (See Chapter 6.) Remarkably, an insurance adjuster will accept your report of pain and discomfort as true if the doctor writes it down, but the adjuster may discount the very same report of pain and discomfort made during the course of your claim if it was not earlier reported to the doctor.

3. Residual or Permanent Injury

If you can show that an injury you suffered in an accident has left any long-lasting or permanent effect—referred to as a "residual injury"—such as scarring or back or joint stiffness, the amount of your damages award can go up significantly. The simple and obvious reason that even a relatively small residual disability or disfigurement can greatly increase your award is that you will suffer from it over a long time. And naturally, the more serious the effect on your life—work, home or recreation—the higher your damages go.

Scars A common permanent residual injury is scarring, from the original injury or from medical repairs. Particularly large and obvious scarring can mean quite a lot in damages, both because of the cosmetic embarrassment it causes and because scar tissue can make an area of flesh less flexible. If there is scarring at any joint or in any other area of the body which flexes—such as the webbing of fingers or toes—it might cause a permanent even though slight loss of mobility, and so might justify higher damages.

The damages for disfigurement go up if the scarred part of the body is normally visible. Scars usually covered by clothes are not considered as important unless they are large enough to cause you embarrassment in your love life or when you want to wear a bathing suit. Scars visible on hands and arms can be considered important if they are large enough that you feel the need to keep them hidden. And any scar on the face and neck—even if small—always increases damages.

Scarring is also one of the few areas in which women sometimes benefit by our society's stubbornly resistant sexism. A woman who receives a permanent scar is normally considered to have been damaged by it far more than a man with an identical scar. Unfortunately, ageism may rear its ugly head here, too. A young single woman is often compensated more for scars than an older married woman, on the assumption that a facial scar may more strongly affect a young single woman's social life. Insurance adjusters are usually socially aware enough to know that they should not openly discuss these kinds of discriminations, especially not directly with the injured person. Nonetheless, you should be aware that these societal prejudices do affect the settlement judgment of most adjusters.

One way to demonstrate to an insurance company how much your scarring is worth is to obtain a medical opinion about the cost of having the scar removed or repaired. Ask your doctor to refer you to a plastic surgeon for an opinion about whether your scar could be removed, and specifically ask how much such a procedure would cost. You can then include both the cost of the examination by the plastic surgeon and the potential cost of repair in the medical costs you use to figure how much your case is worth. Specifically, include the cost of scar removal—whether or not you will actually undergo such a procedure—in your demand letter to the insurance company. (See Chapter 6, Sections B2 and B4.)

Consult a Lawyer If You Suffer Permanent Injury

If you have suffered any injury which is likely to be permanent—a substantial visible scar, a limp, bad back or other disability—you may have a right to very high damages which are beyond the scope of the damages formula discussed in this book. This is particularly true if you may need future medical treatment to cope with your injury.

In such cases, it may be wise to consult with a lawyer who specializes in personal injury cases to get an opinion about whether your permanent injury entitles you to high damages. If the lawyer you consult convinces you that your permanent injury may entitle you to compensation much higher than the range you have calculated by using the formula discussed in this chapter, consider letting him or her, or some other experienced personal injury lawyer, handle your claim for you. (See Chapter 9, Section B.) If the lawyer convinces you that your permanent injury does not justify damages beyond the normal formula range, you can continue to handle the claim yourself.

Back or joint injuries   In general, if you have an injury to a disc in the spine, or a narrowing, displacement or other damage to a vertebra, or a dislocation, ligament or cartilage injury to any joint, you will most likely suffer some permanent effect, even if slight. The pain may subside and the injury may stabilize or "resolve" as the doctors say, but there is a medical likelihood that some pain, discomfort or lack of mobility will continue or will reoccur as you get older.

If you have had such an injury, part of your claim for damages should be for permanent injury and therefore higher compensation. And if you can get your doctor to mention in your medical records the possibility of some permanent or residual effect,you will have documented support for your claim. The simplest way to get your doctor to make a notation about permanent effects is to ask.

Toward the last part of your treatment, ask your doctor's opinion about whether there is a likelihood—doctors rarely speak in anything more definite than "likelihoods"—that you may have recurring or degenerative (showing up later in life) problems as a result of your injuries. If the answer is yes, ask that the doctor note it in your medical records. And if the doctor asks why you want it noted, there is no reason not to say that you want it for an insurance claim you are filing against the person who caused your accident.

Even if your doctor does not note the likelihood of permanent problems, you are still permitted to raise the possibility in your claim to the insurance company, just as you would mention future problems with any injury to a joint.

4. Physical and Emotional Distress

It is not only pain that gives you a right to be compensated, but also any other kind of physical discomfort. Loss of sleep, trouble eating or digesting, stomach upset and the side effects of medication are just some of the physical miseries in addition to pain for which you have a right to be compensated.

Emotional difficulties, too, can be compensated. Physical injuries can cause stress, embarrassment, depression or strains on family relationships—for example, the inability to take care of children, anxiety over the effects of an accident on an unborn child or interference with sexual relations.

As with pain, however, this other physical or emotional suffering can be difficult to demonstrate. Sometimes the discomforts or disruptions are

---

The Proof Is Up to You

Many of the things that can establish the amount of pain and suffering you have experienced and will continue to experience can best be shown if you take charge of documenting them.

If you have pain or discomfort and are being treated by a physician, make sure you fully report it to the physician so that it will be noted in your medical records.

If you believe you need medication to control your pain or discomfort, don't be too brave or too shy or too stubborn to ask for it. You can always choose the dosage once you have it.

If you are suffering continued pain or discomfort but do not have any further medical appointments scheduled, consider scheduling one. It makes good medical sense, and it will document your continued problems.

If your pain or discomfort are interfering with your ability to lead your normal life, write down daily any activities you are unable to do or that you are having difficulty doing because of your injuries.

If your injuries can be seen—wounds, swelling, discoloration—photograph them regularly and indicate in each photograph the date on which it is taken.

---

obvious. If you have a broken arm, you cannot easily care for your small children; if you have a slipped disc in your back, sleeping is going to be a problem. An effective way to show you've suffered physical discomfort is to report it to your doctor, who will then note it in your medical file which you will eventually show to the insurance adjuster handling your claim. Insurance adjusters more readily accept as true something which appears in a medical record than something which you report directly to the insurance adjuster.

If your discomfort or emotional distress is serious enough that you have to seek assistance from someone other than the doctor treating your original injury—a dietician for eating problems, a psychologist or other therapist to cope with pain or stress—these expenses also become part of your medical special damages, and the records of the person assisting you can serve as proof of the problem.

5. Life Disruption

Accident injuries can cause a number of unfortunate results which cannot easily be assigned dollar values but which amount to very real and considerable losses. And since money is the only way these losses can be compensated, they must be figured into your damages compensation. Once again, the damages formula is the way this figuring is done.

Any substantial loss of time, opportunities, pleasures or effort can be compensated by raising the multiplier used in the formula used to arrive at your general damages, just as the multiplier goes up if you have a serious, long-term or permanent injury. For example, a claim based on a soft-tissue injury which might have a multiplier of one and a-half times medical specials could go up to two or three times specials because the injuries caused you to miss a planned vacation or lose out on a special event.

There is no restriction on the types of non-monetary losses that can increase your general damages. Anything important to you that you missed because of your injuries can be included in a claim for compensation. Here are some of the more common kinds of non-monetary losses for which compensation is paid:

Missed school or training   If your injuries have caused you to miss school or training, or studying for school or training, you will have to make that time up at some point. The difficulty you experience in making up that missed time—perhaps you will have to give up a number of evenings and weekends to catch up, or perhaps you will lose an entire semester of school—will determine how significantly your general damages should be increased.

Missed vacation or recreation   If your injuries have caused you to cancel a vacation, family visit or other trip or event, you are entitled to extra compensation because of it. Similarly, if you have had to give up your regular recreation activities for an extended time—if you are a runner or hiker or other exerciser who has been unable to exercise; someone who regularly takes dance class but has been unable to for some time after an accident—you are entitled to compensation for that loss.

Canceled special event   If your injuries made it impossible for you to attend an important or personally meaningful event such as a wedding, funeral, graduation, conference or reunion, you are entitled to compensation for the loss. Of course, in order to have an insurance adjuster take your claim for compensation seriously, it must have been a one-time event which will not be repeated.

D. Lost Income

You are entitled to reimbursement from the person responsible for an accident for any income you have lost because of the accident or your injuries. This includes both income lost because of time spent unable to work and time missed because you were undergoing treatment for your injuries. The right to be reimbursed applies whether you have a full-time or part-time job, regular or occasional employment, an hourly wage or weekly or monthly salary, or you are self-employed.

Income loss is not a part of the amount multiplied in the formula applied to special damages, but is added on after the multiplied amount has been arrived at.

Example *After an accident, your medical expenses total $400, and your income loss is $500. Because your injury was soft tissue only, a formula of two times specials is applied. Only your medical expenses of $400 would be multiplied by two, not your $500 income loss. Instead, the $500 income loss would be added on to the multiplied total. In this example, the formula would be 2 x $400 = $800, plus $500 lost income, for a formula total of $1,300.*

This total only begins negotiations, and it can go up or down depending on the facts discussed in Section F.

1. Sick Leave or Vacation Pay Is Irrelevant

The fact that you were able to take sick leave or vacation pay for the time you missed, and therefore did not directly lose income, does not matter. You were entitled to use that sick leave or vacation time for other periods when you might have needed or wanted it, and therefore using up sick leave or vacation pay is considered the same as losing the pay itself.

To be reimbursed for lost income, you must be able to show two things:
- the time you missed from work because of your accident
- how much money you would have made during the time you missed.

(See Chapter 6, Section A3 for a discussion of how to demonstrate these losses.)

2. Lost Opportunities

In addition to time lost from work, you are entitled to be reimbursed for work opportunities you lost because of the accident and your injuries. Of course, proving that a lost opportunity such as a job interview or a scheduled sales meeting translates as lost income to you is more difficult than actual lost work hours. (See Chapter 6, Section A3.)

But even if you cannot point to specific dollar amounts you lost, the fact that an insurance adjuster knows that lost potential income is a valid part of your claim will move your final compensation amount upward. How much your final compensation is raised will depend on how strong your proof is of lost income opportunity, and how much that lost opportunity might have cost you.

E. Property Damage

If someone is liable to you for your personal injuries, they are also liable for any damage they caused to your property in the same accident. Property damage occurs most frequently in vehicle accidents, not only to the vehicle itself but also to its contents. Anything you were carrying in the car or any equipment you were wearing while riding a cycle at the time of the accident should be included in a property damage claim.

But property damage can occur in other types of accidents as well—the clothes, watch or jewelry you are wearing or any object you happen to be carrying may be damaged. To claim compensation for damaged or destroyed property, you must be able to show that the property was actually damaged and the property damage figure is then included in your demand for compensation, if it has not been settled earlier with an insurance company. Property damage claims are not a part of the damages formula but, like lost income, are added onto the total after the formula has been applied.

1. Figuring the Value of Property Damage

You are permitted to claim the cost of repair for any item damaged in an accident, but only up to the actual cash value (ACV) of the property. Actual cash value is another label for current market value, or what someone would reasonably pay for the used property. However, it does not mean replacement value, or the cost of buying an identical new item. You often hear that a damaged car is a "total" or "total loss." A total refers to damage of such an extent that the cost of repairing the car would exceed its ACV. In the case of a total, an insurance company is required to pay you only the vehicle's ACV. The same thing is true of any other item when the cost to repair it would be higher than its ACV.

In addition to the value of destroyed property and the cost of repairing damaged property, a person liable for your accident may also be responsible for the reasonable cost of temporary replacement property. This includes a rental car or other transportation expenses if your car cannot be driven—and any other property you need to use until your own property is repaired or replaced. The liable person is also responsible for vehicle towing and storage costs. And if you lose work not because of your injuries but because of damage to or destruction of a vehicle, equipment or other work-related property, your property damage claim can include all income lost as a result of that property damage.

Example *In an auto accident, your car is out of commission for ten days while you get estimates and have it repaired. The towing and storage bill was $140 and the cost of repairs was $1,200. While the car was unavailable, you rented a car for $26 per day, using the rental car both for work and for daily non-work transportation.*

Also damaged in the collision was the lap-top computer you had in the trunk of your car and which you use for work. You had the computer checked out for repair, which cost $75, but it turned out the computer was not salvageable. You checked the newspaper classified ads for a replacement computer of the same model and age, and found one for $1,200 and another for $1,300. The total property damages from this accident were:

auto towing & storage	$ 140
auto repair	1,200
rental car	260
computer estimate	75
computer value (ACV)	1,250
TOTAL	$2,925

2. Using Your Own Auto Collision Coverage

If you have had an accident with a hit-and-run or uninsured motorist, the only place you can turn for compensation for your property damage is to the collision coverage of your own automobile policy. Although the process of claiming property damage under your own collision coverage is basically the same as claiming under the liable person's insurance, there are usually tighter rules about how to get estimates and where to get repairs—all of which are spelled out in your policy. (See Chapter 6, Section A4.)

F. Arriving at a Final Compensation Figure

Now that you know how the damages formula can be applied to your injuries, and how lost income and property damage are added to the damage formula total, you are more than half-way home to figuring out the total compensation value of your claim. But the remaining parts of figuring out the value of your claim are also important if you want to settle your case for the full amount you are entitled to—without wasting a lot of time and energy trying to obtain compensation that is unrealistically high.

Basically, the other elements in deciding how much your claim is worth boil down to one thing: how the insurance company believes a jury would decide your claim if it were to wind up in court. And in measuring its chances in court, the insurance company has to figure in its cost of putting up a legal fight, on top of what a jury might award you, compared with the amount your claim could be settled for without going to court.

1. Assigning Fault

The extent each person is at fault is the most important factor affecting how much of the total arrived at by using the damages formula you are likely to receive. The damages formula tells you how much your injuries *might be* worth, but only after you figure in the question of fault do you know how much your claim is *actually* worth—that is, how much an insurance company will pay you.

Example   *The cracked wrist bone you suffer in a slip and fall results in $1,000 in medical specials, but you suffer no permanent injury. Applying the damages formula to your injuries might result in a figure of between $3,500 and $5,000, depending on all the other facts previously discussed in this chapter.*

If your accident was clearly and completely someone else's fault—your car was stopped at a light when someone ran into you from behind—then your claim is likely to be worth the full amount of the formula total, that is, between $3,500 and $5,000.

If, on the other hand, the accident was partly your fault, the amount your claim is worth would be reduced by the degree you were to blame—expressed in "percentage" of fault. (See Chapter 2, Section A3.) So, if you were 25% at fault for the accident, your claim would be reduced by 25% from a $3,500 to $5,000 range to a range of $2,650 to $3,750.

If it appeared that you were mostly at fault, the value of your claim would be greatly reduced, perhaps to nothing but more likely to a very small amount referred to as "nuisance value." (See Section 2, below.)

Of course, as discussed, determining fault for an accident is not an exact science. But in most claims, both you and the insurance adjuster will at least have a good idea whether the insured person was entirely at fault, you were a little at fault or you were a lot at fault. And whatever that rough percentage of your comparative fault might be—10%, 50%, 75%—is the amount by which the damages formula total will be reduced to arrive at a final claim figure. (See Section G, below, for examples of how degrees of fault are applied in different accident situations.)

In claims negotiations, some insurance adjusters will discuss comparative negligence in terms of specific percentages. Others will discuss who was at fault, or who was negligent, or who violated what

rules or laws, but they will never actually put a percentage figure on anyone's degree of fault. Don't worry about it either way. Although it may be useful for you to begin the negotiations by using a specific comparative fault percentage (see Chapter 6, Section B), it doesn't matter how the insurance adjuster phrases things. Just be aware that how much you appear to have been at fault is the crucial element in an insurance adjuster's decision about how much to offer you as a settlement for your injuries.

2.   The Intangibles

In almost every claim there is at least one thing, in addition to the basic facts of the accident and of your injuries, which might push your settlement toward the higher end of the range of compensation. Usually you will never know whether one of these "intangible" factors has actually increased your settlement. But emphasizing these intangible factors in negotiations will at least increase the odds that you will receive as much as possible out of your claim.

a.   Your effectiveness as a witness

One of the most important factors in an insurance adjuster's decision about what your claim is worth is how convincing you are about the accident, your injuries and your other damages. An insurance adjuster is more likely to be sympathetic to your claim if he or she believes you are giving an accurate picture of the accident and your injuries. If you are organized and understand how the claims system works, the insurance adjuster will realize you are unlikely to settle the case for less than it is worth. And, the insurance adjuster knows that if you are both organized and believable, a jury is more likely to give you a substantial award if your claim ever went to court.

b.   An unfavorable insured

There may be something about the person who caused the accident that would increase the likelihood that a jury would favor your story over that person's, or would consider the accident or your injuries in a light more favorable to you. And if an insurance adjuster knows that a jury is likely to award higher or lower damages, then the adjuster is likely to increase or decrease your settlement.

For example, if you have had a traffic accident with someone who was driving too fast in a souped-up car, a jury is more likely to be sympathetic to you than to the other driver. The insurance adjuster knows that. And if you show the insurance adjuster that you know it, too—a specific mention of those circumstances in your negotiations would show it—you may get a faster and easier settlement of your claim. (See Chapter 6, Section B, and Chapter 7.)

Other examples may work either for or against you. If your injury is the fault of a big company or the employee of a big company, chances are a jury would favor you as "the little person." On the other hand, settlement awards against local government entities are usually lower because adjusters for the city or county know that juries do not like to spend taxpayer dollars in high damage awards.

c.   Witnesses

Having one or more witnesses to corroborate your version of the accident, or to support your contentions about how much your injuries have interfered with your life, can increase your settlement. A witness takes your claim out of the "my word against yours" category.

d.   Dramatic advantage

Sometimes something that did not actually affect the amount of fault in an accident or worsen your injuries can increase your settlement because it works emotionally in your favor. If, for example, a police report or a witness says that a person involved in the accident had alcohol on his breath, the odds of your getting a higher settlement go up even though you cannot prove the person was legally intoxicated. Similarly, your seriously damaged car—pictures can be very effective—supports the idea that you were seriously injured even though there might not be any direct relationship between how damaged the car was and how damaged you were.

Another example of a dramatic issue which could increase a settlement is pregnancy. Even if there is no evidence that a fetus has been injured in an accident, and upon delivery it appears that the baby suffered no ill effects, a parent's fear of possible injury can be worth a considerable increase in your settlement. Likewise, the emotional distress caused to you and your small child if the child was riding in the car with you is something to emphasize in your claim for compensation.

Similarly, if you are an older person and the accident or your injuries have made you fearful of certain situations or concerned about the injured part of your body, you may be able to collect a higher damage award even though there is no medical evidence of permanent injury.

e.   Your patience

Because negotiations about a settlement can take time, your ability to be patient and wait for the best possible offer might affect how much you will receive. Insurance adjusters never immediately offer the full amount they are actually prepared to pay. (See Chapter 7, Section B.) If you are in a hurry to get your settlement, you might settle for less than you could have gotten if you had been willing to play out your hand as far as it would go.

While patience is paramount, you must also be wary of the time limits within which you must file a lawsuit should your negotiations prove unsuccessful. (See Chapter 7, Section E.)

3. Nuisance Value

Insurance adjusters think some claims are worth nothing at all. This may be because the person making the claim was completely at fault, or that someone other than the insured person was completely at fault, or that the claimant's injuries were not caused by the accident, or that the claimant had no real injuries at all. In each of these situations, an insurance adjuster may at first completely deny the injured person's claim, saying that the insurance company will not pay any compensation.

In many cases, though, an insurance adjuster's initial refusal to make any settlement will eventually turn into an offer to settle the case for a small amount known as "nuisance value." The term comes from the insurance company's idea that it is better to pay a little bit of money than to have to deal with the nuisance of a claim that will not go away. Insurance adjusters won't usually use the term nuisance value, but when they make a very low offer bearing no relation to the damages formula, that's what they're doing.

As with all other categories in accident settlements, there is no fixed amount for a nuisance value settlement. In claims with medical bills under a thousand dollars, a nuisance value settlement is often equal to the amount of the medical bills—or even half of medical bills—with nothing for income loss, pain and suffering, general damages or anything else.

Where the person filing the claim is not able to show any real injuries—small medical bills, soft tissue injury that no doctor has been able to diagnose—an insurance adjuster will often make a nuisance value offer of $500 or $750. On the other hand, if there are medical bills and lost income in the thousands of dollars, and a serious, painful or permanent injury, all of which would cause the damages formula to come out with a figure of as much as $10,000 to $15,000, a nuisance value settlement could be $2,000 to $3,000 dollars.

Even Nuisance Value Is Negotiable

Even when all you will get out of a claim is its nuisance value, remember that any offer of settlement is negotiable. So if you are forced by the circumstances of your accident to settle for some nuisance value amount, you don't have to take the first amount offered. Nuisance value figures probably won't change too much by bargaining, but if you can get an adjuster to move from $500 to $1,000, for example, it certainly will have been worth that extra phone call or two of negotiation.

G. Examples of How Much Different Claims Are Worth

Several different situations are described below—different accidents, injuries, medical treatments, intangibles—with an explanation of what the appropriate range of settlement amounts might be in each one.

These examples show how several different factors in any one accident operate together to determine a final compensation amount. Even if a particular example does not apply directly to your circumstances, reading through each of them can help you understand how the different elements in your claim will determine how much it is worth.

1.   Auto accident, short-term soft tissue injury, extra damages for missed special event

A car hits Olly's car from behind at a stop sign. Olly's neck snaps forward, but he is otherwise unhurt.

Olly develops a headache and stiff neck. He is examined, X-rayed, put in a cervical collar and told to stay in bed until he can move around comfortably.

Olly misses three days work, as well as his close friend's 50th birthday party in a city a couple of hundred miles away.

The next week, Olly returns to work. His doctor now says Olly can go without the collar. Olly is back to normal in about four weeks.

The cost for Olly's medical treatments—his medical specials—was as follows:

emergency room/doctor visits	$150
X-rays	90
prescription medication	18
cervical collar	35
TOTAL	$293

Because Olly's injuries were soft tissue—that is, did not involve broken bones, wounds, dislocations or other medically observable injury—the damages formula used to figure his claim would be only about 1.5 to 3 times his medical specials of $293. This would be between $450 to $900, plus his lost wages. Olly's pay is $12.25 per hour; he missed three days (3 x 8 hours) of work for a total lost wages of $294.

Olly would be entitled to the full value of his damages because he was in no way comparatively negligent in the accident. Also, losing something special—going to his close friend's 50th birthday—might boost his settlement toward the upper range of his damages, somewhere between $900 and $1,200—including lost wages.

Damage to Olly's car would be settled separately from and in addition to compensation for his injuries.

2.   Auto accident, soft tissue injury, large amount of bills for diagnosis, extensive physical therapy

A car runs through a stop sign and hits a car driven by Mary. Emergency room X-rays show no broken bones, and she is referred to her own doctor.

Mary develops a bad headache and very stiff back. An orthopedist who takes more X-rays and says Mary has lumbar spine strain but no apparent disc injury. The orthopedist prescribes pain medication, muscle relaxants and physical therapy.

After four days, Mary returns to work, but is in a lot of pain again and so misses two more days. Mary begins physical therapy three days a week for two weeks, then two days a week for two more weeks, and ends therapy altogether after five weeks. The orthopedist now says that after a few months she should be fully recovered.

The cost of Mary's medical treatment is as follows:

ambulance	$ 125
emergency room	140
emergency room X-rays	90
Mary's doctor	60
orthopedist	210
second set of X-rays	140
physical therapist	420
medications	35
TOTAL	$1,220

Mary missed five days of work—although because she had sick leave, she was not actually out-of-pocket. The value of her missed work is figured by dividing her monthly gross salary of $2,300 by 21 (the number of work days in the month she missed) then multiplying that figure by 5 (the actual number of days she was out). That comes out to $110 per day, for a five-day loss of $550.

Because Mary had only soft tissue injuries—no observable damage to her spine—and no permanent injury, her damages will be calculated using the low end of the damages formula. Also keeping Mary's damages low is the fact that two-thirds of her medical bills were for diagnosis rather than treatment.

On the other hand, Mary's pain and injury were confirmed by two different doctors, she was given prescription medication and was told that full recovery would take several months. And since she did not undergo long or unusual treatment, all of her bills would be considered legitimate by an insurance company.

A low formula of roughly two to three times medical specials would bring a figure of about $2,000 to $3,500. Added to this would be the amount of Mary's lost wages (in this case, lost sick leave) of $550, for total damages in the range of $2,500 to $4,000. Since the other driver was clearly at fault, Mary's settlement would not be reduced at all by comparative negligence.

3. Bicycle-car accident, hard injury, long recovery period, extensive physical therapy, lost unofficial work time, considerable disruption of daily activities

Walter is on a bike when a car switches lanes and pulls in front of him. Walter runs into the back of the car, falls off his bike and hits the ground.

Hospital X-rays show no fracture of an injured ankle but a cracked left wrist, which is put in a cast. Walter also suffered a concussion, so he is kept in the hospital overnight.

An orthopedist diagnoses strained ankle ligaments and advises Walter to begin physical therapy on the ankle the next week and on the wrist as soon as the cast is removed.

Physical therapy for two weeks returns the wrist to normal light use, but two months of physical therapy on his ankle does not seem to help much. Walter's orthopedist does not believe more physical therapy will help, so Walter stops the therapy. Walter doesn't get on a bicycle again for more than six months.

Walter missed eight days of work and after he returned, because of the cast on his wrist, he fell behind in several projects and had to work three straight weekends to catch up.

The cost of Walter's medical specials is as follows:

ambulance	$ 130
emergency room	280
emergency room X-rays	130
hospital room	240
orthopedist	180
physical therapy (wrist)	160
physical therapy (ankle)	800
TOTAL	$1,920

Since Walter had several significant injuries—broken wrist, concussion, long-term ligament injury —a formula of 4 to 5 times specials would be applied. However, the long ankle physical therapy with no obvious value might drop the formula to 4 times specials rather than 5 times.

Walter's salary is $2,800 per month ($133 per day). He missed eight days of work, for a lost income (whether or not he was actually paid sick leave) of $1,064. Walter also "lost" three weekends when he had to work to make up for lost time on the job. They would also be considered when the settlement amount is calculated.

The amount the insurance company would finally pay would also depend on whether it appeared that Walter had been partly at fault for the accident.

Walter's medical specials of $1,920 would be multiplied by 4 or 5 times, which gets the potential settlement to between $7,500 and $10,000. The fact that much of the treatment was physical therapy might reduce this somewhat, but it would be offset by the long recovery time and the long period which he was unable or afraid to get on a bike. Added would be the $1,064 lost income. And increasing that would be compensation for the extra weekends he had to work.

The total value of Walter's settlement, therefore, would be between $10,000 and $15,000 depending on Walter's comparative negligence.

4.   Non-auto accident caused by employees, permanent hard injuries

Yola parks her car in a lot shared by a shopping center and an office building. Next to their office building, a company softball team is practicing on the building's grassy area, as they regularly do at lunch. One of them bats a ball into the parking lot where it hits Yola in the mouth, breaking her front tooth and pushing it through her upper lip.

Yola's tooth requires a permanent cap, and the hole in her lip leaves a small but visible scar. Her medical and dental special damages were as follows:

emergency room	$ 150
dental work	1,200
doctor	120
TOTAL	$1,470

Yola's broken tooth and gouged lip are each observable "hard" injuries, so the formula to be applied to Yola's medical costs would be in the range of 3 to 5 times specials. Based on the type of injury and the specials, her damages would start in the range of between $3,500 and $7,500.

Because the capped tooth and the scar are both permanent and visible, the range could be closer to $7,500. And if the scar or cap is obvious, the value could go up to between $10,000 and $25,000.

Yola is also entitled to compensation not only for the work she missed after the accident, but also the time she lost going to the doctor and dentist. These lost wages would be paid on top of the settlement amounts discussed above.

Since Yola did not contribute in any way to her injury, her settlement would not be reduced by any comparative negligence.

5.   Slip and fall, commercial property-owner liability, witnesses, hard injury, surgery plus non-traditional treatments, long recovery period

Seiji works in an office building which has an underground parking garage. One evening Seiji is walking across the garage floor when he slips on a grease spot and twists his knee badly.

Seiji's doctor advises ice on the knee and rest, which Seiji does. He stays home from work for three days.

Back at work, Seiji finds grease and oil spots all over the garage floor. And several overhead lights are burned out, leaving a dark area where Seiji fell. Seiji takes pictures of the grease spots and burned-out lights. He also finds out that two other people have slipped and fallen in the garage recently.

Seiji continues to have problems with his knee. An orthopedist examines Seiji, takes X-rays and refers him to a physical therapist. Seiji gets immediate relief after each therapy session, but the knee doesn't get any better, so he stops going to the physical therapist.

Seiji starts going to an acupuncturist who treats Seiji for four sessions but then says he believes Seiji should see a body worker who is a licensed chiropractor mixing both Eastern and Western techniques. The body worker does eight sessions on Seiji's knee but then tells Seiji that there might be cartilage damage and that he should see a knee specialist orthopedist.

The knee specialist does an arthroscopic examination which reveals torn cartilage. The orthopedist repairs the damage by arthroscopic surgery. Seiji misses another week of work and it is another eight weeks before Seiji can resume the running he did every morning before the accident. The total time between the accident and Seiji's knee getting back to near normal is eight months.

The costs for Seiji's treatments are as follows:

doctor	$ 60
X-rays (first set)	110
physical therapy	540
acupuncturist	160
body worker	320
orthopedist (with surgery)	1,280
X-rays (second set)	140
TOTAL	$2,610

Seiji accompanies his claim with pictures of the oil spots and of the burned out lights, plus the fact of the two other people who also slipped and fell. And Seiji demands from the insurance adjuster a copy of the building's schedule for garage clean-up and maintenance. The adjuster soon reports that the company will accept full responsibility for the fall.

However, the insurance company refuses to recognize the acupuncture or body work as legitimate medical treatments. Seiji cannot change the adjuster's mind on acupuncture, but he does show that the body work was just another name for chiropracty and that the body worker is a licensed chiropractor.

Excluding the acupuncture, then, Seiji's medical specials are $2,450. His painful injury which required surgery and a long period of recovery would entitle Seiji to about 5 times the $2,450 specials, around $10,000 to $12,000. If he had any permanent problem with the knee, that figure could double to between $20,000 and $25,000.

6a. Slip and fall on stairs, hard injury, surgery, permanent injury, large comparative negligence

Wanda, 76-years old, goes shopping at Broadmart department store. Coming down some steps from a shoe section, Wanda misjudges an edge and falls. She is taken by ambulance to a hospital where X-rays reveal a badly broken elbow.

Surgery is performed a week later and Wanda spends three days in the hospital and the next week in bed, in great pain. After eight weeks the cast is removed and the orthopedic surgeon refers her to physical therapy.

Because of Wanda's age, physical therapy goes slowly. At the end of three months, her orthopedist switches her to home exercises. He advises her, however, that she will never recover full use of her arm: she will not be able to twist her elbow or wrist far in either direction.

The medical costs of Wanda's treatment are as follows:

ambulance	$ 120
emergency room	210
X-rays (first set)	90
orthopedist—X-rays, surgeries, office	2,860
hospital surgery, three nights	1,650
physical therapy	1,200
TOTAL	$6,130

Broadmart's insurance company denies that it is at all liable for the accident and refuses to pay any settlement to Wanda. Wanda can't remember anything wrong with the stairs which caused her to fall, but she says she wouldn't have fallen if there had been a handrail. The insurance adjuster says that there didn't need to be a handrail because it was only four steps and not a full staircase. Wanda knows she is not very steady on her feet, so she assumes the accident must have been mostly her own fault. When the insurance company offers to settle the case "as a gesture of good will"—meaning "nuisance value"—for whatever amounts Wanda's Medicare coverage did not pay, Wanda accepts the settlement: $1,400.

Now see a different Wanda in the next example.

6b. Slip and fall on stairs, hard injury, surgery, permanent injury, no comparative negligence

Everything in this example is the same as in 6a, except for what Wanda did to investigate the stairs after her accident …and the large settlement she was able to get because of her investigation.

This time, Wanda went with a friend back to the store as soon as she got out of the hospital. They took a ruler, a measuring tape, a notebook and a camera. Wanda pointed out where she had fallen, and Wanda's friend took measurements of the stairs and photos of the stairs and of the lights.

At the local library, Wanda looked at a copy of the city's building code which said that in any staircase of two steps or more, the risers and runs—the step width and height—had to be within certain measurements and that each step had to be the same as the others. Wanda checked the measurements and found that the store's second step was a different height from the one above it and the difference was well beyond the building code limit. Also, stairs of that width in a commercial building were required by the building code to have a handrail in the middle, which the store's stairs did not.

Wanda's claim to Broadmart's insurance company lists these building code violations. Also Wanda uses the photos to emphasize that spotlights on the upper platform shine right into a shopper's eyes, so that going down the stairs you cannot see the steps clearly. And finally, that the all-white carpet which covers the stairs provides no contrast for a person to pick out the edge of one step from the beginning of another.

Because a store must expect elderly people and people with poor eyesight to shop there, stairs have to be safe for them. And if there had been a handrail as the building code required, poor eyesight might not have resulted in an accident.

Since the store's negligence is now established, the seriousness of Wanda's injuries, the long time for her recovery and the permanent residual effects would put the damages formula up to at about the 5 times range, making Wanda's settlement about $30,000 to $35,000.

CHAPTER

6

Processing Your Claim

Using This Chapter

This chapter explains what information you should gather to document your accident and injuries and how to put it together into a convincing written claim—known as a demand letter—for a specific amount of compensation.

Your demand letter will be tailored to your accident, the negotiations and the information you have to support your claim, so you will pick and choose the relevant reading among the discussions of liability, injuries, lost income and property damage included in Section A.

Section B explains how to turn your information into the most effective demand letter—what to include and what to leave out.

Section C presents examples of demand letters based on different accidents and injuries that may serve as models for your own demand letter.

A. Collecting Information

As soon as you have taken the initial steps to protect your interests (explained in Chapter 3), begin gathering the written records and other information to support your claim.

1. Documenting Liability

Gather and organize information concerning who was at fault. Begin as soon after the accident as possible because your memory, and the memories of others who may have information about the accident, will fade with time.

a. Police report of vehicle accident

If police responded to the scene and were aware that you or anyone else was injured, they probably made a written accident report. In the report there may be a notation about the location of the cars, a statement by a witness or some other fact which could prove useful to you. And the insurance company for the other driver will certainly get a copy of the accident report, so you will want to have the same information.

To get a copy of a police report, look in the telephone book for the listings of the specific police department or highway patrol which responded to your accident. It may have a special number to call just for accident reports. If not, call the central office or a local station and ask how to get a copy of your report. The report will be filed either by date and time, street location, drivers' names or car description and license plate number, so have that information ready when you call. Three or four days after the accident, you can usually pick up the report in person or request a copy by mail. Call first, though, to find out whether there is any charge—usually a couple of dollars to cover copying costs.

Sometimes a police accident report will plainly state the reporting officer's opinion that one driver or another violated a specific Vehicle Code section and caused the accident. It may even indicate that the officer issued a citation to the driver at fault. In other reports, careless driving is mentioned somewhere—not necessarily by specifying a Vehicle Code section—although no citation was issued and the officer does not plainly state that the carelessness caused the accident.

Regardless of how specific a report is, if you can find any mention of a Vehicle Code violation or any other suggestion that the other driver was careless, it can be great support in convincing an insurance company that the other driver was at fault. Naturally, the clearer the officer's statement about fault, the easier your job will be in convincing the insurance company.

An accident claim requires only that you present a reasonable explanation of how an accident happened so that an insurance company sees that it is too great a risk to deny your claim and to try to fight it in court. And when you have the written opinion of a police officer who is a supposed expert in traffic collisions and a representative of the state, you have a powerful ally for the reasonableness of your argument.

Many police officers, however, will not discuss fault in their reports unless they either witnessed the accident themselves or took a statement from an independent witness who saw the accident, or the physical evidence at the scene—position of the cars, skid marks, damage—makes the cause of the accident obvious. Even if the report does not mention fault, if there is anything in the report supporting your theory of how the accident happened, focus on that—a comment by the officer, a diagram showing the position of the cars, an estimated speed of the other driver, the reported statement of a witness—in your written compensation demand to the insurance company. (See Section B, below, concerning referring to the police report in your demand letter. See Chapter 7, Section A, for more on how to use a police report in your claim negotiations.)

b. Photographs

If you have any photos of the scene of the accident, you may need to explain to the insurance company what the photo shows, what specific part of the photo shows a fact concerning who was at fault and when the photo was taken. (Chapter 3, Section A2.)

Counteracting an Unfavorable Police Report

An unpleasant surprise may await you in the police report of your accident. The investigating officer may have noted that you appear to have violated a traffic rule or that you were otherwise at fault. One way to try to counteract a bad police report is to telephone the police officer as soon after the accident as possible. Although police do not like to get involved in liability disputes between drivers, the officer who wrote an accident report will probably at least return your phone call.

Politely explain that you are dealing with an insurance company on your own and that you would like to take a couple minutes of the officer's time briefly to discuss the report. Do not try to get the officer to change the report or to say that the other person was at fault. Since the officer would probably prefer not to take sides, use this to your advantage by simply asking the officer whether he or she can say for sure who was at fault in the accident. If the officer says that he or she cannot tell who was at fault, you've already helped yourself.

While the conversation is taking place, write down what the officer says, noting the date and time of the call. Later, in your negotiation with the insurance company, if the adjuster mentions the police report, you can say that you have spoken with the reporting police officer and that the officer has specifically said that he or she cannot state who was at fault. You have now accomplished two things: you have neutralized the bad police report; and you have made the insurance company realize that it is dealing with an organized, resourceful claimant who will not easily disappear without a fair settlement.

c.   Witness statements

If you know of witnesses but have not spoken with them, or you have supportive information from witnesses but they have not yet given you a written statement, contact them again before too much time slips by. (See Chapter 3, Section A2.)

d.   Applicable laws

If you haven't yet checked to see if there are any laws in your state that help to show that another person was at fault, now is the time to do so.

In vehicle accidents, your state's Vehicle Code, also known as the rules of the road, may have a law clearly showing why the other driver was at fault. (See Chapter 2, Section B1.) If so, make a copy of that law to send along with your demand letter. (See Section B, below.)

In staircase or other premises accidents, your local or state building code might have a rule which has been violated by the other person and which contributed to your accident. (See Chapter 2, Section B2.)

e.   Evidence of prior incidents

In some states, you are allowed to get a copy of the driving record of a person with whom you have had a traffic accident. Contact the local or central office of your state's Department of Motor Vehicles to find out if other people's driving records are available. If so, get a copy. The record may show that the other driver has a history of traffic violations or accidents which you can refer to in your negotiations with the insurance company.

In returning to the scene of any accident, you may find out that similar accidents have previously taken place in the same spot. (See Chapter 3, Section A2.) Get a written statement, if possible, from people who have had or witnessed such an accident, or at least get whatever information you can from someone who has heard of previous accidents. If the accident was caused by a defective product, check with *Consumer Reports* magazine to see if the specific brand of product has a history of similar accidents and make a copy of any article that discusses dangers or defects in the product. (See Chapter 2, Section B7.)

2.   Documenting Injuries

The simplest way to show the nature and extent of your injuries is through the records of those who have treated you, although research, photos and witnesses may be persuasive evidence as well.

Pay Attention to the Time

While you should wait to finish your medical treatment and fully recover before sending a demand letter, be aware that the law sets time limits for when you must file a lawsuit for personal injury. Most states give you two years or more from the date of your accident within which to file a lawsuit against those you believe responsible for the accident. (See Chapter 7, Section E for a state-by-state list of the legal time limits, called statutes of limitations.)

For most people, the time limit does not present a problem in preparing and negotiating an insurance claim. However, a few states—**California, Kentucky, Louisiana and Tennessee**—allow only one year from the date of the accident to file a lawsuit. So, if you live in one of these states and more than six months have elapsed since your accident but you are not ready to file a demand letter, consider filing a lawsuit to protect your rights. (See Chapter 7, Section B.)

a. Medical records

Doctors, nurses, physical therapists, chiropractors and other medical providers are all trained to make very detailed notes of everything they observe about your condition and of everything they do and say about your treatment. And you can usually get a copy of your medical records just by asking—although you may have to pay copying costs.

Even in states where there is no specific law giving patients access to their medical records, most medical providers will provide copies to a patient who wants them for an accident insurance claim. If you meet any resistance to obtaining your records, politely explain that you need them to support your accident claim. If office personnel are not helpful, ask to speak directly with the doctor or other health provider who treated you.

An Added Boost From X-Ray Reports

Often, a doctor will send you somewhere outside his or her office to get X-rayed. The bill for those X-rays may be included in your own doctor's bill. But your doctor's medical records might not include the notes of the radiologist—the doctor who reads the X-rays—only your doctor's summary of what the radiologist saw. If your own doctor's records do not indicate any specific injury shown on the X-ray, request a copy of the radiologist's records, particularly if you had X-rays of any part of your neck or back. A radiologist will often find something slightly wrong with your spine which may be causing you pain but which your doctor doesn't specifically mention. You can ask your doctor's office to obtain the radiologist's records for you or you can send a medical records request directly to the radiologist's office.

If you still are refused copies of your medical records, you may get help by sending a check for $5 to: the Public Citizen Health Research Group, 2000 P Street, NW, Suite 700, Washington, DC 20063. Request *Medical Records: Getting Yours*. This booklet explains state and federal laws, how to make a request and how to interpret your file.

If all your efforts at obtaining your medical records fail, you have two courses of action. If the medical record is for diagnosis or minor treatment and you have your other medical records, submit your claim without the missing records. If the missing records are central to demonstrating your injuries and treatment, consider getting help from a lawyer. (See Chapter 7, Section B.)

Request your records from every hospital, clinic, laboratory, doctor, therapist, chiropractor or other medical provider who examined or treated you for your accident injuries. But wait until you have finished the treatment before requesting your records; if not, you'll have to ask again later for a complete and updated copy.

Call the office of each medical provider and ask what the procedure is for getting a copy of your medical records. Some offices will take the information over the phone, but most require a written request. Your written request should ask for billing records (see Section b, below) as well as medical records. Give the date of your accident. It will help the office find the correct records and will keep them from sending you and charging you for the records of visits made before the accident.

Some hospitals, clinics and other medical offices require you to fill out a request on their own forms, or will ask that you sign a document called an Authorization for Release of Medical Records, or something similar. Normally there is no reason not to sign such a form, but read it carefully first to make sure that it does not permit your medical information to be released to anyone other than you. Never sign any form authorizing the release of medical records to anyone other than you, your lawyer if you decide to hire one, or to your own insurance company if your policy requires it.

SAMPLE REQUEST FOR MEDICAL RECORDS AND BILLING

Augustine Muk
122 Rumblewood Avenue
Coagula, CA 00000
(510) 999-9999

January 13, 199X

Elizabeth True, M.D.
777 Sunset Street, Suite 666
Coagula, CA 00000

Attention Medical Records
Re: Patient, Augustine Muk
Accident: November 11, 199X

To Whom It Concerns:

I was treated by Dr. True in November and December, 199X for injuries suffered in an accident on November 11, 199X. Please provide me with copies of all medical records and billing records concerning my treatment following this accident.

Please contact me at the above phone if you have any questions concerning this request.

Very truly yours,

Augustine Muk

When you get your medical records, make sure they are complete, and include all visits related to your accident injuries. If they are not complete, call the office of the medical provider with the dates of the visits for which the records are missing. Check, too, that the records do not include listings of examinations or treatments unrelated to your accident. Set aside these irrelevant records so that you do not mistakenly send them to the insurance company along with the correct ones.

b. Medical billing

The clearest evidence of what your claim is "worth" is the billing records showing how much it cost to treat your injuries. Make sure you have a copy of a bill for every medical service you received. If any bill was sent directly to a health insurance company, or for any other reason you do not have a copy, request a copy from the medical provider so that you can include it when you make your demand for compensation.

Treatment by an HMO or Prepaid Plan

If you belong to a health maintenance organization (HMO) or other prepaid health plan, you are not usually charged a specific sum for visits or treatments, and so there is no actual bill. But every HMO and health plan has a list of charges for each service it provides. If you request it, the business office at your HMO or health plan will give you a list of its charges for each of the examinations, treatments, medicines and other services provided you. Insurance companies consider these charges the same as if they were bills you had actually paid.

Most HMO and health plan contracts provide that if you recover compensation from a third person for injuries treated by the HMO or covered by the prepaid health plan, it has right to be repaid the amount of the charges. In exchange for giving you a list of charges for your treatment, the HMO or health plan might require you to sign a medical lien against your future compensation. This lien requires that you repay the HMO or health plan when you are compensated for your injuries. However, there are ways, once you have reached a final settlement of your claim, to negotiate with the HMO or health plan so that you repay it only a reduced amount of its charges. (See Chapter 8, Section D3.)

c.   Medical reports

Read copies of your medical records carefully to see that all your injuries have been mentioned. Unless your medical records show an injury, an insurance company is not going to take the injury very seriously in calculating your compensation. Therefore, if your medical records do not reflect all your injuries, you may want to contact your doctor about preparing a brief medical report which specifically describes the extent of your injuries, your treatment and recovery. And although you may also have been treated by medical providers other than doctors, insurance companies pay much more attention to a report if it comes from a doctor rather than from a non-physician.

Also, since the amount of time you take to recover from your injuries, plus any permanent residual effects, can greatly increase the amount of your compensation, check whether your medical records accurately reflect these things. If not, ask your doctor to prepare a brief medical report about these aspects of your injuries.

Your medical records may mention what insurance adjusters refer to as a preexisting injury—an injury that already existed in the same area of your body which was again injured in the accident—a "bad" knee, for example, twisted again in the accident. If so, you only have a right to be compensated for the amount of injury caused by the accident, not for the level of injury which existed before it. It is not always easy to tell from medical records alone, however, how much of an injury already existed and how much came from the accident.

Doctors are familiar with the insurance question of pre-existing injuries and, while it is far from an exact science, are used to giving an estimate—expressed in percentages of injury—of pre-existing and accident-caused injury. If a pre-existing injury becomes an issue in your claim, explain the problem to your doctor. If a substantial percentage of your injury was caused by the accident, ask the doctor to prepare a brief report stating that fact.

Requesting a Medical Report

When you speak with your doctor, explain what you would like the medical report to cover: length of recovery, inability to perform certain functions, existence or probability of permanent or disabling effects. Speak to the doctor directly. Most doctors will try to have a nurse or other assistant take non-treatment information, but if you speak only with the assistant, the doctor may not precisely understand what you need, and you will wind up paying for a useless report. Also, explain why you want the report; most doctors are familiar with the accident claim process and will understand.

Also, ask the doctor for a brief report only. And find out ahead of time how much the doctor will charge. Some may charge $50 to prepare a brief report, but doctors are known to charge $300 to $500 for a full report. Since you will be paying for the report out of your own pocket, make sure you get your money's worth. Unless it seems the doctor can say something useful to you in a report, don't bother to ask for one.

The report should be addressed "To Whom It Concerns," but it should be given only to you and not sent directly to an insurance company. That way you can make sure it says something worth sending, and doesn't say anything that minimizes your injuries, before you make it a part of the negotiating process.

Medical Reports and No-Fault Insurance

In a number of states, a person covered by no-fault (Personal Injury Protection) automobile insurance can file a claim for compensation if he or she has suffered injuries which go over a certain threshold—defined as either a certain amount of medical bills or a permanent, disabling or disfiguring injury. If you cannot qualify under your no-fault coverage because the amount of your medical bills do not meet the monetary threshold, you may need to show that your injuries have had some permanent effect. Your medical records alone may do this, but if they do not state clearly that your injury is disabling or permanent as defined by your no-fault policy, a separate statement or report written by your doctor may be your only way of proving that.

d. Medical research

An inexpensive and sometimes very effective source of information to highlight the seriousness and effects of your injuries is the general medical books in your local library, a nearby law library, or the library of a local hospital. Most local libraries have one or two medical encyclopedias such as *Current Medical Information and Terminology* or an illustrated medical dictionary which give both the common and technical names of conditions and parts of the body. A law library will also have a copy of the *Lawyers Medical Cyclopedia* which defines medical terms specifically with legal claims in mind.

Check in a medical encyclopedia or dictionary under the medical terms you find in your medical records describing your injuries—for example, "comminuted fracture" or "root compression." There may

be information in the book explaining such injuries which was not included in your personal medical records, particularly concerning long-term and permanent effects. If so, copy the information so that you can refer to it in your demand letter. (See Section B.)

Another source of medical research is your doctor. Without requesting a costly written medical report, you can ask him or her questions about the exact extent of your injury and the prognosis for long-term or permanent problems. Often, during treatment, a doctor fails to explain in detail the extent of your injury, or will not mention possible long-term effects because they are too uncertain.

However, if you ask—either during a visit or on the phone—the doctor may give you that kind of valuable additional information which you can then put into your demand letter. The medical details of an injury—and the fact that you know the details— often give the injury more status in the eyes of an insurance adjuster. And the mere mention of possible long-term or permanent residual effects from your injury might increase the compensation you are offered.

e. Injury photos and witnesses

As suggested, you may have taken photographs of your injuries at different times after the accident. (Chapter 3, Section A2.) If so, arrange the photos in chronological order, picking out the four or six photos which most clearly show the extent of your injuries and how long they lasted. Send copies of these photos along with your demand letter.

People other than your doctors may have witnessed your pain and discomfort resulting from the accident. Non-family members are particularly useful witnesses because they do not have a direct personal interest in helping your claim. For example, your employer or a co-worker might be able to confirm not only how much time you missed from work but also how much pain and discomfort you were in, and for how long, after you returned to work.

If so, a brief note or letter from that witness describing the nature and duration of your pain and discomfort could be useful for your claim negotiations.

Also, there may be witnesses or documents to verify that you have been unable to participate in some family or other personal or social obligation or event, or that you have missed some business or educational opportunity. Such documents might be an invitation to or notice of an event. If no written evidence exists, a simple letter from anyone involved addressed "To Whom It Concerns" describing the obligation, opportunity or event would be helpful.

The extent to which your injuries have disrupted your regular daily life—unlike special events—does not have to be proven by document or other witness. Proof of your injuries plus a description in your demand letter of the normal activities you have missed will be enough. (See Section B2.)

3. Documenting Lost Income

If you are regularly employed by someone else, collecting information about your lost income is simple. Ask your supervisor, boss or personnel office to write a letter on company stationery. The letter should include: your name, your position, your rate of pay, the number of hours you normally work and the number of hours or days you missed following the accident. The letter need not indicate whether you took sick leave, vacation time or a leave of absence.

If you are irregularly employed or are self-employed, proving lost income is more complicated. You have to show how much work time you lost and what you might have earned had you been able to work. You can use any evidence you have of a drop in billing or invoices, a calendar showing appointments you had to cancel and any letters or documents showing meetings, conferences or other appointments you were unable to attend.

After you have demonstrated how much work you missed, you have to show how much you might have earned. If you had been working a relatively

steady amount immediately before the accident, you can show an average for the period by putting together copies of your billing, invoices, payments received or other evidence of money earned. Then, depending on the average amount you were working and how much you were earning, you can calculate how much income you are considered to have lost for the time you were unable to work.

If you work sporadically—some weeks or months earning most of your income and other weeks or months earning little or nothing—you can show the value of lost work time through evidence of what you make during an entire year, then dividing that into a weekly or monthly average.

The best evidence of your yearly income is your personal income tax return for the previous year. You only need to show the part of your tax return which gives your year's gross income; the rest of the return —deductions, exemptions—is irrelevant and an insurance company has no right to see it. If you had particularly low earnings during the previous year, include two or three years of returns to demonstrate how much you usually earn. If you also have some evidence of income for the current year showing a similar earning pattern, include that as well.

4. Documenting Property Damage

You have a right to be compensated not only for your injuries but also for any personal property damaged or lost in the accident. (See Chapter 5, Section E.) This applies most often to vehicle accidents, in which you can claim the cost of repairing the car, or its actual cash value if totaled, and any contents which were damaged, as well as the cost of alternate transportation during repairs.

But you also have the right to compensation in any other type of accident in which your personal property is damaged. So, for example, a fall might cause a watch to break, or a piece of jewelry to be lost or damaged, or something you were carrying to be damaged or destroyed. Whatever the item, you must provide some evidence of its existence and value.

a.   Vehicle damage

A property damage claim against another person is usually handled by the other person's insurance company immediately after the accident and separately from any personal injury claim. In a vehicle damage claim, you are not required to get any specific number of repair estimates. However, getting more than one written estimate makes it less likely the insurance company will argue that the repair costs were too high. Also, you do not have to accept the insurance company's estimate of repairs based on its own inspection. Unless you can actually get the car competently repaired somewhere for that amount, the company's estimate is meaningless.

If the car is so badly damaged that it cannot be driven, you don't have to have more than one written estimate—although the insurance company will probably want to have one of its own inspectors take a look at the car to see if it has been totaled. "Totaled" doesn't necessarily mean that the car can't be fixed, but that the repairs would cost more than the car is worth. In that case, the insurance company only pays you the car's actual cash value (ACV), and will not pay to have the car fixed. The car's ACV is determined by comparing it with the current sale price of similar year, make and model cars in the area and by referring to the *Kelly Blue Book* which is available at your local public library. (See Chapter 5, Section E.)

It is reasonable for the insurance company to examine or inspect your car, but do not allow that inspection to hold up the repairs. If the insurance company does not inspect the car within a couple of days after the accident and you already have two independent written estimates, there is no legal reason to delay getting your car fixed. If you are able to pay for the repairs yourself, you can get the car fixed and then ask the insurance company to reimburse you later. Of course, if you get your car fixed at the most expensive shop, the insurance company may only be willing to pay you one of the lower estimates.

Or, you can submit a claim under your own vehicle insurance coverage and let your insurer collect from the other person's insurance company. If you take this route, however, you will have to abide by the rules of your own policy, which may be more restrictive than a liability claim against the person at fault for the accident. (See Section b, below.) And if your own policy has a deductible, you must collect that amount from the other driver's insurer.

Getting the car fixed before you agree on an amount with the insurance company removes some of the incentive for the insurance company to settle quickly because once you have your car back, the insurer no longer has to pay for alternative transportation. If the company stalls in paying you car repair money, remind the adjuster that the company is responsible for alternative transportation—a rental car, public transportation, even a taxi when necessary—and that those alternative costs are adding up every day. That often results in a quick settlement offer.

When you do finally settle with the insurance company about your vehicle damage, make sure the settlement includes your costs of alternative transportation. Prove what those costs were by providing the insurance company with copies of receipts from a rental car or taxis. Also make sure that the settlement includes any damaged or destroyed personal property that was in the car. (See Section A4c.)

b.   Damage claims under your own policy

If you make a claim under your own collision coverage—either because the other driver was uninsured or because the insurance company for the other driver is stalling payment and you do not want to wait to get your car fixed—the process is basically the same as for a claim against another person. But because your own insurance company's obligations to you are determined by your policy, the rules might be slightly different. Sometimes your own insurance company can insist that at least one of the estimates be at a shop it names, or that you permit one of its own inspectors to examine the car before repairs are made; under other policies it simply means that you must get a required number of estimates—usually two—before making repairs. Your policy may also have a limit on the amount it will pay for alternative transportation, or a limit on how much personal property in the vehicle is covered, or a deductible you must pay out of your own pocket.

To find out your company's rules, check the terms of the collision coverage in your policy. Although your policy may say that the company can require an estimate at a shop of its own choosing, you do *not* actually have to get the car repaired there. You and your insurance company will reach an agreement about how much it will pay for repairs, but where you get estimates does not determine where you get the car fixed. That is your decision.

Read the Fine Print

Once you accept a property damage settlement, you are forever prevented from claiming that there is still more damage to your car. So make sure that your repair estimators have checked for possible hidden damage—cracked or bent frame, cracked block— before you accept a property damage settlement.

Double check your property damage settlement check and any accompanying Release to make sure it says "Property Damage Only." Do not deposit any check or sign any release that reads "General Release" or any paper that does not clearly indicate "Property Damage Only." Get the insurance adjuster to mark "Property Damage Only" on the check and to write you a letter confirming that this settlement is only for the property damage, and not the personal injuries, in your claim.

If you make a claim for property damage under your own policy, your insurance company will then have the right to get that money back from the person who was responsible for the accident, or from his or her insurance company. Your insurance company will send you a document called something like "Right of Subrogation" which will give it the right to collect from the other person whatever your company has paid you. If you are paid by your own company for your property damage, you cannot also collect property damage compensation from the other person or his or her insurance company.

c. Non-auto property damage

You can recover for any of your personal property that is lost, damaged or destroyed in an accident, either in a claim against the person at fault or under your own collision coverage if the property was in your car. But an insurance company does not have to pay you the cost of replacing the item. Instead, it only has to pay you the "actual cash value" (ACV), which is the item's current market or resale value.

The first step in demonstrating your loss is to prove that the item existed and was damaged. If you still have the item, it's easy: give identifying information to the insurance adjuster and, if the adjuster wants it, a photo of the item. If the item was lost or completely destroyed, you will have to try to prove it existed some other way. A photo showing you with the item is useful, and a receipt, credit card slip or other proof of purchase also establishes ownership. If you have no other proof, you can offer to the insurance company a written statement by someone who knows that you had the item.

Proving actual cash value is more difficult. Even if the item can be repaired, actual cash value is important because the insurance company will not pay for repairs which cost more than the item is worth. The first place to begin establishing ACV is to prove how much you or someone else paid for the item. If you have some proof, it will also establish how old the item is, which affects current ACV.

Older means less valuable, unless it is the kind of item that maintains or increases its value, such as antique jewelry. The condition of the item also affects ACV. A stained and worn leather coat, for example, is not as valuable as a clean and unbattered one.

Items of Great Sentimental Value

The emotional significance of an item—a wedding ring or a family heirloom, for example—cannot be fairly measured by its market value. For such losses, there are two avenues for you to pursue. One is to explain to the insurance company the significance of the item to you and to ask for a settlement amount that takes the emotional value into account. If the insurance adjuster offers you an amount you believe is fair, you can simply settle the matter like any other personal property claim.

If an insurance adjuster will not compensate you for your special attachment to the item, you can take the item out of your property claim and instead include the loss in your personal injury claim. Laws vary from state to state about whether such an emotional loss is part of general damages, part of property damage, or part of a separate legal claim for emotional distress. But regardless of how the law categorizes such a claim, you can include it in your demand to the insurance company for personal injury general damages. If the emotional loss is an easy one to understand—a wedding ring, for example—emphasize the loss in your negotiations and an insurance adjuster will almost certainly take it into consideration when making an offer of settlement.

You can also prove current market value by showing what people are selling the same item for. Check the classified ads of local newspapers to see if the same item—of the same age and condition—is for sale.

Finally, the price of a new replacement item is also useful in determining ACV, particularly if your item was relatively new. If the item is almost new and its value does not diminish much with careful use—a good camera, for example—the current selling price will at least give you a reasonable starting place at which to begin negotiating with the insurance company about the item's ACV.

B. Preparing a Demand Letter

The demand letter is the centerpiece of the negotiation process. In it, you set out to the insurance company your strongest arguments concerning:

- why the other person is legally responsible
- what your injuries were and are
- why you qualify to make a third party claim under no-fault, if that applies
- what your medical treatment was and how much it cost
- what your income loss was, and
- what other damages you suffered.

The letter concludes with a demand on the insurance company for a lump sum to settle your entire claim.

The insurance company uses this demand letter to compare your claim with the information it has about the case, and then to make a counter-offer of settlement. The process of back-and-forth negotiating from there on—usually a combination of phone calls and letters—will determine how much your claim will be settled for. (See Chapter 7.)

Because a demand letter is the beginning of the negotiation process, make your claim as strong and convincing as possible. Even if you know of weaknesses in your argument, do not discuss them in the demand letter. If an insurance adjuster spots a weakness, he or she can bring it up during negotiations and you can deal with it then. If the insurance adjuster does not bring up the weakness in your argument, you are under no obligation to do so.

The demand letter not only sets out your theory of the case and the range of your demand, but it can also demonstrate to the insurance company your understanding, organization and preparation of your claim. In other words, a good demand letter—clear, organized, including all useful information—sets the tone for a good settlement. This section discusses what goes into a good demand letter and how to arrange and forcefully argue the information. (See Section C for sample demand letters for different accident and injury situations.)

1. Letters To More Than One Insurance Company

There may be more than one person or business liable for your injuries, and therefore more than one insurance company which might have to deal with a claim from you. By the time you prepare your demand letter, you will probably have received a notice from one or both insurance companies indicating which company will provide the primary coverage—the one with which you will settle your claim)—and which will provide only excess coverage. (See Chapter 3, Section B.) You only need to send your demand letter to the primary company.

But if you have not received a notice of primary coverage when you are ready to make your settlement demand, prepare two demand letters—each one tailored to the particular liable conduct of that company's insured. After sending both demand letters, you should receive a response from one or both insurance companies indicating which one assumes responsibility for primary coverage. That insurance company will then be the one with which you negotiate.

If you have not received written acknowledgement of primary coverage by the time you are ready to begin settlement negotiations, you will need to resort to other negotiation tactics. (See Chapter 7, Sections B and C.)

2. What To Emphasize in Your Demand Letter

Before beginning to write your demand letter, review your notes from the days and weeks following the accident to remind yourself of the details of the accident—your pain, discomfort, inconvenience, disruption of life and treatments.

Use the chart below to remind yourself of the things that can increase or decrease the amount a claim is worth. If anything in the chart applies to your claim, include it in your demand letter.

a. Liability

A demand letter begins by describing how the accident happened and why the insurance company's insured was at fault. In plain language, briefly describe where you were and what you were doing immediately before the accident, then how the accident took place:

"I was driving north in the right-hand lane along 4th Avenue at about three o'clock in the afternoon. When I was more than halfway through the intersection with Broadway, your insured entered the intersection in the center eastbound lane on Broadway and slammed into the passenger side of my car."

Include all points that might indicate that the insured was at fault for the accident. Put your strongest argument first:

"I clearly had the right of way at the intersection. The insured had a stop sign on Broadway and I had no stop sign on 4th Avenue."

Factors Affecting Compensation

THINGS THAT SIGNAL A HIGHER MULTIPLIER TO BE APPLIED TO MEDICAL EXPENSES INCLUDE:

- hard injury—broken bone, head or joint injury, wounds, vertebrae injury, nerve damage (Chapter 5, Section B1)

- expenses primarily for treatment (Chapter 5, Section B2)

- treatment by a medical doctor, clinic, hospital (Chapter 5, Section B2)

- prescribed medication (Chapter 5, Section C1)

- ong treatment (Chapter 5, Section B2)

- long recovery (Chapter 5, Section C2)

- permanent injury—scar, stiffness, weakness, loss of mobility (Chapter 5, Section C3)

- physical or emotional distress resulting from the injury (Chapter 5, Section C4)

- daily life disruptions—such as missed school or training, missed vacation or recreation, canceled special event (Chapter 5, Section C5)

FACTORS THAT SIGNAL A LOWER MULTIPLIER TO BE APPLIED TO MEDICAL EXPENSES INCLUDE:

- soft tissue injury—sprain, strain, bruise (Chapter 5, Section B1a)

- large part of expenses for diagnosis rather than for treatment (Chapter 5, Section B2)

- treatment by non-M.D. providers (Chapter 5, Section B2)

- no medication prescribed (Chapter 5, Section C1)

- brief treatment (Chapter 5, Section B2)

- short recovery period (Chapter 5, Section C2)

- no residual or permanent injury (Chapter 5, Section C3)

- no physical or emotional problems other than original injury (Chapter 5, Section C4)

FACTORS LIKELY TO GET YOU HIGHER COMPENSATION AFTER THE FORMULA IS APPLIED INCLUDE:

- no comparative negligence by you (Chapter 5, Section F1)

- your organization and calmness (Chapter 5, Section F3e)

- the insured is not credible or sympathetic (Chapter 5, Section F3b)

- witnesses in your favor (Chapter 5, Section F3c)

- some "dramatic" advantage (Chapter 5, Section F3d)

FACTORS LIKELY TO GET YOU LOWER COMPENSATION AFTER THE FORMULA IS APPLIED INCLUDE:

- comparative negligence by you (Chapter 5, Section F1)

- disorganization or impatience (Chapter 5, Section F3e)

- a sympathetic insured (Chapter 5, Section F3b)

- no witnesses for you, or witnesses who favor the insured (Chapter 5, Section F3c)

And add other facts that might lead to an even stronger case against the insured:

"Furthermore, since the insured struck my car on the rear side panel, it is obvious that I was already well into the intersection when he entered. Also, the extent of the damage to my car indicates that your insured was moving at a substantial rate of speed, which would mean that he never even stopped at the stop sign."

If you have any outside support for your theory, make sure to include it here. In a vehicle accident case, repeat any helpful remark in a police report. In a premises liability case, quote a building code section which has been violated. Information received from any source about similar accidents should be included, although you do not have to give the identities of your sources at this stage. If you have information that the other driver has a bad driving record, mention it here.

If you have any witnesses who support your version of the accident, let the insurance company know how many of them back up your story. If you have a good written statement from a witness, quote the best part of the statement. You do not have to reveal the identity of a witness in the demand letter; instead, write that you will make the identity of the witnesses known to the insurance company "at the appropriate time." (See Chapter 7, Section B2f.) Be sure to let the insurance company know that you are aware of other information, or intangibles, that could help you should the case ever get to court. (See Chapter 5, Section F3.) For example, if there was any evidence that another driver's breath smelled of alcohol, or there was an empty beer bottle in the car, even if he or she was not cited for drunk driving, mention it in your demand letter:

From the beer cans on the floor of your insured's automobile, observed by my passenger as well as by me, it also appears that your insured may have been drinking and driving."

"Another intangible may be how gruesome your damaged car looked. If it was badly smashed, describe that. And include a photo if you have one, to highlight how serious the collision was. If the car was spun all the way around, mention it. If it had to be towed away, mention that. Likewise, if you have a photo of a hole you tripped in or a dangerous-looking object that injured you, include the photo and refer to how obviously dangerous it is just from looking at the picture. If you not only fell, but fell down several stairs, mention it.

Words Can Be Your Best Ally

One of the most important but overlooked effects of language in negotiating a claim is how strong words—instead of merely the most direct words—can get across to an adjuster the emotional impact of the accident and your injuries. In your claim, highlight the dangerous carelessness of the other person, the pain you suffered and the seriousness of its consequences. So, for example, a car does not *hit* another car, it *slams* into it. Or a car did not *merely* have the right of way, it *clearly* or *obviously* had the right of way. A knee is not merely *twisted* but has *suffered a strained collateral medial ligament*. An injury is not just *painful*, but is *extremely* painful. A wound doesn't merely leave a scar, but a very *disfiguring scar*.

Of course, you have to be careful not to get so colorful with your language that an insurance adjuster will mistrust what you say. But within that reason, bear in mind that while you are writing in your demand letter that carefully chosen words can be a very effective tool for helping an adjuster understand what you have been through.

If property had been in a dangerous condition for a long time, mention that the owner or manager of the property was negligent not only for allowing the danger to occur, but also for failing to inspect or otherwise reasonably look after the property. (See Chapter 2, Section B2.)

b.   Comparative negligence

In many accidents, there is some question about whether your own carelessness contributed to the accident even though the other person was primarily at fault.

Raise the issue in your demand letter by denying that you were at all comparatively negligent. This denial shows the insurance company that you are aware of the rules and have thought about the issue. It allows you briefly to state your argument in writing so that you don't have to discuss it for the first time on the phone with the insurance adjuster—a situation which is more difficult for you to control.

Do not admit any fault. Even if you believe that you might have been partly at fault for the accident, do not admit that in your demand letter. Mention only the reasons why you were not at fault. Although you must consider your own negligence in deciding what a fair settlement is, it is not your job to make the comparative negligence arguments for the insurance company. So, for example, if there was a traffic accident, point out that the police report confirms that you violated no traffic laws and that it mentions no careless driving on your part. If you tripped or slipped and fell on stairs, indicate that you were walking normally, that your shoes had normal heels and soles, and that you were watching your step.

Your discussion of comparative liability should wind up with a statement that it is clear that the insured was fully liable for the accident.

c.   Your injuries and treatment

In describing your injuries and treatments, do not be too shy. Emphasize your pain, the length and difficulty of your recovery, the negative effects of your injuries on your daily life and any long-term or permanent injury—especially if it is disabling or disfiguring, such as permanent stiffness, soreness or scarring.

Of course, do not make things up or be overly dramatic. Insurance adjusters are regular people who are susceptible to the kid-who-cried-wolf phenomenon; they will simply turn a deaf ear to claims they believe are false. To support your claim of injury, pain and disability, wherever possible, use the terms which appear in a medical record, particularly official medical terms wherever they are available: "narrowing of disk spacing" is stronger than "strained back."

The easiest way to describe your injuries, treatment, recovery and long-term or permanent effects is to go step-by-step chronologically, from how the injury occurred, to your pain and what you did about it immediately after the accident, through all the medical examinations and treatments you received, through all the stages of your pain and disability during recovery and ending with any long-term or permanent effects. (See Section C for examples.)

d.   Other losses

Most of what you recover for your injuries is compensation for pain, discomfort and disruption in your daily life. But sometimes you suffer extra or unusual discomforts, embarrassments, inconveniences or losses. (See Chapter 5, Section C.) Review your notes to remind yourself of the kinds of things you went through, or had to miss or give up, because of your injuries. Mention them in your demand letter, and do not be shy about saying how important those things are to you.

Qualifying for a No-Fault Claim

If you are covered by a no-fault (Personal Injury Protection) automobile insurance policy, you may first have to meet one of certain qualifying thresholds before being allowed to file a liability claim for compensation. (See Chapter 4, Section A4.) What those thresholds are depends on the state in which you live and the particular provisions of your policy, and might include a certain amount of money spent on medical treatment, or on your injury being "serious," "permanent" or "disabling" as defined by your state's no-fault law.

If you are covered by a no-fault policy, check the listings of no-fault laws in Chapter 4, Section A4, as well as the terms of your own policy, to see what threshold you must meet to proceed with your claim against the other person's insurance company.

If you are relying on the nature and extent of your injuries—rather than on the amount of money your treatment cost—to get your claim over the no-fault threshold, include in your demand letter a paragraph explaining why you meet the threshold. This explanation should appear immediately after the description of your injuries.

If you are relying on the amount of your medical expenses to get over the threshold, immediately after you have listed those expenses you can simply state that the total qualifies you for a third-party claim.

e.   Medical expenses

Immediately following your description in the demand letter of all your medical treatments, include a list of each medical provider who treated you and the total amount charged by each. (See Section C for examples.) If you were treated by an HMO or other prepaid plan, list the charges it provided you with in place of actual bills. List all medical costs, regardless of whether you paid them, your own or your employer's insurance paid them, or they were part of a health plan. Make sure the list matches the medical billing records you have, copies of which you will be sending to the insurance company along with the demand letter. (See Section h, below.)

If you were in a vehicle accident and you have no-fault insurance coverage requiring you to meet an expense threshold, a list of your medical expenses plus copies of the bills in your demand letter gives the insurance company notice of your right to pursue your claim against its insured.

f.   Lost income

Make a brief statement of the amount of time you missed from work because of your injuries, and refer to whatever letter you have from your employer verifying your pay and missed time. Then multiply the time missed by your rate of pay to get a total figure for lost income. You do not have to explain why you were unable to work. If the insurance company wishes to challenge your claim that you were unable to work, it will do so during negotiations.

Don't try to convince the insurer in your demand letter that your injuries made you miss work. Lobbying too strongly may signal that this is a subject for disagreement and negotiation. And you do not have to discuss whether you took sick leave, vacation time, or unpaid time off. The time you missed and the amount you are paid are the only things that matter.

If you are irregularly or self-employed, explain how you arrived at the total figure for lost income. Your income is impossible to predict exactly, so you do not have to claim that the figure you give is exact. Just explain what basis you used for figuring your rate of income—a weekly amount based on your previous year's income as shown on your tax return, for example, or a monthly amount based on the months immediately preceding the accident—and refer to whatever documents you have to back up that income and your missed work.

If the insurance company wants to dispute your figures or the method you used, let it bring up the matter during negotiations. Don't worry about convincing the insurer in your demand letter that the method you are using is the best or only method possible.

g. Your settlement demand figure

In the last paragraph of your letter, demand a specific sum of money as total compensation for your pain, suffering, lost income and other losses. Before naming the amount, very briefly repeat the strongest part of your argument and any special facts—particularly dangerous behavior by the insured, extreme pain, extensive treatment, a long period of recovery, permanent injury—which should increase your compensation.

To arrive at the final number, review how the damages formula works. (See Chapter 5, Section A.) Then plug in the figures for your medical treatment and lost income and choose a higher or lower range of the formula—whichever is more realistic given the nature of your injuries and the difficulty in proving who was at fault. When you apply a high or low end of the formula to the amount in your case, you will arrive at a range of figures which would be a fair settlement amount. Whether you believe your settlement is worth a figure at the higher or lower end of that range then depends on several additional

facts (discussed in Chapter 5, Section F3): how obvious is the other person's fault, your comparative negligence, existence of witnesses, sympathy or dramatic advantage for you or against the other person, your willingness to be patient through the negotiation period.

Deciding what you think would be a fair settlement, however, does not mean putting that amount in your demand letter. The demand letter is only the beginning of a negotiation process similar to bargaining at a swap meet. You start too high, the insurance adjuster will start too low, and then you both bluff and counter-offer until you agree on a number somewhere in between. How much bluffing and counter-offering depends on your personality and that of the insurance adjuster you are dealing with, and on how many variables there are in your claim, such as unclear liability or uncertain long-term injury.

The demand letter begins the negotiating process with a request for compensation considerably higher than the amount you would be satisfied accepting. Do not make the number outrageously high because the insurance adjuster will know that it is a meaningless number and it will not get the real negotiation process started. The adjuster will just come back with an equally meaningless low number and you will be back at square one. So, the number in your demand letter should be higher than what you think your claim is worth, but still believable. A general rule is 75% to 100% higher than what you would actually be satisfied with. For example, if you think your claim is worth between $1,500 and $2,000, make your first demand for $3,000 or $4,000; if you think your claim is worth $4,000 to $5,000, make your first demand for $8,000 or $10,000.

An insurance adjuster does not know how much you know about what the claim is worth. So, making a high first demand announces that you know your claim should not be settled for a small sum. And it also gives the adjuster room to maneuver downward while keeping the figure within a fair settlement range.

Watch the Time

If more than six months have gone by since your accident, check on the time within which you must file a lawsuit to protect your rights. (See Chapter 7, Section E.) If the time limit for filing a lawsuit is coming up within the next three months or so, remind the insurance adjuster of this in your demand letter. It will signal to the adjuster that you are aware of the time limit, and since insurance adjusters want to settle claims before a lawsuit is filed, it might help get you a prompt reply to your demand.

h. Supporting documents

Along with your demand letter, send the insurance company copies of documents, records, letters, bills or other writings supporting the things you describe in your letter. Keep the originals for your own files. Although no one's claim has all of the documents listed below, use the following list to remind yourself of the documents that might support your claim. When you send these documents along with your demand letter, arrange them in the same order as they are referred to in the letter.

Supporting documents to include with your demand letter

- a police report, copy of a traffic law or building code or any other document which supports your contention that the insured person violated a law or legal rule, such as a statement or report about prior accidents
- photos of the accident scene
- witness statements supporting your description of how the accident happened

- any other document supporting your contention that the other person was at fault in the accident
- photos of your injury
- your medical records, arranged by medical provider—that is, all your records from Dr. X together in chronological order, then all records from Dr. Y together
- bills, billing records or lists of charges for all medical treatment—regardless of who actually paid for it—arranged chronologically by medical provider in the same order as the medical records
- documents showing your income loss, and
- documents showing other losses you suffered, such as the invitation to a wedding you missed, the schedule of the dance classes you could not go to and will not be able to attend for another six months.

C. Sample Demand Letters

In this section are six samples showing the form a demand letter takes and how it can be tailored to different accident and injury situations. There are no special words you have to use, and each demand letter will be a little different. The main thing to remember is to include your strongest arguments that the accident was fully the other person's fault and that your injuries caused you pain, discomfort, inconvenience, perhaps long-term or permanent effects and income loss, as explained in Chapter 5. Refer to all medical treatments you received for your injuries.

Each demand letter starts with a reference to the name of the insured, your name, the claim number given by the insurance company when you first notified it of your injuries and the date of the accident—sometimes called "date of loss." Make sure to include this information at the beginning of all correspondence with an insurance company.

The sample demand letters here are written to support claims for the accidents and injuries described in the examples in Chapter 5, Section G. When you read a sample demand letter here, you can refer back to the corresponding example at the end of Chapter 5 to see how the demand letter emphasizes the strongest parts of the injured person's argument. You can also see the relationship between what the claim seems to be worth, as discussed in the example, and the compensation amount requested at the end of the corresponding sample demand letter.

Within each sample demand letter are explanations highlighted in bold print of why something was included or excluded in the letter, or why certain wording was used to describe one of the elements of the claim. And at the end of each sample letter is a list of the supporting documents the injured person would include with that letter.

1. Auto accident, short-term soft tissue injury, extra damages for missed special event

---

SAMPLE DEMAND LETTER

Oliver Simon Ball
135 Southwood Lane
London, CT 12345

March 15, 199X

Roberta Butler
Claims Adjuster
All Risk Insurance Company
4800 Covent Boulevard
Gainsville, CT 00000

Re: Your Insured, Matthew White
    Claim No.: G 765-93
    Claimant: Oliver Simon Ball
    Date of Loss: January 13, 199X

Dear Ms. Butler:

As I informed you by letter of January 17, 199X, I was injured in an automobile accident with your insured Matthew White on January 13, 199X in Highgate, Connecticut. I was headed west on Hornsey Lane and stopped at the stop sign at the intersection with Highgate Hill Road. While I was stopped, your insured slammed into the back of my car. *(The words "slammed into" are more dramatic than the simple word "hit" and set the stage for a serious and painful injury.)* The force of the blow threw me forward against my shoulder restraints and my head snapped forward and back. *(Describing exactly how you were injured makes it easier for the adjuster to understand the injuries that resulted.)*

In the middle of that night I woke with a severe headache and extremely stiff neck, so in the morning I went to the emergency room of Highgate Medical Center. *(Notice that Olly's headache is "severe" and his neck "extremely" stiff, which sounds more serious than a headache and stiff neck.)* There I was examined and X-rays were taken of my neck and back. The doctor diagnosed a cervical strain, fitted me with a cervical collar and advised bed rest. *(Olly describes it here as "cervical strain" even though it could also be called "whiplash.")* Because of the severe pain, he also prescribed pain relief medication. *(The fact that medication was prescribed shows that the treating doctor took the injury seriously.)*

I was in considerable pain for the next five days, forced not only to miss three days of work, but also the 50th birthday party in Boston of an old and dear friend. On Monday of the next week I returned to work, but still with pain and stiffness and wearing a cervical collar, which made doing my job very difficult. *(Mentioning continued pain shows that even though Olly went back to work, his injury was not yet healed.)* After another week, the doctor advised that I could remove the cervical collar. I continued to have quite a bit of soreness and stiffness for another two weeks, interfering with my sleep and making it impossible to do any recreation or to drive unless absolutely necessary. *(Good to mention disruptions in sleep and other daily life matters to show that ability to return to work does not end the effects of the injury.)* I continue to suffer occasional stiffness and sleep disruptions. *(Mentioning continuing problems may nudge the insurance adjuster to settle the claim quickly rather than risk that Olly will have to return for more medical treatment which would increase his medical specials.)*

The medical expenses for my treatment, as shown in the enclosed medical and billing records, are:

Highgate Med. Center (emergency room)	$150
Highgate Med. Center (X-rays)	90
Cervical collar	35
Prescription medication	18
TOTAL	$293

As mentioned, a result of the accident, I also missed three days of work. As the enclosed letter from the personnel office of Battersea Grocery indicates, my wage loss was $294 (24 hours at $12.25 per hour).

Because of the negligence of your insured, I went through a period of extreme pain and discomfort which lasted for several weeks. This discomfort still continues. Not only was my normal daily life disrupted, but I was forced to miss the 50th birthday party of a very dear friend whom I rarely get to see. *(Repeat of a loss which does not have a dollar value but which must be compensated anyway.)* As a result, I demand compensation for my injuries and general damages in the amount of $2,500. *(Olly's claim is probably worth only about $1,000, but in his demand letter he begins negotiations by asking for more than twice the amount he would be willing to settle for.)*

I hope to hear from you soon, no longer than 30 days from the date of this letter.

Very truly yours,

Oliver Simon Ball

Supporting documents to be enclosed:

- Police accident report
- Medical records from the hospital
- Bills from the hospital
- Receipt from prescription medication
- Letter from Olly's job showing income and work days missed
- Written invitation to his friend's 50th birthday party or other evidence of the event.

2. Auto accident, soft tissue injury, large amount of bills for diagnosis, extensive physical therapy

---

SAMPLE DEMAND LETTER

Mary Graham
812 Octavia Street, Apt. #4
Chicago, IL 00000

June 30, 199X

Oscar Salinas
Claims Adjuster
High Life Insurance Company
1000 Throughway Boulevard
Chicago, IL 00000

Re: Your Insured, Anthony Stacatto
   Claimant: Mary Graham
   Claim No.: 93-8822 TX
   Date of Loss: January 13, 199X

Dear Mr. Salinas:

As you are aware, I was injured in an automobile accident with your insured, Anthony Stacatto, on January 13, 199X at the intersection of 12th Street and Loop Lane, Chicago. I was traveling east on Loop Lane, and as I entered the intersection with 12th Street, your insured came through a stop sign on 12th Street and smashed into my car just behind the driver's seat, barely missing a direct hit on me. *(Even though a direct hit on Mary did not occur, the near miss increases the sense of emotional trauma Mary suffered.)* The power of the collision spun my car all the way around and left it facing west almost all the way to the curb. *(The power of the impact shows how fast the other driver was going, which supports both how negligent he was and also how seriously Mary is injured.)* I have enclosed the police report of the accident which states that I had the right of way, and a diagram that shows where your insured struck my car and the final resting place of the car. The enclosed photograph showing the severe damage to my car indicates how strong the collision was. In addition to violating my right of way, your insured also admitted to the police officer that he failed to see and stop at the stop sign.

I was badly battered by the collision and was taken by ambulance to the emergency room of Providence Hospital. Immediately after the accident, I had pain and stiffness in my back and a headache which was rapidly getting worse. After X-rays, I was released and advised to see my private physician. During the night, my headache became severe and I was unable to move my back. First thing in the morning I was taken to my personal physician, Ann Lindley, M.D., who referred me to an orthopedist, Martin Chuzzlewit, M.D. Dr. Chuzzlewit examined me and discovered an inflammation of the lumbar spine. He prescribed pain and muscle relaxant medication, advised immediate bed rest and referred me to physical therapy. *(It is important to point out that the orthopedist referred Mary to physical therapy rather than her deciding to go on her own; in the mind of an insurance adjuster, that makes the physical therapy treatments more medically legitimate.)*

I was forced by the pain to remain in bed for the next four days. I attempted to return to work the following Monday but the pain once again forced me to bed for another two days. *(Good to mention that Mary tried to return to work; it shows that she was not just using her injury as an excuse for a holiday.)* I began physical therapy at the Bendright Clinic, which I continued for a period of five weeks, during which I remained in considerable pain and discomfort. After completing the physical therapy, I returned for an examination by Dr. Chuzzlewit who advised me that I would have residual pain and stiffness for another few months. *(The doctor confirms long period of recovery.)*

The medical specials for my treatment are as follows:

A-One Ambulance Co.	$ 125
Providence Hospital	230
Ann Lindley, M.D.	60
Martin Chuzzlewit, M.D.	210
Loop Radiology Group	140
Bendright Physical Therapy	420
Prescription medication	35
TOTAL	$1,220

As a result of the accident, I missed a total of five days of work as a teacher at Grover Cleveland High School. My monthly gross salary is $2,300, and the number of school days in January were 21, so per diem pay for January was $110. In total, I lost $550 in wages.

Because of the unlawful and dangerous driving *(reminding the insurance company that the insured's driving would look very bad if the claim ever made it to court)* of your insured, I suffered excruciating back pain requiring some five weeks of physical therapy and which has taken months to subside. I continue to suffer occasional pain and stiffness now, some six months after the accident. Also, the trauma of so narrowly missing a direct hit by your insured's car has made me fearful of driving and causes me daily anxiety when I have to drive anywhere. *(Since driving is an important part of most people's lives, being afraid to get in a car may raise the value of the claim.)* To compensate me for the severity of the shock, the long period of treatment and the continuing pain and discomfort I suffer, I demand the sum of $7,500.

I look forward to your prompt reply on this matter.

Yours truly,

Mary Graham

Supporting documents to be enclosed:

- Police accident report and diagram
- Photos of Mary's smashed car
- Medical records from all hospitals, doctors and physical therapists Mary was treated by
- Bills from ambulance, doctors, hospital and physical therapy and receipt from prescription medication
- Letter from the school district showing Mary's employment, wages and work days missed

3. **Bicycle-car accident, hard injury, long recovery period,
   extensive physical therapy, lost unofficial work time,
   considerable disruption of daily activities**

SAMPLE DEMAND LETTER

Walter Blancmange
666 Crescent View
Palo Alto, CA 00000

June 15, 199X

Maria Teeuw
Claims Adjuster
Continental Insurance Company
900 Cramer Avenue
San Francisco, CA 00000

Re: Your Insured, Sameer Mehendale
     Claimant: Walter Blancmange
     Claim No.: AQ 65393
     Date of Loss: January 13, 199X

Dear Ms. Teeuw:

As you have been notified, I was injured in an accident with your insured Sameer Mehendale on January 13, 199X in the city of Palo Alto, California. On that date, at about ten o'clock on a clear morning I was riding my bicycle in the right lane of Amstel Road, a four lane street, when your insured in his large Oldsmobile cut over (*"cut over" rather than "changed lanes"*) from the middle lane into my lane without properly looking, forcing me into a collision with (*"forcing me into a collision" rather than "I ran into the back of"*) the rear of his car. As you are aware, the rules of the road in California give a bicyclist the same right to occupy a lane of traffic as an automobile.

Since I was already in the right lane when your insured moved into it, cutting me off, he clearly violated my right of way and was fully at fault for the accident. Although I was unable to stop in time to avoid a collision, I was traveling within the speed limit and in a proper position to the right side of the right lane, and was therefore not at all comparatively negligent. (*A full description of all the reasons the insured was completely at fault.*)

The collision knocked me off my bicycle, into the car's bumper and to the ground. I was knocked unconscious and was taken to the hospital by ambulance. (*Being knocked unconscious is a dramatic detail, and it is a good idea to mention it.*) At the hospital, it was discovered that I had numerous injuries, including a concussion, a fractured left ulna and damaged ligaments in my right ankle. My injuries were so extensive that I was admitted to the hospital and the left wrist was placed in a cast. (*Walter was probably kept overnight in the hospital more for observation of his concussion than for his other injuries, but it is certainly truthful for him to state that it was the "extensiveness" of his injuries which put him in the hospital.*)

Upon release from the hospital, I was unable to put weight on my right leg and my broken wrist permitted me to use only one crutch. I was in great pain not only in my ankle and wrist but also in my back and neck. I suffered from severe headaches. I was confined to bed for a week following the accident. (*Having to spend a week in bed would probably not show up in the medical records, so it is a good idea to mention it here.*)

My broken wrist remained in a cast for three weeks, followed by two weeks of physical therapy as prescribed by my orthopedist, Dr. Kiek Bak. Dr. Bak also prescribed physical therapy for the damaged ligaments of my ankle, but even after two months of therapy and four more months of recovery and exercises the ankle is still stiff and painful when rotated or when weight is put on it. Dr. Bak cannot say whether the ankle will ever return to its pre-accident condition. *(Good to note the doctor's opinion on the likelihood of permanent injury.)*

My medical special damages for the required treatment are:

Lifesaver Ambulance Service	$ 130
Amstelhof Mem. Hospital	280
Amstelhof Mem. Hosp. (X-ray)	130
Amstelhof Mem. Hosp. (inpatient)	240
Kiek Bak, M.D. 180	
Jolle Demmers (phys.ther./wrist)	160
Jolle Demmers (phys.ther./ankle)	800
TOTAL	$1,920

As a result of the accident, and this complicated recovery, I have been unable to ride my bicycle since the accident. And riding the bicycle was not merely an occasional recreation. I rode it as inexpensive and practical local transportation and as my major source of exercise. Long evening and weekend rides have also, for many years, been a source of pleasure and relief from stress. I am now 54 years old. Because of the accident and the uncertainty it has caused about when and how well I will again be able to ride, all these important elements of my life are in serious jeopardy. *(An emphasis here on how life has been seriously disrupted by the injuries.)*

As a further result of the accident, I missed eight days of work in my capacity as an editor for Sunlight Software. As the enclosed letter from the Sunlight personnel office indicates, my salary is $2,800 per month ($133 per day). My lost income, therefore, was $1,064. In addition, I fell behind on a project with a deadline and was forced to work at home for three consecutive weekends for which I received no compensation. At $133 per day, those extra six days of work add a further $798 in lost income. *(Put a specific dollar amount on the make up work which resulted from the accident.)*

Through the clear negligence of your insured, I suffered serious multiple injuries, including head trauma, a fracture and ligament damage from which I have not fully recovered six months after the accident. *(Even though it is not certain, the possibility of permanent injury is an important factor and should be emphasized.)* Further, a major source of health and satisfaction in my life, regular and long-distance bicycle riding, may have been permanently taken from me. As a result, I demand the sum of $30,000 in recompense for my injuries and their consequences.

Yours sincerely,

Walter Blancmange

Supporting documents to be enclosed:

- Police accident report
- Photo of battered bicycle
- Photos of Walter on previous long bicycle trips
- Photos of injuries
- Medical records from all hospitals, doctors and physical therapists
- Bills or record of charges from ambulance and all hospitals, doctors and physical therapists
- Letter from employer indicating salary and missed work time, plus extra weekends Walter had to work

4. Non-auto accident caused by employees, permanent hard injuries

---

SAMPLE DEMAND LETTER

Yolanda Mercurio
24 Park Place
Seattle, WA 00000

October 15, 199X

Reginald Chen
Claims Adjuster
All-Safe Insurance Company
3400 Salmon Boulevard

Seattle, WA 00000

Re: Your Insured, Gorgon Mortgage Company
    Claimant: Yolanda Mercurio
    Claim No.: 4876-93
    Date of Loss: June 13, 199X

Dear Mr. Chen:

This letter constitutes a demand for compensation from your insured, the Gorgon Mortgage Company, for serious and permanent injuries I sustained on June 13, 199X as a result of the reckless behavior of employees of the Gorgon Mortgage Company committed on Gorgon property. *("Reckless" behavior sounds worse than "careless" behavior.)*

On that date at about 1:45 p.m., I had just parked my car in the outdoor parking lot of the Soundbite Shopping Center when I was struck in the mouth by a softball. The softball came from property adjoining the parking lot, owned by your insured, thrown or batted by employees of your insured during practice on that property of a softball team sponsored by your insured. Because your insured provided a place on its property for its employees to practice softball in a dangerous spot next to a public parking lot, your insured is liable for the consequences.

Further, through your insured's sponsorship of the team made up of employees, and its permission for them to practice during the working day, they are clearly playing softball in their capacity as employees and your insured is legally responsible for their actions as employees. *(These are the reasons why the employer is liable for the acts of the employees even though the accident occurred as the result of activity not normally associated with their work.)*

The softball had traveled a full thirty or forty yards from the field, and so had tremendous velocity. The force of the blow directly on my mouth broke my front tooth and drove the broken tooth through my upper lip. *(A graphic description of a nasty injury.)* I was knocked to the ground in terrible pain. there was a tremendous amount of blood and I was driven to the hospital emergency room. To close the wound, hospital attendants had to put stitches in both the inside and on the outside of my lip. The enclosed photographs were taken the day after the accident and show the broken tooth, the wound and the tremendous swelling. *(A picture of the unsightly injury can be very effective.)*

The stitches in my lip were removed by my own doctor after a week, but as the enclosed photograph shows, the wound has left a scar on the outside of my upper lip. My doctor says that although it will reduce somewhat over time, a scar will remain permanently visible. *(Emphasis on the permanent nature of the injury.)*

My broken tooth was temporarily treated by my dentist until the lip wound healed, and then a cap was fitted over the tooth. The cap is uncomfortable and it has affected what I can eat because of my concern for biting into anything hard. Also, it is obvious that the cap is not a real tooth, and since it is my front tooth, it causes me considerable embarrassment. Now, every time I start to smile I become self-conscious, thinking about my false tooth as well as my scar. *(Emphasis on the emotional distress caused by the injury.)*

The problem with the false tooth will only get worse over time. It will discolor differently from the normal teeth around it and will have to be replaced at regular intervals for the rest of my life. Also, because it is fit over my broken tooth, there is the potential for movement, gum disease and other future dental problems which can prove painful, inconvenient, disfiguring and expensive. *(Discussion of future problems suggests to insurance adjuster that claim should be settled sooner rather than later when such long-term problems might actually start to appear.)*

The medical expenses for the treatment of my lip and my tooth, so far, are: *(The words "so far" remind the adjuster that if the claim is not settled soon, more medical bills might have to be put into the formula.)*

Puget Sound Medical Center	$ 150
Fiona Brown, M.D.	120
Elton Limpet, D.D.S.	1,200
Total	$1,470

My injuries also caused me to lose time from work. I am a self-employed graphic artist. For the three months immediately prior to my accident I averaged $2,204 per month, as my enclosed billing records indicate. As a result of the accident, I lost a day and a half of work right after the accident, plus another day and a half during medical treatments, for a total of three days. At $105 per day ($2,204/month divided by 21 work days per month) my income loss for those three days was approximately $315. *(Includes explanation of how self-employment income loss was calculated.)*

Because I was unable to go on any job interviews until my mouth had healed and my tooth was fixed, my income for the following two months dropped to an average of only $850 per month—an additional $2,700 in income loss as a result of the accident.

Through the irresponsible actions of your insured and its employees, I have suffered a painful injury which has left a permanent scar on my face and a permanently disfigured and unstable front tooth. Because of the visibility and permanence of the injuries, and the inevitable future work on the tooth, I demand the sum of $25,000 compensation.

Sincerely yours,

Yolanda Mercurio

Supporting documents to be enclosed:

- Photo of the scene
- Photo of Yolanda's injuries immediately after the accident
- Photo of Yolanda's scar
- Photo of Yolanda's capped tooth
- Medical records from hospital, doctor and dentist
- Bills from hospital, doctor and dentist
- Yolanda's business billing records showing how much she made during the months immediately before and after the accident

5. **Slip and fall, commercial property-owner liability, witnesses, hard injury, surgery plus non-traditional treatments, long recovery period**

SAMPLE DEMAND LETTER

Seiji Kurosawa
236 Sunset Grove
Fontana Beach, FL 00000

September 15, 199X

William Casey
Claims Adjuster
Atlantic Risk Insurance Company
2400 Causeway Boulevard
Miami, FL 00000

Re: Your Insured, Medellin Investments
   Claimant: Seiji Kurosawa
   Claim No.: T11889 PX
   Date of Loss: January 13, 199X

Mr. Casey:

As you are aware, I was injured in a fall on January 13, 199X in the underground parking lot of a building at 6750 Palm Avenue, Miami, owned by your insured, Medellin Investments. The accident occurred at about 6:00 p.m. when I was heading for my car parked in the garage. I am an employee of the South Florida Import-Export Exchange which leases offices in the building from your insured. As I crossed the dark garage floor, I slipped on a patch of oil, badly twisting my left knee and falling to the ground.

That night my knee swelled greatly and in the morning I went to see my physician, Dr. Rose Parker, who advised that I stay off the leg for the next several days. I went home and rested the leg, missing the next three days of work.

The following Monday, I returned to work and examined the garage where I had fallen. As the enclosed photographs taken that day show, there were grease and oil spots all over the floor, some of which had obviously been there for quite a while. To make matters worse, several of the overhead lights were burned out, leaving dark areas on the floor and hiding the oil and grease spots. Since there were several lights burned out, it is clear that no one had checked or replaced the bulbs for quite some time. Obviously, your insured fails to maintain the garage in a reasonably safe manner, and instead is maintaining a real hazard there. *(Seiji demonstrates that he investigated near the time of the accident.)*

The situation in the garage is so dangerous that at least two other people in the building have recently slipped on oil spots in the garage. *(Seiji informs the adjuster that witnesses are available to support his claim of danger in the garage. If he has good written statements from them, he ould identify the witnesses here and refer to enclosed witness statements.)* Further investigation may, of course, show that others have slipped in the garage as well.

The swelling in my knee subsided after about a week but continued to be painful and to catch when bent. I was examined by an orthopedist, Dr. Ralph Brancusa, who began me on physical therapy in his office. Although I obtained some relief from the soreness, the physical therapy did not eliminate the catch inside my knee when I bent or twisted it. I therefore voluntarily ended the physical therapy sessions. *("Voluntarily ended" demonstrates that Seiji did not continue treatment any longer than necessary.)*

I received acupuncture treatment from Dr. William Chan, which relieved some of the pain in the knee. *(Shows that non-traditional treatment had positive results.)* I was referred by Dr. Chan to a chiropractor, Lilly Sing Rhee, for manipulation to treat the catch in the knee. Ms. Sing Rhee stopped treatment after a short time and suggested that I return to an orthopedic surgeon.

I was referred by my physician to Dr. Walter Frisch, an orthopedic surgeon. Dr. Frisch X-rayed the knee and performed an arthroscopic examination which revealed torn cartilage, which Dr. Frisch repaired arthroscopically.

Following the arthroscopic surgery, I missed another week of work, then resumed walking and began home exercises prescribed by Dr. Frisch. After another approximately eight weeks, I was able to begin running again, my regular daily exercise that I was unable to do for almost eight months because of the accident. *(Emphasizes long time for recovery.)*

My medical expenses for this treatment are:

Rose Parker, M.D.	$ 60
Ralph Brancusa, M.D. (including X-rays)	650
William Chan	160
Lilly Sing Rhee	320
Walter Frisch, M.D. (including X-rays)	1,420
Total	$2,610

As the enclosed letter from my employer, South Florida Import-Export Exchange, indicates, I missed eight days of work (three immediately after the accident, five more after surgery), for a total of $1,120 ($140/day) in lost wages.

Because of the obvious negligence of your insured in failing to properly maintain its building, a dangerous hazard was created which resulted in serious cartilage damage to my knee, requiring surgery and an eight month period of recovery and rehabilitation. Because of the seriousness of the injury and the long time for its recovery, I demand $20,000 in compensation.

Because the statute of limitations requires me to file a lawsuit against your insured in this matter within three months from now, I look forward to resolving this claim in the near future. Please provide me with a response within 14 days from your receipt of this letter. *(Demands prompt reply.)*

Very truly yours,

Seiji Kurosawa

Supporting documents to be included:

- Photos of garage showing grease spots and burned-out lights
- Statements of others who have fallen there
- Medical records and bills from all doctors and other medical providers
- Letter from employer stating wages and work time missed

6. Slip and fall on stairs, hard injury, surgery, permanent injury, large comparative negligence

(Corresponds to Example 6b in Chapter 5.)

SAMPLE DEMAND LETTER

Wanda Shore
21566 Riverside Drive
Los Angeles, CA 00000

September 15, 199X

Roger de la Rue
Claims Adjuster
Twentieth Century Insurance Adjuster
6400 Century Boulevard
Los Angeles, CA 00000

Re: Your Insured, Broadmart Stores
    Claimant: Wanda Shore
    Claim No.: 93-1033 BS
    Date of Loss: January 13, 199X

Dear Mr. de la Rue:

I was injured on January 13, 199X in the West Hollywood Broadmart store. I fell coming down some stairs in the women's shoe section where I had been shopping. I landed on my right arm, shattering my elbow. *(Wanda describes her elbow as "shattered" rather than simply broken, establishing the seriousness of her injury.)*

Liability

Two weeks after the accident, with assistance, I visited the store again to examine the stairs on which I had fallen. In at least four separate ways, the stairs present an unreasonable hazard to a customer. First, the lack of handrails is a violation of law. The Los Angeles County Building Code Section 1225 requires that all commercial sets of stairs have handrails every 88 inches. Since this open stairway is over eleven feet wide, it should have had handrails on each side and one in the middle. It had no

handrails at all. At my age, 76, I always use a handrail when one is available, and in this case a handrail would have prevented a serious fall.

Also, the county building code requires that riser heights be the same to within one-quarter inch. The riser heights of the second and third stairs, on which I fell, differ by a full inch (6 $\frac{1}{8}$ inches to 7 $\frac{1}{8}$ inches). This violation of the code proved dangerous because when I came down the stairs, the third step down did not meet my foot at the same point as did the previous step, throwing me off balance. *(Wanda specifically explains why the violation of the building code caused her accident.)*

As the enclosed photographs show, the color of the carpeting contributes to the danger. The third step is covered with the same dark red carpet as on the bottom floor, while the platform and the first two steps down are covered in white carpet. Looking down onto the red third step, it is difficult to see that it is a step at all rather than the beginning of the floor. *(Photograph explained instead of merely included.)* The third step should have been white like the other two. And finally, display spotlights set up around the stairs shine directly into your eyes as you come down, making it extremely difficult to see the steps clearly.

For all these reasons, the stairs presented a hazardous condition to a customer and directly caused me to fall. The building code violations alone establish the store's liability, and when the other factors are added it becomes even more clear how dangerous the stairs were.

Injury and Treatment

I was taken by ambulance to the Mt. Pleasant Hospital Emergency room where they took X-rays and put my arm in a temporary cast. I was in terrible pain and was given a Demerol injection and more Demerol to take orally. *(Mention of the specific strong drug verifies the amount of pain Wanda suffered.)* The next day I went to see Dr. Barton Groback, an orthopedic surgeon, but my arm was so swollen that he could not examine it. He gave me more prescription pain medication, and for the next several days, I was in so much pain that all I could do was stay in bed. Even the slightest movement brought on excruciating pain. *(Great pain emphasized again.)*

When I returned to Dr. Groback the next week, he took more X-rays and scheduled me for surgery. He operated on January 24, 199X, and I spent three days in the hospital, then another week in bed, in great pain. I stayed in a cast for eight weeks, during which I required help just to care for myself. For the first two weeks after the operation I was in great pain. And for most of the eight weeks I was in a cast I was forced to stay around the house.

After the cast was removed, I began physical therapy treatments to regain movement and strength in my arm. I went to physical therapy for three months, and since then I have been doing daily exercises given to me by Dr. Groback. Despite all the therapy and the exercises, however, I still have much less strength in the arm than before the accident and I cannot bend the elbow much or twist my arm in either direction. Dr. Groback says that I will have to keep doing the exercises just to keep the arm at its present level, but that I will never recover full use of it. He also says that over time I may develop arthritis in the elbow joint, making it even less movable and more painful. *(Mention not only of long recovery and permanent injury but possibility of further problems later on.)*

The costs of my medical treatment are as follows:

Osprey Ambulance Service	$ 120
Mt. Pleasant Hospital (E.R.)	300
Barton Groback, M.D.	2,860
Mt. Pleasant Hospital (surgery)	1,650
Flexall Physical Therapy	1,200
TOTAL	$6,130

Because of the many dangers on the stairs, including two violations of the building code which led directly to my fall, I suffered a shattered right arm which required surgery and many months of rehabilitation, and which has resulted in a permanent loss of some use of my arm. Because of the great pain I have suffered, and the permanent disability the injury has caused, I demand $60,000 as compensation.

As you are aware, if this matter is not settled before January, I will be forced to file a lawsuit against Broadmart stores to protect my legal interests. *(A reminder to the insurance adjuster that Wanda may file lawsuit soon, something the adjuster does not want her to do because it may get lawyers involved.)* I hope, therefore, for your prompt attention to this matter.

Very truly yours,

Wanda Shore

Supporting documents to be included:

- A copy of the building code sections which regulate construction of stairs
- Photos of the stairs
- Photos of Wanda's arm at different stages of treatment and recovery
- Medical records and bills from ambulance and all hospitals, doctors and physical therapists

CHAPTER

7

Negotiating a Settlement

Using This Chapter

This chapter explains how you can take the final negotiation process from a first demand for compensation to a settlement of your claim.

- Read Sections A and B to understand how insurance adjusters operate and what you can do and say to ensure fair and speedy negotiations.

- Read Section C for strategies on how to break a negotiating stalemate.

You are now on the doorstep of settling your claim. If you have presented an organized demand letter and supporting documents (as discussed in Chapter 6), the negotiation process will probably consist of nothing more than a few brief phone calls with a claims adjuster. During the first of these calls, you and the adjuster will each make your points about what the proper settlement amount should be. Then the adjuster will make an offer to settle your claim for an amount lower than what you asked for in your demand letter. You will counter with a figure higher than the adjuster's offer but lower than that in your demand letter. And after two or three phone calls, you will agree on a settlement figure somewhere in between.

Settlement negotiations which begin with a thorough demand letter are usually just that simple. Occasionally, though, negotiations take a bit more work. It may be because the adjuster has questions about liability, your injuries, your medical treatment

or your lost income. Or perhaps you have not provided all necessary documents. Or you may just run into a difficult adjuster. This chapter helps you handle any of those situations by explaining who claims adjusters are, how the negotiation process works and what to do if you cannot quickly and easily get a reasonable settlement offer.

A. Adjusters: Who They Are and How They Work

Insurance claims adjusters come with different titles, such as claims specialist, claims representative or independent claims analyst, but they all do the same job. Understanding who claims adjusters are and how they work lets you see that they have no real advantage over you in the negotiation process, and that by having a good understanding of the facts of your own claim, you may well have an advantage over them.

1. Insurance Adjusters

When you have filed a claim against someone you believe was responsible for your accident, the negotiation process normally will be with a claims adjuster for that person's liability insurance company, referred to as the insurance carrier.

Occasionally, a claim is not handled by an insurance company's own adjuster, but instead is referred to a firm of independent insurance adjusters. Insurance companies often do this if they do not have a local claims office in a particular area. But independent claims adjusters representing an insurance company operate the same as in-house claims adjusters. The only difference is that they may have a lower authority limit within which to settle a case and therefore must have your settlement amount approved by a claims supervisor at an insurance company office. The negotiation process, however, is exactly the same.

Public entities, such as state governments or large cities which receive lots of claims, often have their own claims adjustment offices. The negotiation process with these government claims adjusters works exactly the same as with private insurance adjusters. The only notable difference in negotiating with a government claims adjuster is that if a claim eventually winds up in court, judges and juries tend not to be overly generous in awarding damages with public money. For this reason, government entity adjusters tend to be tighter with settlement money than private insurance adjusters. If you have a claim against a public entity, expect your settlement to be 10% to 25% lower than if it were against a private party.

It also sometimes happens that even though you have not filed a lawsuit, you may find an attorney negotiating with you about your claim instead of a claims adjuster. Self-insured corporations and some insurance companies without a local claims office will sometimes use either their own staff attorney or a local attorney as a claims adjuster. And government entities sometimes have assistant city, county or state attorneys who deal directly with accident claims even before they get to court.

If an attorney is handling your claim instead of a claims adjuster, don't panic. In the claims negotiation process, a lawyer cannot do anything different from a non-attorney claims adjuster. A lawyer may bluff a little more than a claims adjuster about the law regarding negligence and liability, but there are easy techniques to call that kind of bluff. (See Section B4.)

Often, a lawyer handling a claim will actually be easier to deal with than a claims adjuster. Many lawyers realize that in smaller cases, it's better for the company to settle with you promptly rather than spend a lot of time, and therefore a lot of the company's money, trying to get you to settle for a little bit less.

If you file a claim under your own automobile collision, uninsured or underinsured motorist coverage, you do *not* negotiate a settlement with your own insurance agent. All an agent can do is refer your claim to the claims department—and then it is completely out of the agent's hands. You will then negotiate a settlement with a claims adjuster who will be acting as the company's representative, not yours. (See Section B3.)

2. How Adjusters Settle Claims

The job performance of insurance adjusters is judged not only by how little of the insurance company's money they spend in settlements but also in how quickly they settle claims. Most adjusters get between fifty and a hundred new claims a month across their desks. So, they have to settle that many claims—known as "clearing" or "closing" a claim file—each month just to stay even. Another of the things their performance is rated on is how many claims they can personally settle without having to involve supervisors or insurance company lawyers. So an adjuster usually wants to settle a claim without much delay. Once an adjuster knows that you understand the range of how much your claim is worth, the adjuster will not usually stall your claim.

And during negotiations, you will find that you know much more about your claim than the adjuster does. Except for those assigned to the largest cases, insurance claims adjusters have no special legal or medical training. And most have neither the time nor the resources to investigate or study your claim very carefully. The result is that while an adjuster will know a little bit more than you about the claims business in general, he or she will not know your particular claim nearly as well as you do.

You were there during the accident. You know what your injuries are, how much and where they hurt, how long they have taken to heal; and you will have put in the time to understand how the accident happened and to demonstrate through photos and medical records and other documents what your damages were. The insurance adjuster, on the other hand, has only a couple of minutes a week to look at your file. As long as you are organized and understand the process, you are the one with the negotiating advantage.

Once an adjuster realizes you understand how much your claim is worth, he or she has the authority to come to an agreement with you on the telephone for what the final settlement amount should be. Once you and the adjuster agree on an amount, the adjuster simply sends you the paperwork to finalize the settlement. (See Chapter 8, Sections A and B.) But adjusters' authority to settle claims on their own is restricted to certain dollar limits. The limits depend on how much experience the adjuster has—less experienced adjusters, perhaps a $5,000 to $10,000 authority; more experienced adjusters, maybe $10,000 to $20,000.

An adjuster will not tell you what his or her authority is unless he or she is ready to make an offer higher than that authority. If so, the adjuster will have to ask for approval from a superior—usually called a claims supervisor or claims manager. This is neither unusual nor difficult. But if the adjuster does need to check with a supervisor about your settle-ment offer, get a date by which you will hear back from either one and then send a letter to the adjuster confirming that date.

B. How the Negotiation Process Works

Negotiating a final settlement is a little like bargaining for something at a flea market. You and the buyer (the adjuster) both know roughly how much an item (your damages) is worth. You know how much you are willing to take for it and the adjuster knows how much the insurance company is willing to pay. But neither of you knows how much the other side is willing to pay or receive. So you go through a process of testing each other, a dance of bluff and bluster that goes like this, usually in just two or three phone calls:

- You ask for a high amount in your written demand letter.
- The insurance adjuster tells you what's wrong with your claim—that there is a question about liability, or that your lengthy physical therapy was unnecessary.
- You respond to these arguments.
- The adjuster makes a low counter-offer to feel out whether you are in a hurry to take any settlement amount.
- You concede a little bit concerning the adjuster's arguments and make another demand slightly lower than the one in your demand letter.
- The insurance adjuster increases the company's offer.
- You either accept that amount or make another counter-demand.

It is usually as simple as that. The main facts determining how an accident settlement comes out are how well you have prepared all stages of your claim—investigation, supporting documents and demand letter, how much you are willing to settle for and how much of a hurry you are in to settle. The rest of this chapter explains how the unwritten rules of negotiation operate, including some of the legiti-mate negotiating responses you can expect from adjusters, plus some of the improper tactics a few adjusters might try as a way to get you to settle for less than is reasonable.

1. Conducting Negotiations

Negotiations with the insurance claims adjuster will begin shortly after the adjuster receives your demand letter. Usually the adjuster will telephone you within a week or two after receiving your demand. The length of time between demand letter and response depends on how busy the adjuster is and how much time the adjuster needs to go over your claim and perhaps to speak with the insured about the accident.

Keys To Successful Claims Negotiation

How you act during settlement negotiations can go a long way toward making the process run smoothly and quickly, with a minimum of stress or aggravation for you, and resulting in a satisfying settlement. Here are some of the basic rules about dealing with a claims adjuster.

BE ORGANIZED. If you follow the steps mapped out in Chapters 5 and 6, you will already be organized when you begin the negotiation process. Keep up the habits you've already developed. If you have a conversation with the adjuster, make a note of what was said. If either you or the adjuster have said that you will or will not do a certain thing, or that something is to occur by a certain date, write a confirming letter and send it to the adjuster. Keep a copy of everything you send. If you have agreed to provide the adjuster with information, do it promptly.

BE PATIENT. Although you may have already had to wait a considerable time to get all your medical and income records, try not to be in too great a hurry to settle your claim. One of the tactics claims adjusters use is to make a low initial settlement offer and see if you are too impatient to continue negotiating. If you can stand to wait, do not jump at a first offer because holding off for a little while often increases your settlement amount. After some time passes, it will be the adjuster who will want to settle your claim as soon as possible, and then you will be able to get the full value of your claim.

BE PERSISTENT. The flip side of being patient is to be persistent. Don't let the adjuster sit on your claim. If the adjuster has said that he or she will do something—make you another offer, check with a supervisor—get a specific date by which it will be done. Put everything agreed upon in a confirming letter, and when that date rolls around call and politely demand a response. If you have asked for information, or for a new settlement offer, set a reasonable deadline by which you would like the response. Don't pester an adjuster by calling every day, but make sure the adjuster knows you are out there and that you will be regularly and thoroughly following up on your claim.

BE CALM AND STRAIGHTFORWARD. Insurance adjusters are overworked and underpaid, and they hear a lot of stories every day. They are also human, which means they don't respond well to abuse or to hysterics, but do respond well if they believe what you say. So, even if you get an inconsiderate or unsympathetic adjuster, keep your cool and don't get into a personal battle; there are other and better ways to deal with an uncooperative adjuster. (See Section C.)

Your job is simply to show the adjuster that you know how the process works and that your claim is an honest one. Let the adjuster know you believe in the facts you have presented, and avoid high emotions. If you show the adjuster you are making a good faith claim, you will likely get a good faith settlement offer in return.

a. Reservation of rights letter

The first thing you might receive from an insurance company is called a "reservation of rights letter." This letter informs you that the company is investigating your claim but that it is reserving its right not to pay anything on your claim if it turns out that the accident is not covered under the policy—for

example, because the place where an accident occurred might be a neighbor's responsibility rather than the homeowner against whom you filed a claim, or because in an uninsured motorist claim the accident was entirely your fault.

A reservation of rights letter is intended to protect the insurance company so that you cannot later claim that because it began settlement nego-tiations with you, it acknowledged that the policy covers the accident. It also serves to plant the idea in the insured's mind that the insurance company might not cover the loss at all, intimidating some people into taking a quick and small settlement.

Do not be intimidated by a reservation of rights letter. The insurance company still must investigate your claim and negotiate with you fairly. Of course, if there is good reason to deny coverage altogether under the policy, the insurer is legally free to do so. But a reservation of rights letter does not change how

the insurance company will respond to your claimThat will be determined by the facts of your accident and your injuries.

b.   Delayed response from the insurer

If you do not hear from an adjuster within two weeks of sending your demand letter, call the claims depart-ment and ask when you can expect a response. If an adjuster says that he or she hasn't had a chance to review your demand yet, be polite but ask for a specific date—two more weeks, perhaps—by which the adjuster will contact you with a response. How-ever long you believe is reasonable, confirm the date with a brief written letter.

If you haven't heard from the adjuster by the date mentioned, telephone and firmly remind him or her of the promises made. If, after that, you still do not get a prompt response to your demand, you may have to go over the adjuster's head to a supervisor. (See Section C5.)

c.   Have a settlement amount in mind

As part of putting together your demand letter, you figured out a range of what you believe your claim is worth. Within that range, and before you speak to an adjuster about your demand, decide on a minimum settlement figure that you would accept. This figure is for your own information, not something you would reveal to the adjuster. But once the figures and discussions start going back and forth, it helps if you already have your bottom line in mind. That way, you don't have to make a snap decision if an adjuster makes you a take-it-or-leave-it offer on the phone. You will know whether it meets your minimum level or not.

However, you do not have to cling to the figure you originally set for yourself. If an adjuster points out some facts you had not considered but which

---

SAMPLE CONFIRMATION LETTER

> Allen Wright
> 345 Tenth Street
> Olean, NY 00000
>
> June 15, 199X
>
> Allison Lavelle
> Claims Adjuster
> Great Lakes Insurance Co.
> Syracuse, NY 00000
>
> Re: Your Insured, Robert Lee
>   Claimant: Allen Wright
>   Claim No.: 93-HQ1234
>   Date of Loss: January 13, 199X
>
> Dear Ms. Lavelle:
>
> This letter confirms our telephone conversation today during which you agreed to respond by July 1, 199X to my settlement demand letter dated June 1, 199X. I look forward to your response by July 1.
>
> Thank you for your attention to this matter.
>
> Sincerely,
>
> Allen Wright

clearly make your claim weaker, you may have to revise your minimum figure down somewhat. And if the adjuster starts with an offer at or near your minimum, you may want to revise your minimum upward.

d. Do not jump at a first offer

It is standard practice for insurance adjusters to begin negotiations by first offering a very low settlement amount—or, sometimes, denying liability altogether. With this tactic, the adjuster is trying to find out whether you understand what your claim is worth and to see if you are so impatient to get some money that you will take any amount that is quickly offered.

When a first offer is made, your response should depend on whether it is a reasonable offer but too low—or it is so low that it is just a tactic to see if you know what you are doing. (See Section e, below.) If the offer is reasonable, you can immediately make a counter-offer which is a little bit lower than your demand letter amount. That shows the adjuster that you, too, are being reasonable and are willing to compromise. A little more bargaining should quickly get you to a final settlement amount you both think is fair. In these negotiations, don't bother to go over all the facts again. Just emphasize the strongest points in your favor—the insured was completely at fault, you had a very painful injury, reasonable medical costs, long-term or permanent physical effects.

e. Get the adjuster to justify a low offer

If in your first conversation, the adjuster makes an offer so low that it is obviously just a negotiating tactic to see if you know what your claim is really worth, do not immediately lower the amount you put in your demand letter. Instead, ask the adjuster to give you the specific reasons why the offer is so low

and make notes of what he or she tells you. Then write a brief letter responding to each of the factors the adjuster has mentioned. Depending on the strength of any of the adjuster's reasons, you can lower your demand slightly, but before lowering your demand very far, wait to see if the adjuster will budge after he or she receives your reply letter.

The next time you speak with the adjuster, begin by asking for a response to your reply letter. The adjuster should now make you a reasonable offer upon which you will be able to bargain and arrive at a fair final settlement figure.

Only You Can Decide How Much Is Fair

There is no rule to go by in deciding whether a particular settlement offer is enough. Some people want to get as much as they possibly can out of a claim no matter how long it takes, and are willing to argue and bargain and bluff on and on and on. Other people want just to get a minimum amount of money as quickly as possible. Most people fall somewhere in between.

Deciding when a settlement offer is acceptable depends completely on your attitude toward the accident, and your injuries, on your tolerance for the claims process, and on your judgment about whether more bargaining is likely to produce a higher offer. Once you are within a certain range that you know is reasonable, how much is enough is completely up to you.

**SAMPLE REPLY LETTER TO
UNREASONABLY LOW INITIAL OFFER**

Angel Ruiz
123 Peach Street
Denver, CO 00000

June 15, 199X

Victor Rubinion
Claims Adjuster
Rocky Mountain Insurance Company
Denver, CO 00000

Re: Your Insured, Richard Leonard
      Claimant: Angel Ruiz
      Claim No.: 93-HQ1234
      Date of accident: January 13, 199X

Dear Mr. Rubinion:

In our telephone conversation today, you relayed
Rocky Mountain Insurance Company's offer to settle
my claim for $1,000. However, none of the reasons you
gave is supported by the facts.

First, you said that since your insured was already in
the intersection when our cars collided, I had a duty to
avoid hitting him and that therefore I was just as much
at fault. However, the police report makes clear that
your insured had a Yield sign and I had the right of
way.

Second, you claimed that I suffered "only a soft tissue"
injury which did not justify either the physical therapy I
underwent or my settlement demand. If you look at
the record of my X-rays, you will see a narrowing of a
cervical vertebra. Therefore, your characterization of
my injury as "minor" and as "soft tissue" is completely
unjustified.

Because of the slight possibility of some minor
comparative negligence in the accident, however, I
am willing to reduce by five percent my settlement
demand of $15,000. Therefore, I demand the sum of
$14,250 as settlement of the claim.

Please provide me with Rocky Mountain's response
within fourteen days after you receive this letter.

Very truly yours,

Angel Ruiz

f. Emphasize emotional points in your favor

During negotiations, mention any emotional points
supporting your claim. If, for example, you have sent
the adjuster a particularly strong photo of a smashed
car or a severe-looking injury, refer to it. If there was
a bottle of beer found in the other party's car, refer
again to the possibility of alcohol use. If other accidents had occurred in same way, remind the adjuster.
If your injury interfered with your ability to care for
your child, mention that your child suffered as a
result. Even though there is no way to put a dollar
value on these emotional factors, they can be very
powerful in getting an insurance company to settle
an accident claim.

Reducing Your Demand: Once Is Enough

Do not reduce your demand more than once until you
have a new offer from the adjuster. Never reduce your
demand twice without an intervening increased offer
from the adjuster; it's simply not good bargaining.

   If the adjuster comes up with more reasons for a
low offer, go over each one. Once you have dealt with
all the adjuster's arguments, you will either get a
reasonable offer or you will have found out that no
reasonable offer is coming and you will have to try to
put some additional pressure on the insurance
company. (See Section C.)

g. Put the settlement in writing

When you finally get to that moment of agreeing to a
settlement offer, or the adjuster's agreeing to your
counter-offer, immediately confirm the agreement in
a letter to the adjuster. The letter can be short and
sweet.

SAMPLE SETTLEMENT CONFIRMATION LETTER

Michael Filippi
1747 Lemming Way
Mendota, WI 00000

April 24, 199X

Esther Berganian
Claims Adjuster
All Claims Insurance Company
Boston, MA 00000

Re: Your Insured, Cynthia Berquette
     Claimant: Michael Filippi
     Claim No.: PI-23469
     Date of accident: April 2, 199X

Dear Ms. Berganian:

This letter confirms today's telephone conversation in which we agreed to settle the injury claim for $5,000, not including property damage which was previously settled.

You have informed me that you will prepare and send to me settlement and release documents within 10 days from this date.

With best regards,

Michael Filippi

---

2. The Subjects of Negotiations With an Adjuster

During negotiations, an insurance adjuster has a right to ask questions and dispute facts in an attempt to limit your right to compensation. Questions or disputes might concern:

- **Coverage**   whether the insurance policy in question actually covers the accident

- **Liability**   who was at fault for the accident and what was the degree of your comparative negligence
- **The extent of your injuries**   whether an injury was disabling, or had a long-term permanent effect, and
- **The nature and extent of medical treatment**   whether the type and duration of procedures or therapies were medically necessary.

You should meet an adjuster's reasonable questions and inquiries with reasonable answers. But some questions and arguments are not legitimate—and are intended unfairly to influence you to settle the case for less than it is truly worth. (See Section 3, below.)

Specific legitimate and improper conduct by adjusters is discussed in this section. But for situations not covered here, there is a simple rule to follow: If the question, request or argument seems reasonably necessary for the adjuster to get an accurate picture of your claim, be reasonable in your response. And if you are not certain about whether a question, request or argument is reasonable or not, tell the adjuster precisely that—"I'm not certain that this is a reasonable request"—and allow him or her to explain why it is reasonable.

In deciding the reasonableness of questions or requests for information, consider both sides of the negotiating process. Bear in mind that, except in claims against your own insurance company, a claims adjuster has no legal right to see or receive anything specific, or to get you to answer anything particular, unless a lawsuit is filed and served on the insured. On the other hand, the claims adjuster is not legally obligated to settle a claim unless he or she has sufficient information to understand the accident, your injuries and your damages. You have to balance your rightful reluctance to give too much information against the insurance company's right to evaluate your claim.

The following discussion of specific arguments, questions and requests from claims adjusters will give you a feel for what is reasonable and what is not.

a.   Denying coverage

A claims adjuster might contend that the insurance policy involved does not cover your accident. The reasons given might be:

- the policy lapsed
- the nature or location of the accident was not covered—particularly if it is a homeowners' policy
- the person who caused the accident is not covered, or
- you do not qualify to make a third-party claim under your state's no-fault vehicle insurance law.

However, an adjuster's contention that there is no coverage does not end settlement negotiations. Instead, the coverage question simply becomes one more element in your negotiations.

First, ask the adjuster to give you a written explanation of the insurance company's reasons for claiming there is no coverage. This will reveal whether the adjuster is just bluffing, and will give you a chance to respond to the reasons more specifically.

If the adjuster does not agree to give you a written explanation, write a letter to the adjuster confirming your conversation, the denial of coverage and the adjuster's refusal to explain in writing. This letter may pressure the adjuster to give you the information because an insurance claims supervisor will not like such a letter in the insurance company's file. If you eventually go to the insurance commission or file a lawsuit to pursue your claim, such a letter in the claim file would show the insurance company's lack of cooperation.

Also ask the claims adjuster to provide you with a copy of the insured's policy—or at least the portions on which the adjuster relies in denying coverage—so that you can read it for yourself. If the adjuster refuses, write a letter to the adjuster confirming the refusal so that it becomes a part of your claim file. Then, if the adjuster still refuses to negotiate with you about settlement, you will have to use other pressures to get negotiations moving. (See Section C.)

In many cases, an adjuster will initially contend that there is no coverage but as soon as you indicate that you will not abandon your claim, the adjuster will begin to negotiate a settlement, anyway. If, after that, you cannot reach a satisfactory settlement, because of the coverage question or any other problem, you will have to move into other negotiating strategies. (See Section C.)

Don't Be Swayed by a Lawyer's Letter

In claiming that there is no insurance coverage for your accident, an adjuster may tell you that "the lawyers" have said there is no coverage. The adjuster may even send you a copy of a letter from a company lawyer stating that there is no coverage for your accident.

Do not be impressed. A company lawyer's opinion that there may not be coverage for your accident is no more binding than anyone else's opinion. Whether or not there is coverage depends on the terms of the policy, and a policy can often be read in several different ways, depending on the facts. If the matter goes to court, ambiguities in a policy are resolved in favor of coverage.

So, even if there is a lawyer's opinion, ask to see the language of the policy on which the lawyer and adjuster are relying. The policy language concerning the question of coverage, like the questions of liability and of damages, should become a matter of negotiation between you and the claims adjuster.

If the adjuster seems to you to be correct that there is no coverage at all and refuses to negotiate for a settlement, you may be able to turn to insurance which covers someone else responsible for the accident. For example, if the city claims there is no coverage for a cracked sidewalk because sidewalk maintenance is the legal responsibility of each property owner, you will file a claim against the insurance company for the owner in front of whose property you fell on the sidewalk. (See Chapter 4, Section B.)

The End of Your Negotiating Road

Sometimes, an insurance adjuster will not budge from a denial of coverage and on that basis refuses to make any settlement offer. If there is no one else who was responsible for the accident, it is probably worth your time to consult with an attorney to see if the lawyer can find some technical way around the apparent lack of coverage. (See Section C4 of this chapter and Chapter 9, Section B.)

---

b. A claim beyond auto policy limits

Although most state laws require that automobile liability insurance be sufficient to cover most accidents, in some states, the amount of total coverage required by laws is quite low—$5,000 or $10,000 total per accident victim; $10,000 to $20,000 total for all injured people per accident. The total amount which can be paid under a given insurance policy coverage is referred to by insurance adjusters as the "policy limits." Per person and per accident policy limits are often referred to together as "10/20" or "15/30"—meaning $10,000 per person and $20,000 per accident or $15,000 per person and $30,000 per accident.

Your demand may be for $15,000, for example, but the claims adjuster tells you that the insured's policy limits are only $10,000. If the adjuster tells you that the insured's policy limits are below what you are demanding, request that the adjuster put the policy limits in writing.

Policy limits are the maximum you can recover from that particular insurance company, but low limits may at least make your settlement negotiations simpler. You can demand a policy limits settlement from the insured's company if your claim is worth at least that much—without having to argue with the adjuster about exactly how much more than the limits the claim is worth.

If you accept a policy limit settlement, the insured person's insurance company will require that you release the insured from all liability. (See Chapter 8.) Accepting the policy limits would mean the end of your claim. So, if your claim is worth far more than the insured's policy limits, check with a personal injury lawyer before settling. The lawyer can determine whether the insured has personal assets beyond his or her insurance coverage that might be available to compensate you through a lawsuit. If so, the lawyer can advise you whether it is worth pursuing such a lawsuit.

In a vehicle accident claim, if you have under-insured motorist coverage in your own policy, you can settle with the insured's insurance company for policy limits and then pursue a claim for the rest of your damages under your own underinsurance coverage. You will negotiate with your own insurer about how much your total claim is worth, exactly as you would if it were a third party's insurance company. And when you settle on a full compensation amount, your underinsurance coverage will pay the difference between this total figure and the amount of policy limits you already received from the other insurance company. (See Chapter 4, Section A3.)

c.   No legal liability

Occasionally an adjuster will tell you "the law" says that you, and not its insured, are liable for the accident. Most of these adjusters are talking through their hats. They have a general idea of what the law is on certain liability subjects, but rarely do they know the law in any detail.

If an adjuster claims that the law is on the insurance company's side, demand proof. Ask the adjuster to send you the statute, rule or regulation which the adjuster claims applies to your situation. If the adjuster does not send you any documentation of the law, then tell the adjuster that you cannot consider something which is undocumented. If the adjuster does send you something, make sure it is a copy of an actual legal rule or law and not merely an insurance company's own memo, or a letter from a lawyer, or some other unofficial opinion about the law.

When you get a copy of an official rule or law, read it carefully. Often what you will be sent is just a general statement of law which can be applied differently in different situations and does not answer the question of who was at fault for your accident. For example, a traffic law may state that the driver to the right has the right-of-way at a four-way stop intersection, but that doesn't answer whether you got to the intersection first and had the right to go through the intersection before the other car, or whether the other car was careless in failing to stop at the stop sign.

If, despite your arguments, an adjuster continues to rely on an interpretation of a law which denies all liability by the insured, and refuses any settlement at all, you will have to turn to other negotiating procedures. (See Section C.)

d.   Relying on the police report

In traffic accident cases, an adjuster will sometimes argue that nothing in the police report confirms your description of how the accident happened. You can point out that nothing in the police report contra-

dicts your version of what happened, and that the police officer did not witness the accident, but only arrived after the event.

You have a more difficult problem if the police report specifically contradicts your version of whose fault the accident was. If the claims adjuster points out something in the police report which indicates that you were at fault for the accident, and suggests that you have no claim at all because it, there are several ways to respond:

- Remind the adjuster that the police report is not actual evidence since the police officer did not see the accident happen.
- Point out that the officer issued you no citation after the accident.
- Note that the reporting officer does not state any opinion about who was at fault.
- Remind the adjuster that the officer's report is based solely on a rough reconstruction of the accident, done without precision, based on limited facts and resting on speculation.

These are all ways of saying to the adjuster that the police officer's accident report is useless as legal evidence of what actually happened. (See Chapter 6, Section A1.)

An attack on the legal value of a police report may or may not immediately get the claims adjuster to back off relying on the report in your negotiations. But it will at least let the adjuster know that you know the police report is of limited help should your claim eventually wind up in court. And an adjuster who knows you will not drop your claim just because of a bad police report will get back to bargaining with you. Of course, you may have to lower your demand somewhat because of the report.

e.   Request to examine evidence

An insurance company against which you have filed a claim has a right to see evidence you have which shows something about how the accident happened or how badly you were injured. You can either provide a photo of evidence, or if the adjuster requests, arrange for the adjuster or other representative of the insurance company to view the evidence in person. *Do not*, however, let the insurance company take away from you, even temporarily, any piece of evidence you have. Once the evidence is out of your hands, you cannot be sure that it won't be changed, modified or lost.

If the insurance company says it cannot do the examination while the evidence remains in your possession, tough luck. If the claim ever becomes a lawsuit, the insurance company can go to court to ask for an order entitling it to make such an examination. But until a claim becomes a lawsuit, the insurer has no right to take evidence out of your possession.

f.   Request to know your witnesses

Simply mentioning in your demand letter that you have supporting witnesses may be enough to convince the insurance company that you can prove the other side was at fault. This is particularly true if you have directly quoted from or sent a written witness statement along with your demand letter.

However, an insurance adjuster may ask you for the names and addresses of your witnesses to speak with them directly. It makes no sense at this point for you to refuse to identify a witness you have already told the insurance company about. Refusing to give the insurance company the name and address of a witness, or refusing to ask the witness to contact the insurance company, will appear to be an unreasonable lack of cooperation which will result in suspicion and lack of cooperation in return. It will also completely undercut the value of having the witness. If you won't let the insurance company verify what the witness says, the insurance company isn't going to be very impressed that you have such a witness.

Accident witnesses have privacy rights, however, and unless there is a formal lawsuit with subpoenas issued by a court, a witness who does not want to speak to an insurance company does not have to. And if a witness has instructed you not to give out his or her identity to the insurance company, tell that to the adjuster. However, if a witness refuses to speak to the adjuster, the adjuster is probably not going to give much weight to what the witness claims to have seen, which makes that witness almost useless for the negotiation process.

A witness who agrees to speak with the insurance company has the right to control where, when and how that contact takes place.

- The witness can contact the adjuster rather than having his or her phone number given out.
- The witness does not have to give a written statement.
- The witness does not have to be interviewed in person.
- The witness does not have to sign any statement drawn up by the adjuster.
- The witness does not have to return to the scene with the adjuster or anyone else.
- The witness does not have to give any more personal information than he or she wants to; and
- Once the witness speaks with the adjuster, the witness does not have to speak with anyone else from the insurance company or have to repeat the conversation with the adjuster.

Even though a witness is not legally obligated to speak with the adjuster, you are not permitted to instruct the witness not with speak to the insurance company; that would improperly interfere with the company's right to gather evidence. You can discuss with the witness what is important in the case, and stress the points you would like him or her to make clear to the adjuster, but you cannot tell the witness what to say or not say. It is certainly all right for the witness to tell the adjuster that you and the witness have discussed the accident, but the witness should be able to tell the adjuster in all honesty that you have not tried to tell the witness what he or she must say.

Ask for the Adjuster's Witnesses

If the adjuster asks you to identify your witnesses, ask that the adjuster do the same for you. If the adjuster denies knowing of any witnesses, write a letter confirming that. If the adjuster refuses to discuss witnesses, or to identify them, write a letter confirming the refusal and state that since the adjuster refuses, you must also refuse to reveal your witnesses.

If the adjuster gives you the identities of witnesses you did not previously know about, do not depend on the adjuster's version of what the witnesses say. Directly contact them and find out what they have to say. You may be pleasantly surprised that the witness does not support the insured's version of events nearly as strongly as the adjuster claims the witness does. (See Chapter 3, Section A.)

g. Request for medical records

Although you will have sent copies of all your relevant medical records along with your demand letter, the adjuster might ask for some additional record you have not provided. For example, if X-rays were taken but there are only the records from your doctor and not from the radiologist, the adjuster might ask for the radiologist's records. Or, if there is an indication of a pre-existing injury, an adjuster might ask to see medical records concerning that injury.

It is up to you to decide whether the request is reasonable. If it seems to be, tell the adjuster that you will provide the records if the insurance company is willing to pay for them. There is often a small fee from the doctor's office for copying records. If the adjuster agrees to pay for the records, confirm the agreement in writing. Then request the records yourself and review them before sending them on to the adjuster, removing any records which do not pertain to accident injuries.

Unfortunately, some adjusters like to get additional medical records just to snoop around in your medical history to see if there is anything they can use against you or to embarrass you. If the request for additional medical records seems unreasonable—that is, is not related to the injuries you suffered in the accident—do not comply. Ask the adjuster to explain why the additional records are needed. If the answer doesn't convince you, politely inform the adjuster that you do not believe the records are relevant to your claim and that providing them would intrude into your privacy. Remind the adjuster that if the claim winds up in court, the lawyers will be able to argue over this issue, but that at this point you can see no reason to allow prying into your personal medical history. Be firm with an adjuster. There is nothing wrong or suspicious about protecting your privacy.

Do Not Sign Your Rights Away

Whatever you decide about providing an adjuster with additional medical records, *never* sign an agreement or verbally authorize an adjuster to directly obtain any of your medical records. Always obtain records yourself. Review them to make sure they only pertain to your claim and do not unnecessarily reveal the rest of your private medical history.

h. Request for medical report

The records that doctors regularly keep may not explain fully enough some medical issue important to your claim. For example, your medical records may not make it clear how much of an injury is the result of an accident or is from a pre-existing injury. Or, the prognosis for length of recovery may not be included. Or, the doctor may have told you something about long-term effects from your injury, but not included it in your medical records.

Either you or the adjuster or both might want a report from your doctor to clarify some medical issue. If the claims adjuster indicates that he or she wants a report and the request seems reasonable, do *not* allow the adjuster to contact your doctor directly. Tell the adjuster you will consider the request and will give an answer within a certain amount of time—a week or two. Then contact your doctor and find out whether the doctor would write a report favorable to you. (See Chapter 6, Section A2c.) Also find out how much the doctor would charge for the report.

If the doctor indicates that the report might do you some good, you can contact the adjuster and agree to request a report if the adjuster agrees to pay for it. If the adjuster says yes, send a confirming letter.

i. Request for medical examination

Once in a while, a claimant and an adjuster will have widely different opinions about the seriousness of an injury. Most disagreements arise over long-term or permanent effects which the adjuster does not believe are as serious as you describe them to be. Usually this difference of opinion can be resolved in negotiations. You and the adjuster each compromise and meet at a settlement figure somewhere in the middle. But sometimes the difference of opinion can be so wide that the adjuster will ask if you would be willing to be examined by a doctor, designated by the insurance company, to provide another medical opinion about your injury. Because the insurance company has to pay a doctor for such an exami-

nation, cost-conscious adjusters do not request them very often.

Although these second opinions are referred to by insurance people as an "independent medical examinations" (IME), they are anything but independent. The doctors who conduct the examinations are chosen—and paid—over and over again by the insurance company because they almost never find anything seriously wrong with an insurance claimant.

An IME is usually a bad idea for an insurance claimant. Fortunately, you are not required to submit to an IME, except, sometimes, under your own automobile policy. (See Section 3, below.) If an adjuster asks if you are willing to have an IME, politely refuse on the grounds that you do not wish to be examined by a doctor you do not know and whose opinion you have no way of judging. Remind the adjuster that if your claim later winds up in court, the insurance company can then follow the appropriate legal procedures to request an IME.

3. Special Rules for Negotiating With Your Own Insurer

A claim filed under the uninsured or underinsured motorist coverage of your own automobile insurance policy is referred to as a "first-party" claim. The rules for proceeding with a first-party claim are determined by the specific terms of your policy. And often your policy requires a bit more from you than you would have to provide in a third-party claim.

In general, your own policy will require that you cooperate with your insurance company during the claim. Of course, what cooperation means is subject to different interpretations, and usually comes down to what is reasonable under the circumstances: your right to privacy balanced against the company's right to get enough information to process your claim.

Most policies spell out the main points of cooperation you are required to provide, such as:

Timely notification Your policy may provide a specific time limit within which you must notify the company of your claim. Even if you have missed this time limit, however, your insurance company cannot deny your claim unless it shows that it has been prejudiced by the late notice. (See Section 4b, below.)

Authorization for release of medical records   You must sign an authorization permitting your insurance company to directly obtain medical records concerning your injuries.

Authorization for release of personnel and other income records   If you have claimed income loss, you must sign an authorization permitting the insurance company to obtain directly from your employer information concerning your income and your work record.

Independent medical examination   If your insurance company requests that you have an IME, read the policy carefully to see what the terms are. In general, make sure there is only one examination, that the insurance company agrees in writing to pay for it and that it is arranged at your convenience, not just the doctor's. Also, get a statement from the claims adjuster in writing, in advance, of the limits of the examination. You only have to undergo an examination of the injuries you claim, and not a general physical exam.

If you have any dispute with the adjuster for your insurance company over submitting to a medical examination, providing information or following policy rules, do not take the adjuster's word as gospel. Read the policy. If you don't have a copy, the adjuster must provide you with one. And if you reach a stalemate with your own company's adjuster about any point of negotiations or about the amount of the settlement offer, you may have to switch negotiation strategies. (See Section C.)

4.   Improper Settlement Tactics

Claims adjusters are hired to save their companies' money. And although most adjusters do their jobs within the rules, there are a few who will try break those rules if they think they can get away with it. This section alerts you to a number of the improper negotiating tactics that some adjusters use, and explains how to respond if an adjuster tries one on you.

a.   "Settle with the other company"

When beginning negotiations, an adjuster may tell you to contact the insurance company for another person or business involved in the accident because that other person or business was more responsible that its insured. Politely remind the adjuster that until one company or the other commits itself in writing to be the primary insurance carrier, you are entitled to proceed against either responsible party and that you are doing so against that adjuster's insured. (See Chapter 6, Section B1.)

b.   "You waited too long"

If there was any delay between your accident and when you notified the insurance company in writing of your intention to file a claim, an insurance adjuster might try to intimidate you by telling you that you waited too long and that the delay might now disqualify your claim.

In fact, in third-party claims there is no time limit other than the Statute of Limitations within which you must file a notice of claim. (See Section E.) The exception is for a claim against the government. (See Chapter 3, Section C.) If the adjuster for a third party contends that you delayed "too long" or asks why you waited to file your claim, remind the adjuster that there is no time limit for filing a liability claim and politely demand that the adjuster move onto actual settlement negotiations.

If you are filing a claim under your own insurance coverage, your policy may require that a notice of injury be filed within a specific number of days or within a reasonable time after the accident. But even if you have delayed before filing a notice of claim, the insurance company must honor your claim unless the claim was so late that it prejudiced the insurance company's ability to investigate the claim.

It is up to an insurance company to prove any prejudice caused by the delay—for example, that it was unable to investigate the scene of the accident, or that evidence was destroyed. And it is very rarely able to do so. You do not need to prove that there was no prejudice. And, of course, if the insurance company was notified of the accident by its own insured, it has no reason to complain about your delayed claim.

Tell the claims adjuster the reasons for the delay in notifying the insurance company: you didn't know who the responsible party might be; you were not provided with adequate insurance information; your injuries made it impossible for you to investigate for a while. But do not concede that the time was unreasonable. And do not permit the adjuster to put you off your claim. This tactic of suggesting that you filed your claim too late is just an attempt to make you nervous enough that you will jump at any small settlement offer out of fear of losing your claim entirely.

Unless the adjuster offers to prove specific prejudice to the insurance company, ignore any comments about a delayed claim. If the adjuster continues to deny your claim altogether, you will have to move on to other negotiating tactics. (See Section C.)

c. "You weren't out of pocket"

As mentioned several times, whether you paid for medical care out of your own pocket or it was paid for by your health or other insurance is none of the claims adjuster's business. And it is none of the adjuster's business whether or not your lost time at work was covered by sick leave or vacation pay. Under what is known as the "collateral source rule," it is improper for a claims adjuster to consider other sources of payment in determining a reasonable settlement amount—or even to ask you about such other payments.

The reasoning behind the collateral source rule is simple. A person who causes injuries should not benefit because you have taken the precaution of paying for health or other medical insurance coverage—nor by the fact that by working steadily you have earned the right to sick leave or vacation time.

If an adjuster so much as breathes anything about other sources of medical or income payments, remind him or her that the collateral source rule prohibits such questions. Inform the adjuster that you will consider any further reference to collateral payment sources to be bad faith settlement tactics. You are not likely to hear about collateral sources again. But if by some strange chance you do, report the matter to the adjuster's superior and to the State Department of Insurance. (See Sections C and D.)

C. What To Do When You Can't Get a Settlement

Most adjusters want to handle a claim simply and without unnecessary time and energy. But there are always a few adjusters—because of personality, negotiating style, or company policy—who are willing to bluff or stall well past the time all the documents have been examined and all the arguments have been made on both sides.

These adjusters will often make an extremely low initial offer and then stick to it without giving any justification. They hope that their tactics will either intimidate or frustrate you into accepting a settlement much lower than your claim is worth.

This section suggests several things you might do to get a troublesome adjuster to make you a fair settlement offer. Some of the suggestions involve nothing more than matters to raise in your communications with the adjuster; others involve going over the adjuster's head. And if all else fails, you may have to consider going to court—either on your own to small claims court or with a lawyer through the slow and costly process of standard court litigation. (See Chapter 9, Sections A and B.)

1. Persistence

You may be able to move an adjuster off a stubbornly-held position simply by regularly—every week or ten days—calling or writing to ask when the adjuster will make a fair and reasonable settlement offer. By reaffirming that you will be both patient and persistent and will not fold up your claim, you may get the adjuster to come up with a fair settlement offer.

2. Suggestion of Bad Faith

Key phrases in the insurance industry sometimes make adjusters sit up and take notice. When you are negotiating a settlement with your own insurance company as part of uninsured or underinsured motorist coverage, "bad faith" can be one such phrase. Because your policy is a paid-for promise by your insurance company to provide you with insurance protection, the company has a duty to provide that protection and settle claims in good faith.

Insurance companies for third parties also have a duty of good faith toward an injured person, but that duty is much less than the duty owed by your own company. A claim of bad faith against a third party's insurance company only arises if it has engaged in outright lies or fraud. If you believe a third-party

---

Check the Time

Every state has a law, called the statute of limitations, restricting the time a person injured in an accident can sue. After that time has passed, no lawsuit can be filed by the injured person to seek compensation for his or her injuries.

If the time limit has passed and you have failed to file—or have a lawyer file on your behalf—a lawsuit against the person or business legally responsible for your accident, their legal responsibility ends. And their insurance company will no longer settle a claim with you.

In most states, you have two years or more from the date of the accident to file a lawsuit. And since settling a claim doesn't normally take nearly that long, you don't usually have to be concerned about the timing. However, in California, Kentucky, Louisiana and Tennessee, the statute of limitations is only one year from the date of the accident. (See Section E for a state listing of time limits.)

If you have not yet settled your claim by two months before your state's time limit, consider filing a lawsuit. Consult an attorney who specializes in personal injury cases about getting the formal lawsuit papers filed. Filing the papers does not mean that you have to hire the lawyer to take over your claim. (See Section C4.) Nor does it necessarily mean you have to move forward right away with an actual court case. Filing a lawsuit does, however, protect your right to proceed with your claim and with a court case if that later becomes necessary.

insurer has engaged in such outrageous behavior, contact the State Department of Insurance (see Section 6, below) and an experienced personal injury attorney (see Chapter 9, Section B).

An adjuster for your own insurance company is not negotiating in bad faith just because you and the adjuster have a difference of opinion about how much your claim is worth. However, bad faith may exist if the adjuster for your own company has refused to give you any specific reasons for a very low settlement offer or has said or done something which might amount to an improper settlement tactic. (See Section B4.)

If you believe the adjuster for your company is negotiating in bad faith, use the term in conversation with the adjuster. If you get no satisfactory response, you may want to put your accusation of bad faith in writing. In a bad faith letter to the insurance company, specifically refer to the conduct of the adjuster which you believe amounts to bad faith. (See sample letter claiming bad faith.)

A written accusation of bad faith often gets prompt attention and, if justified, may rapidly provoke a change in the adjuster's settlement position. If an insurance company is proved to have acted in bad faith, it may be liable to pay damages to the insured well above the injury compensation amount. The rules about what is and is not bad faith vary from state to state, and it is extremely difficult to win bad faith damages in court. Nonetheless, in settlement negotiations, the mere possibility of a fight over bad faith often can help nudge a reasonable settlement offer out of an insurance company.

SAMPLE LETTER CLAIMING BAD FAITH

Alice Mendoza
123 Broadway
Redhook, IL 00000

June 15, 199X

Ronald Firth
Claims Adjuster
Metropolitan Insurance Co.
St. Louis, MO 00000

Re: Your Insured, Alice Mendoza
    Claimant: Alice Mendoza
    Claim No.: 93-HQ1234
    Date of accident: January 13, 199X

Dear Mr. Firth:

This letter concerns the discussions you and I have had over the past several weeks concerning settlement of the uninsured motorist claim referenced above. You have made only one offer of settlement in the amount of $500. This offer bears no reasonable relationship to my injuries, since my medical expenses alone total $1,550. Yet you refuse to provide me with any explanation for your position.

The only conclusion I can come to is that Metropolitan Insurance Company is refusing to negotiate in good faith.

If no fair and reasonable settlement offer, or explanation for the lack of such offer, is made by July 1, 199X, I will be forced to take further steps regarding Metropolitan's apparent bad faith.

Yours truly,

Alice Mendoza

3. Threat of a Lawsuit

Adjusters do not like lawsuits. A lawsuit usually means that lawyers will soon get involved, costs will go up and the claim file may be taken away from the adjuster and given to an insurance company lawyer or to another adjuster, which may mean a blemish on the adjuster's work record. Also, a lawsuit can get the insured person upset, which can mean lost business for the insurance company. Since a claims adjuster wants to avoid all this, you might be able to loosen the insurance company purse strings by suggesting that if a fair offer is not made by a certain date, you will be forced to file a lawsuit and to hire an attorney to handle the claim for you.

4. Consulting an Attorney

Although most lawyers are paid for handling personal injury cases by taking a percentage of your settlement, some are willing to consult with you on an hourly basis while you continue to handle your claim yourself. If you and a claims adjuster are at an impasse, particularly if there is some legal question about liability over which you and the adjuster disagree, you might want to meet for a couple hours with a lawyer who specializes in personal injury cases.

Bring with you all your papers, documents, notes and correspondence. After a brief review, the lawyer might be able to point out some particular fact, rule or tactic you can use in your next contact with the adjuster. The lawyer may also be able to help you file a lawsuit to protect your rights within the limits of your state's statute of limitations. (See Section E.)

Injecting some new idea or legal theory into the negotiations can sometimes get an adjuster finally to make a serious settlement offer. You may even want to let the adjuster know that you have consulted with an attorney and that if a fair settlement offer is not made, you will be forced to let the attorney take over your claim.

If you decide to consult with a lawyer on an hourly basis, make sure you know ahead of time how much the lawyer will charge per hour, and be sure to set a limit, in writing, on the number of hours you want the lawyer to spend reviewing your claim. (See Chapter 9, Section B2.)

5. Speak With the Adjuster's Supervisor

If you are unable to settle your claim with the adjuster assigned to it, there are other people within the insurance company from whom you might get a more reasonable offer. The adjuster has an immediate supervisor, and there is also usually an overall claims manager within the claims department. If you have reached an impasse, or if the adjuster fails to act promptly on your claim, politely suggest that the difficulties might be overcome if you both got another opinion, and ask to speak with the claims supervisor. Merely asking the adjuster to bring the supervisor into the picture may jar the adjuster into changing the settlement offer.

If the adjuster promises to contact the supervisor for a review of the file, allow some time for that. The adjuster may come back with a better settlement offer. But if the adjuster is going to discuss the matter with the supervisor, agree on a specific date by which the adjuster will report back to you on the results.

If the adjuster does not agree to speak with the supervisor, ask for the supervisor's name. Call or write to the supervisor, mention the number of contacts you have had with the adjuster and explain that the adjuster has yet to make a reasonable settlement offer and has failed to give you satisfactory reasons for the low offer. If the adjuster has delayed or used improper settlement tactics, mention that, too. Then ask that the supervisor review the file and either handle the matter personally or refer it to a new adjuster.

If you cannot get a reasonable settlement offer from the supervisor, ask him or her to write to you the reasons for the insurance company's settlement position. This statement of the company's position may be helpful to you in any further steps you have to take. One of those steps is to contact the claims manager, who is the boss of the adjusters and supervisors. Get the name of the claims manager from the supervisor and repeat the process with the manager, describing the problem you have had with the adjuster and the supervisor. To avoid further hassles with a persistent claimant, the claims manager might authorize an increase in the settlement offer.

6. Contact the State Department of Insurance

Every state has a Department or Commission or Bureau of Insurance that oversees the insurance companies in the state. And each department has a consumer complaint division which will sometimes pressure an insurance company to settle a claim. For the most part, these state departments of insurance are in the pockets of the big insurance company lobbies, but the consumer complaints divisions are a little better than the larger policy-making parts of the agencies.

The mere mention of a complaint to the state department of insurance may bring the adjuster around to making a new settlement offer. Even though state departments of insurance don't often do anything more than write a letter of inquiry to the insurance company, adjusters would rather not have to deal with a complaint and don't want one in their personnel file.

If mentioning the possibility of a complaint to the state department of insurance doesn't get any movement from the adjuster or supervisor, file an actual complaint. Before making your written complaint to the state department of insurance, call to find out where to send it. (See Section D for a list of state departments of insurance.) Then, send a letter of complaint which includes:

• the date of the accident and people involved in it
• a general description of your claim

• the insurance company's claim number
• details of the difficulties you have had with the claims adjuster—delays, no fair settlement offer, improper settlement tactics
• the number of conversations you have had with the adjuster and supervisors trying to settle the matter, and
• copies of all your correspondence, including your demand letter, so the insurance department investigator will understand exactly what the claim is based on.

The quality, quantity and speed of response from state Departments of Insurance varies greatly from state to state. In a few states, notably California, every complaint gets at least some attention from the department's Consumer Affairs Office. In other states, however, your complaint may only get action if the office spots obvious and extreme improper conduct, or if it has received numerous other complaints about the same adjuster or insurance company. Most Departments of Insurance keep a registry of complaints and if any one company has too many, the company may have some trouble with the Department of Insurance or with consumer groups when they try to have new rates or policies approved by the state.

The state insurance department probably will at least send a form letter to the insurance company informing it of your complaint. The company will then have to respond to the state insurance department within two weeks.

Your complaint to the state insurance department can accomplish several things. First, someone in the claims department of the insurance company other than the adjuster who handled the claim will become aware that there is a claimant who intends to do whatever it takes to get a fair and reasonable settlement, and that may inspire someone to take another look at your claim and come up with a reasonable settlement offer. Also, because a complaint with the state insurance department adds an extra layer of work for the insurance company, the company will want to try harder to settle your claim.

SAMPLE LETTER TO THE DEPARTMENT OF INSURANCE

Anton Simchek
2284 West Hawthorne Boulevard
Los Angeles, CA 90000
213/777-0000

November 1, 199X

Office of Consumer Complaints
California Department of Insurance
66666 Wilshire Boulevard
Los Angeles, CA 90000

Re: Claimant: Anton Simchek
       Insurance Co.: Pacific All-Risk
       Claim No.: 1X-29987-PI
       Date of accident: January 12, 199X

To Whom It Concerns:

I was injured in an automobile accident on January 12, 199X with Corrine Pass, who is insured by Pacific All-Risk Insurance Company. I notified Pacific All-Risk of the accident on January 14, 199X. On April 22, 199X, I submitted a demand letter, plus copies of my medical records and billing to Pacific All-Risk, for compensation for my injuries.

On May 28, 199X, I received a telephone call from John McCarthy, a claims adjuster from Pacific All-Risk. Mr. McCarthy at first denied that Ms. Pass was at all liable for the accident. In a phone call of June 6, 199X, Mr. McCarthy admitted that Ms. Pass had some liability for the accident and offered to settle my claim for $750, despite the fact that I suffered a broken wrist as well as back injuries and my medical bills were $1,250.

I have had six conversations with Mr. McCarthy and with John Taylor, Mr. McCarthy's supervisor, between June 6 and November 1, 199X. They have made no other settlement offer and refuse to give any reason for their failure to make a reasonable offer.

I believe that Pacific All-Risk is negotiating in bad faith. I hope that you will investigate this matter and convince Pacific All-Risk to make a good faith offer of settlement.

Enclosed are copies of all correspondence between me and Pacific All-Risk, plus copies of documents supporting my claim.

Yours truly,

Anton Simchek

The state insurance department may also lean on the insurance company on your behalf—although this usually only happens when there are obviously unfair settlement tactics, other clear evidence of bad faith, or a pattern of complaints about the same company. You may also benefit by getting a state insurance department investigator to answer some questions for you about your claim and, perhaps, to give you an experienced opinion about the validity of the insurance company's arguments regarding your claim.

7. If All Else Fails

If you have tried all the steps suggested here but still have no success getting a reasonable offer of settlement from the insurance company, consider two other options.

One is to take your claim to small claims court and try to get a settlement there. Small claims court is simple, relatively fast and does not involve lawyers. On the other hand, the amount of money you can recover in small claims court is limited in every state. (See Chapter 9, Section A3.)

The other alternative is to hire a personal injury lawyer to represent you in pursuing your claim, perhaps all the way through a lawsuit. That path, however, will cost you a lot of your compensation money—anywhere from 25% to 50% of whatever your final settlement turns out to be.

The advantages and disadvantages of each process, along with an explanation of how they work, is discussed in Chapter 9, Sections A and B.

D. Listing of the State Departments of Insurance

As discussed in Section C6, if you are unable to get a fair and reasonable offer settlement offer from an insurance company, or if you are subject to any improper negotiating tactics, you may be able to find help at your state's Department of Insurance consumer complaints office. Listed below are the addresses and telephone numbers for each state's Department of Insurance. When you call or write, explain that you are having a problem with a third-party personal injury claim—or first party if your claim is under your own insurance policy—so that the Department of Insurance can direct you to the right office within the Department.

ALABAMA

Alabama Insurance Department
135 South Union Street
Montgomery, AL 36130-3401
205/269-3550

ALASKA

Alaska Insurance Department
800 East Diamond, Suite 560
Anchorage, AK 99515
907/349-1230

ARIZONA

Arizona Insurance Department
Consumer Affairs and Investigation Division
3030 North Third Street
Phoenix, AZ 85012
602/255-4783

ARKANSAS

Arkansas Insurance Department
Consumer Service Division
400 University Tower Building
12th and University Streets
Little Rock, AR 72204
501/686-2945

CALIFORNIA

California Insurance Department
Consumer Services Division
Claims Service Bureau
3450 Wilshire Boulevard
Los Angeles, CA 90010
800/927-4357 (within state)

COLORADO

Colorado Insurance Division
1560 Broadway, Suite 850
Denver, CO 80202
303/894-7499

CONNECTICUT

Connecticut Insurance Department
Post Office Box 816
Hartford, CT 06142-0816
203/297-3800

DELAWARE

Delaware Insurance Department
841 Silver Lake Boulevard
Dover, DE 19901
302/739-4251

DISTRICT OF COLUMBIA

District of Columbia Insurance Department
613 G Street, NW; Room 619
Post Office Box 37200
Washington, DC 20013-7200
202/727-8017

FLORIDA

Florida Department of Insurance
State Capitol; Plaza Level Eleven
200 East Gaines Street
Tallahassee, FL 32399-0300
800/342-2762 (within state)
904/922-3100

GEORGIA

Georgia Insurance Department
2 Martin Luther King, Jr. Drive
Room 716, West Tower
Atlanta, GA 30334
404/656-2056

HAWAII

Hawaii Department of Commerce and
Consumer Affairs
Insurance Division
Post Office Box 3614
Honolulu, HI 96811-3614
808/586-2790

IDAHO

Idaho Insurance Department
Public Service Department
500 South 10th Street
Boise, ID 83720
208/334-4250

ILLINOIS

Illinois Insurance Department
320 West Washington Street, 4th Floor
Springfield, IL 62767
217/782-4515

INDIANA

Indiana Insurance Department
311 West Washington Street, Suite 300
Indianapolis, IN 46204
317/232-2395

IOWA

Iowa Insurance Division
Lucas State Office Building
East 12th and Grand Streets
Des Moines, IA 50319
515/281-5705

KANSAS

Kansas Insurance Department
420 Southwest 9th Street
Topeka, KS 66612-1678
913/296-3071

KENTUCKY

Kentucky Insurance Department
229 West Main Street
Post Office Box 517
Frankfort, KY 40602
502/564-3630

LOUISIANA

Louisiana Insurance Department
Post Office Box 94214
Baton Rouge, LA 70804-9214
504/342-5900

MAINE

Maine Bureau of Insurance
Consumer Division
State House, Station #34
Augusta, ME 04333
207/582-8707

MARYLAND

Maryland Insurance Department
Complaints and Investigation Unit
501 St. Paul Place
Baltimore, MD 21202-2272
410/333-6300

MASSACHUSETTS

Massachusetts Insurance Division
Consumer Services Section
280 Friend Street
Boston, MA 02114
617/727-7189

MICHIGAN

Michigan Insurance Department
Post Office Box 30220
Lansing, MI 48909
517/373-0220

MINNESOTA

Minnesota Insurance Department
Department of Commerce
133 East 7th Street
St. Paul, MN 55101
612/296-4026

MISSISSIPPI

Mississippi Insurance Department
Consumer Assistance Division
Post Office Box 79
Jackson, MS 39205
601/359-3569

MISSOURI

Missouri Division of Insurance
Consumer Services Section
Post Office Box 690
Jefferson City, MO 65102-0690
314/751-2640

MONTANA

Montana Insurance Department
126 North Sanders, Room 270
Post Office Box 4009
Helena, MT 59604
800/332-6148 (within state)
406/444-2040

NEBRASKA

Nebraska Insurance Department
Terminal Building
941 O Street, Suite 400
Lincoln, NE 68508
402/471-2201

NEVADA

Nevada Department of Commerce
Insurance Division, Consumer Section
1665 Hot Springs Road
Capitol Complex, Suite 152
Carson City, NV 89701
702/687-4270

NEW HAMPSHIRE

New Hampshire Insurance Department
Life and Health Division
169 Manchester Street
Concord, NH 03301-5151
603/271-2261

NEW JERSEY

New Jersey Insurance Department
20 West State Street
Roebling Building
Trenton, NJ 08625-0325
609/292-4757

NEW MEXICO

New Mexico Insurance Department
Post Office Drawer 1269
Santa Fe, NM 87504-1269
505/827-4500

NEW YORK

New York Insurance Department
160 West Broadway
New York, NY 10013
212/602-0203 (New York City)
800/342-3736 (within state, outside NYC)

NORTH CAROLINA

North Carolina Insurance Department
Consumer Services
Post Office Box 26387
Raleigh, NC 27611
919/733-2004

NORTH DAKOTA

North Dakota Insurance Department
Capitol Building, 5th Floor
600 East Boulevard Avenue
Bismark, ND 58505-0320
701/224-2440

OHIO

Ohio Insurance Department
Consumer Services Division
2100 Stella Court
Columbus, OH 43266-0566
614/644-2673

OKLAHOMA

Oklahoma Insurance Department
Post Office Box 53408
Oklahoma City, OK 73152-3408
405/521-2828

OREGON

Oregon Department of Insurance and Finance
Insurance Division/Consumer Advocate
440-7 Labor and Industry Building
Salem, OR 97310
503/378-4484

PENNSYLVANIA

Pennsylvania Insurance Department
1321 Strawberry Square
Harrisburg, PA 17120
717/787-2317

RHODE ISLAND

Rhode Island Insurance Division
233 Richmond Street, Suite 233
Providence, RI 02903-4233
401/277-2223

SOUTH CAROLINA

South Carolina Insurance Department
Post Office Box 100105
Columbia, SC 29202-3105
803/737-6140

SOUTH DAKOTA

South Dakota Insurance Department
Consumer Assistance Section
500 East Central
Pierre, SD 57501-3940
605/773-3563

TENNESSEE

Tennessee Department of Commerce and Insurance
Policyholders Service Section
500 James Robertson Parkway, 4th Floor
Nashville, TN 37243-0582
800/342-4029 (within state)
615/741-4955

TEXAS

Texas Board of Insurance Complaints Division
1110 San Jacinto Boulevard
Austin, TX 78701-1998
512/463-6501

UTAH

Utah Insurance Department
Consumer Services
3110 State Office Building
Salt Lake City, UT 84114
801/530-6400

VERMONT

Vermont Department of Insurance and Banking
Consumer Complaint Division
120 State Street
Montpelier, VT 05602
802/828-3301

VIRGINIA

Virginia Insurance Department
Consumer Services Division
700 Jefferson Building
Post Office Box 1157
Richmond, VA 23209
804/786-7691

WASHINGTON

Washington Insurance Department
Insurance Building
Post Office Box 40255
Olympia, WA 98504-0255
800/562-6900 (within state)
206/753-7300

WEST VIRGINIA

West Virginia Insurance Department
Post Office Box 50540
2019 Washington Street, East
Charleston, WV 25305-0540
304/558-3386

WISCONSIN

Wisconsin Insurance Department
Complaints Department
Post Office Box 7873
Madison, WI 53707
608/266-0103

WYOMING

Wyoming Insurance Department
Herschler Building
122 West 25th Street
Cheyenne, WY 82002
307/777-7401

E. Listing of State Statutes of Limitations

Every state has a law called the Statute of Limitations which sets limits on the time within which a person injured in an accident can file a lawsuit. After that time has passed, no lawsuit can be filed by the injured person to seek compensation for his or her injuries.

In addition, a lawsuit against a government entity can be filed only if a timely formal claim has first been filed. (See Chapter 3, Section C.)

The following are the Statutes of Limitations for personal injury lawsuits in all 50 states. The law of the state where an accident happened is the one that controls, regardless of what state you live in. The time begins on the date of the accident.

Watch the Time

Laws frequently change. If you are getting close to one year from the date of your accident, double check the Statute of Limitations in your state to see its latest version. You can find the statute at your nearest law library; ask the law librarian for assistance in finding the latest statute. For your reference, next to each state listed below is the section number of the Statute of Limitations for personal injury cases.

ALABAMA
2 years (Ala. Code §6-2-38)

ALASKA
2 years (Alaska Stat. §09.10.070)

ARIZONA
2 years (Ariz. Rev. Stat. Ann. §12-542)

ARKANSAS
5 years (Ark. Stat. Ann. §16-56-115)

CALIFORNIA
1 year (Cal. Code of Civ. Proc. §340)

COLORADO
2 years (Colo. Rev. Stat. §13-80-102)

CONNECTICUT
2 years (Conn. Gen. Stat. Ann. §52-584)

DELAWARE
2 years (Del. Code Ann. §8107, §8119)

DISTRICT OF COLUMBIA
3 years (D.C. Code Ann. §12-301)

FLORIDA
4 years (Fla. Stat. Ann. §95.11)

GEORGIA
2 years (Ga. Code Ann. §3-1004)

HAWAII
2 years (Hawaii Rev. Stat., §657-7)

IDAHO
2 years (Idaho Code §5-219)

ILLINOIS
2 years (Ill. Ann. Stat., §13-202)

INDIANA
2 years (Ind. Code Ann. §34-1-2-2)

IOWA
2 years (Iowa Code Ann. §614.1)

KANSAS
2 years (Kan. Stat. Ann. §60-513)

KENTUCKY
1 year (Ky. Rev. Stat. §413.140)

LOUISIANA
1 year (La. Civ. Code Ann. art. 3492)

MAINE
6 years (Me. Rev. Stat. Ann. art. 14, §752)

MARYLAND
3 years (Md. Ann. Code §5-101)

MASSACHUSETTS
3 years (Mass. Gen. Laws Ann. art. 260, §2A,4)

MICHIGAN
3 years (Mich. Comp. Laws §600.5805)

MINNESOTA
2 years (Minn. Stat. Ann. §541.07)

MISSISSIPPI
3 years (Miss. Code Ann. §15-1-49)

MISSOURI
5 years (Mo. Ann. Stat. title 35, §516.120)

MONTANA
3 years (Mont. Code Ann. §27-2-204, 207)

NEBRASKA
4 years (Neb. Rev. Stat. §25-207)

NEVADA
2 years (Nev. Rev. Stat. Ann. §11.190)

NEW HAMPSHIRE
3 years (N.H. Rev. Stat. Ann. §508:4)

NEW JERSEY
2 years (N.J. Stat. Ann. §2A:14-2)

NEW MEXICO
3 years (N.M. Stat. Ann. §37-1-8)

NEW YORK
3 years (N.Y. Civ. Prac. R §214)

NORTH CAROLINA
3 years (N.C. Gen. Stat. §1-52)

NORTH DAKOTA
6 years (N.D. Cent. Code §28-01-16)

OHIO
2 years (Ohio Rev. Code Ann. §2305.10)

OKLAHOMA
2 years (Okla. Stat. Ann. Title 12, §95)

OREGON
2 years (Or. Rev. Stat. §12.110(1))

PENNSYLVANIA
2 years (42 Pa. Con. Stat. Ann. 42, §5524)

RHODE ISLAND
3 years (R.I. Gen. Laws. §9-1-14)

SOUTH CAROLINA
3 years (S.C. Code Ann. §15-3-530)

SOUTH DAKOTA
3 years (S.D. Comp. Laws Ann., §15-2-12.2, 15-2-14)

TENNESSEE
1 year (Tenn. Code Ann. §28-3-104)

TEXAS
2 years (Tex. Civ. Prac. & Rem. Code. Title 2, §16.003)

UTAH
4 years (Utah Code Ann. §78-12-25(3))

VERMONT
3 years (Vt. Stat. Ann. Title 12, §512)

VIRGINIA
2 years (Va. Code, §8.01-243)

WASHINGTON
3 years (Wash. Rev. Code Ann., §4.16.020)

WEST VIRGINIA
2 years (W. Va. Code §55-2-12)

WISCONSIN
3 years (Wis. Stat. Ann. §893.54)

WYOMING
4 years (Wyo. Stat. Ann. §1-3-105)

Finalizing Your Settlement

Once you accept an offer, or a claims adjuster accepts an amount you propose, you have a verbal agreement with the insurance company for a full and final settlement of your claim. This chapter explains:

- how the verbal agreement is processed into a written one by the insurance company
- how and when you will receive your settlement money
- what to do in case of delay, and
- how to deal with a prepaid medical plan with a lien against some of your settlement money.

A. Confirming the Offer and Acceptance

As soon as you and an insurance adjuster agree on a settlement amount, you must take two more steps to make it final. First, ask the adjuster to send you a letter confirming the settlement. If you do not receive that letter within a week, call and remind the adjuster to send it. Also, immediately send your own brief confirming letter to the adjuster, keeping a copy for yourself.

Although it seems that nothing could go wrong at this point, on rare occasions, something does. The adjuster with whom you settled could lose his or her notes about the settlement negotiations. Your claim file could get lost. Or the adjuster may quit or be transferred before preparing the settlement documents. Don't risk having to start the negotiation process all over again. Send the confirming letter—and keep a copy for yourself.

SAMPLE SETTLEMENT CONFIRMATION LETTER

Thomas Tucker
123 Peach Street
Greensville, GA 00000

June 15, 199X

Elton Jack
Claims Adjuster
Great Southern Insurance Company
Atlanta, GA 00000

Re: Your Insured, Mark deVille
Claimant: Thomas Tucker
Claim No.: 9X-HQ1234
Date of Loss: January 13, 199X

Dear Mr. Jack:

This letter confirms our telephone conversation today during which you agreed on behalf of Great Southern Insurance Company to settle my claim for the sum of $3,500, excluding property damage amounts previously paid. I agreed to accept that amount in settlement of all personal injury claims I have against your insured, Mark deVille, arising out of an accident on January 13, 199X.

This letter also confirms that within 14 days you will send me documents reflecting this settlement, and that upon my endorsement and return to you of those documents, Great Southern Insurance Company will send me a check in that amount.

Thank you for your continued cooperation in this matter.

Very truly yours,

Thomas Tucker

B. Formal Settlement Document

Within a couple of weeks of reaching a final settlement amount with the adjuster, you will receive by mail a document entitled Settlement and Release, or Release of All Claims. This release serves two purposes. First, it puts in writing the insurance company's agreement to pay you a certain amount of money to settle your claim against its insured. And second, it commits you to a final settlement of all claims from the accident. Once you sign this release, you give up your right to seek any additional compensation from this person—regardless of what you may later discover about how the accident happened or how serious your injuries are.

Because of the slow internal workings of insurance claims departments, the settlement document does not always arrive immediately. Often the adjuster has to have the final settlement figure approved by a supervisor, or the file must be sent to another part of the office to be prepared. And sometimes the delay is due to just plain inefficiency.

Call the adjuster if you do not receive the settlement document within two weeks of your final agreement. If your file has been lost in the shuffle somewhere, ask the adjuster to track it down and let you know that the documents are being processed.

When you receive the settlement document, your check will not be included. You will not receive the money until you sign the settlement document and return it to the insurance company—where it will be processed through the next bureaucratic step. That will probably take another two to four weeks. Before you return the signed release form to the insurance company, make a copy for your files. If there is any delay in processing the settlement and getting your check, you will need a copy of the release as a reference.

1. Contents of a Settlement and Release

Although settlement documents differ somewhat in form and language, all releases contain essentially the same things: the names of those involved; the date of the accident (sometimes referred to as date of claim); the settlement amount; and the fact that this settlement fully and finally ends the entire matter.

Most of the legal language in a release serves one purpose: It makes clear that no matter what else happens, this settlement and release completely ends your rights against the insured and anyone else the insured is legally responsible for—an employee, a child or other relative. The settlement takes the insurance company off the hook for any further compensation if you later find out something you didn't know before about how the accident happened, or discover that an injury takes longer than expected to heal, or does not heal completely, or some other physical problem develops that may be connected with the accident.

A release also states that the settlement is not an admission of any liability or fault on the part of the insured, that it is intended only to avoid litigation. Although this statement may be a little aggravating to you, do not worry about it. These "no admission of liability" clauses came into use in big cases where personal or business reputations were at stake and the individuals or companies did not want to admit publicly that they had done anything wrong. Now they are just a standard part of every release form.

Finally, some insurance companies require that your signature on the release form be notarized.

2. Sample Settlement and Release

The sample settlement below contains a typical amount of legal lingo to say that this is a final settlement. Thankfully, many releases are simpler than this one. Explanations of legal lingo appear in bold print in parentheses

SAMPLE SETTLEMENT DOCUMENT

SETTLEMENT AND RELEASE OF ALL CLAIMS

Claimant RHONDA SIMPSON (hereinafter referred to as Claimant), in consideration of payment of THREE THOUSAND FIVE HUNDRED and no/100ths dollars ($3,500) by Metropolitan Insurance Company (hereinafter referred to as Company), on behalf of MOLLY GARDNER (hereinafter referred to as Insured), does hereby fully, completely, irrevocably and forever release said Insured, his/her agents, servants and employees from any and all liability, claims or causes of action, whether known or unknown, arising out of the matters occurring on or about January 13, 199X and as set forth in a claim filed with the company by Claimant and against the Insured, and identified by Company and Claimant as Claim No. 9X-HQ1234. *(This language makes certain that the case is now finished, even if you later discover more injuries or need more treatment.)*

It is understood and agreed that this settlement is the compromise of a disputed claim and that the payment made is not to be construed as an admission of liability on the part of the Insured hereby released, and that said release denies any and all liability arising out of the matters set forth in the above-described claim and intends merely to avoid litigation in this matter and to buy the Insured his or her peace. *(This is simply a public relations paragraph so that if anyone asks the insured person whether he or she was at fault for the accident, the response can be that it was never admitted. It does not affect your compensation at all.)*

It is further understood and agreed that all rights under Section 1542 of the Civil Code of the State of California, and any similar law of any state or territory of the United States or other jurisdiction, are hereby waived. Said Section reads as follows:

> "Section 1542. Certain claims not affected by general release. A general release does not extend to a claim which the creditor does not know or suspect to exist in his favor at the time of executing the release, which if known by him must have materially affected his settlement with the debtor." *(Some state laws say that a settlement does not necessarily settle a claim for damages if you do not know what all the damages are. This language says that you know all your damages and agree to end the claim forever.)*

Claimant further declares and represents that no promise, inducement or agreement not herein expressed has been made to Claimant, his agents, servants or employees, and that this Settlement and Release of All Claims contains the entire agreement between the parties hereto and that the terms of this release are contractual and not a mere recital. *(This section makes clear that you are not permitted to later claim that you had a different oral agreement with an adjuster or someone else in the insurance company to give you more money or to reopen your claim.)*

THE UNDERSIGNED HAS READ THE FOREGOING SETTLEMENT AND RELEASE OF ALL CLAIMS AND FULLY UNDERSTANDS IT.

Dated:

_____

(Signature of Claimant)

If there is something in your release form that you do not understand, do not sign it until you get a satisfactory explanation. Call the adjuster and ask what the particular language means, and if you can get an explanation that satisfies you, ask the adjuster to put the explanation in writing. If you do not get a satisfactory explanation from the adjuster, move up through the ranks of the claims department and then to the state Department of Insurance. (See Chapter 7, Section C).

C. What To Do If the Check Doesn't Arrive

You should receive your settlement check within two to four weeks after you return the signed release to the insurance company. Ask the claims adjuster how long it usually takes them to process checks. Some insurance companies have a local office issue the check and do it quickly. Others require that the check be issued by a regional or home office, which may be in another state and may take a little longer.

All too frequently, however, a settlement check does not arrive as soon as it is supposed to. This usually means nothing more serious than a paperwork logjam in the insurance company office. But there are some things you can do to help speed up the process.

Call the adjuster Although in most companies the adjuster does not prepare the check, if it has not arrived when promised, ask the adjuster to find out what the delay is. Since their job is essentially done, adjusters do not have much motivation to track down the final paperwork, so if you want results, ask politely.

If the check is late, do not let the adjuster put you off by just telling you, without checking on it, that the papers are in the works. Remind the adjuster that the check is already overdue. Ask that he or she find out where it is in the process and if there is anyone else you should contact about speeding things up. Most adjusters will make some effort to find out

what is going on—if for no other reason than they know that until the check arrives, you will keep calling.

Contact the head of the claims department If more than four weeks have passed and you still do not have your check, step up the pressure. Call the adjuster, tell him or her that your check has still not arrived and ask for the name of the head of the claims department. Call the head of the claims department, give that person your claim number, the name of the adjuster you dealt with, the amount of your settlement and the date you returned the settlement document to the company. Then firmly but politely demand that a check be issued immediately.

Whatever the supervisor's response, immediately write a letter, either confirming the supervisor's promise or making a demand for immediate payment; send a copy of the letter to the adjuster. After they have received this letter, call the supervisor again to ask the status of your payment.

Contact the state insurance department As discussed, every state has a Department or Commission or Bureau of Insurance that oversees insurance companies operating in the state. (See Chapter 7, Section C.) And each has a consumer complaint division which can pressure an insurance company claims department that grossly mishandles a claim. However, a Department of Insurance will not get involved with a late settlement payment until more than 30 days after you returned the completed settlement documents—and only if you have made several unsuccessful contacts with the claims department to find out why the check is delayed.

If you have made several attempts to get your settlement payment but have not received the money after more than 30 days, contact your state Department of Insurance consumer complaints office. (See the listing in Chapter 7, Section D.) Telephone first, so that you can send copies of your papers to the right office—and not suffer yet another bureaucratic delay. Then send copies of your settlement confirmation letter, your signed release form and any follow-up letters you have sent to the insurance company. Also explain in a cover letter how many times you have spoken with the insurance company about receiving your settlement check and what it has told you about the delay.

If the state Department of Insurance calls the insurance company to investigate the matter, it shouldn't be long before the settlement check is in your mailbox.

D. Liens on Your Settlement Money

A lien is a legal claim against money you might receive from a particular source, such as compensation for your injuries in an accident. Holders of such a lien might be your own auto insurance company if it paid you anything for medical bills under your own medical payments coverage, and your health plan or HMO which covered your medical treatment. Although technically you must repay the full amount of these liens as soon as you receive your settlement, sometimes you can negotiate something less than full repayment.

1. Lien by Your Own Auto Insurance

If you were involved in a vehicle accident and claimed immediate payment of some of your medical bills under the medical payments coverage of your own automobile insurance policy, you may now be obligated to repay that money out of your settlement amount. (See Chapter 4, Section 3c.) Virtually all policies include a repayment provision.

If you have received a notice of lien or other document from your own insurance company describing its right to reimbursement, you must repay that money as soon as you receive your settlement check. If your policy requires repayment but you have never received any notice of lien from your own insurance company, you can keep all your settlement money and wait to see if your company requests repayment. But do not think the lien amount is yours just because you do not hear from your insurance company right away. If you do not repay your insur-

ance company and sometime later it requests repayment, you will have to pay the money back even if you have already spent it.

2. Lien by an HMO or Other Prepaid Health Plan

If you were treated for your injuries by a Health Maintenance Organization (HMO) or other prepaid health plan, it may have sent you a Notice of Lien claiming the right to be repaid a certain amount out of your settlement. (See sidebar on HMOs, Chapter 6, Section 2c.) Although it never charged you any specific sum for visits or treatments, the HMO or health plan gave you a list of charges for each service it provided—and you used those charges in your claim as the equivalent of a bill showing your medical expenses.

However, as part of its contract with you, many HMOs and other prepaid health plans provide that if you recover compensation from a third person for injuries treated by the HMO or covered by the prepaid health plan, it has a right to be repaid for its services. And when it provided you with a list of the charges for your medical treatment following the accident, it probably required you to sign—or at least sent you notice of—a lien against your future compensation. This lien now requires that you repay the HMO or health plan the total amount stated in the list of charges.

3. Reducing Your HMO or Health Plan Repayment

It is possible, though, for you to negotiate with the HMO or health plan so that you only repay a reduced amount of the lien. Most large HMOs and health plans are used to this practice—known as "compromising" a lien—so they will understand what you want to do and most will be prepared to negotiate a compromise with you.

An HMO or other health plan is likely to be willing to compromise with you for a couple of reasons. First, the charge listed for your treatment was not an amount it would have collected if you had not filed a claim. Normally, it would have treated you and received nothing beyond the monthly payment you or your employer makes to the health plan. So, by filing a claim and collecting compensation against which the health plan has a lien, you are actually giving the health plan a bonus payment. You do not need to remind the health plan office of this fact, but it underlies the willingness to compromise.

A stronger reason for the willingness to compromise is that the HMO or health plan has a right to be reimbursed only to the extent you were compensated for medical treatment from a third party. But your lump sum claim settlement includes payment for your pain and suffering and for general damages—including permanent injuries—as well as for your medical bills. Since there is no clear-cut way to determine how much of your settlement is for your medical bills and how much for pain and suffering and general damages, it would be difficult for the health plan to prove that you were fully reimbursed for all its medical charges. It is therefore often willing to be convinced that you only received a partial reimbursement for medical bills and that as a result it should only receive partial reimbursement of the lien.

The willingness of the HMO or health plan to accept a compromise amount instead of its entire lien depends on how much your total settlement was in relation to your total medical bills and to the charges made by the HMO or health plan. If your settlement amount is no more than two or three times your total medical bills, you can argue that your settlement only partially paid your medical bills and that the rest of the settlement was general damages. Particularly if your HMO or health plan charges amount to a high percentage (25% to 33%) of your total settlement, you can contend that your settlement actually covers only a portion of your HMO or health plan charges.

As soon as you have reached a settlement figure, contact the HMO or other health plan's business office, or whatever office sent you the lien, and ask to speak to someone about compromising a personal injury lien. Explain that your total settlement is only a small amount, and that when general damages are considered, the settlement did not fully cover all your medical costs. If your comparative negligence also reduced your settlement amount, explain that as well to the person negotiating the health plan's lien. Then offer to pay 50% of the total lien amount. Many HMOs and health plans commonly reduce their liens by 50% if there is no large settlement amount; others will reduce the lien by 33%.

E. Taxes on Your Settlement Money

Since your settlement amount is for the pain and suffering you endured, it is not technically income and you do not usually owe any state or federal income taxes on it.

But there are exceptions. If your settlement specifically reimburses you for out-of-pocket lost income, you could be liable for income taxes on that part of your settlement. If your settlement reimburses you for out-of-pocket medical costs for which you took a medical deduction from your income taxes, you could owe taxes on those amounts. If you took no deduction, you owe no taxes on the medical reimbursement part of your settlement.

But as with most tax questions, these are gray areas, subject to interpretation and differing opinions. And since there is no clear or accurate way to separate out of your lump sum settlement award how much is for lost income, how much for reimbursement of medical bills and how much for general damages, that interpretation is up to you. If the IRS or state tax people audit you, there is usually no specific basis for an auditor to assign a particular portion of a personal injury settlement to lost income. And in most cases, they will not even bother to look at a personal injury insurance payment unless you

The Last Resorts:
Lawyers and Courts

despite the most thorough preparation and persistent negotiation, it is possible your claim could reach a dead end. The insurance company might stubbornly deny your claim, contending that its insured was not at fault. Or it may offer you such unreasonably low compensation that you are unwilling to settle without more of a fight. If the negotiating strategies discussed here (see Chapter 7) have not produced a reasonable settlement and you believe that further negotiations on your own will not bring a better offer, consider taking your claim to Small Claims Court, or hiring a lawyer to negotiate further, perhaps taking your claim to formal court.

This chapter explains what claims you might be able to take to Small Claims Court without a lawyer and how to choose and work with a lawyer if your claim is not appropriate for Small Claims Court.

A. Taking Your Claim to Small Claims Court

Every state has a Small Claims Court that provides a simple, quick, inexpensive and informal procedure for resolving cases involving relatively small amounts of money. In some states, Small Claims Court is called Conciliation Court, Justice Court or the Small Claims Division or Docket of the Municipal or District Court.

If Small Claims Court turns out to be a practical alternative for you, the documents you have already collected and the work you have already done in presenting your demand to the insurance company will be almost all of the preparation you will need to have your case heard there. Once you get to Small Claims Court, you will make exactly the same arguments you made to the claims adjuster, only this time it will be a neutral judge listening. And finally, the value of your claim—both for personal injury and for

any property damage—will be calculated by the judge exactly the same way as you have calculated it using the same factors discussed here (See Chapter 5, Section A.)

States With Short Lawsuit Deadlines

As discussed in Chapter 7, each state puts a limit, called the Statute of Limitations, on the time within which you must file a lawsuit against someone you believe was responsible for your accident. After that time has passed, you are forever barred from filing a lawsuit. And if you failed to file a lawsuit within that time, you cannot collect an insurance claim arising out of that accident.

California, Kentucky, Louisiana and Tennessee have short time limits: only one year from the date of the accident. So, if your accident was in one of those states, either file a lawsuit in Small Claims Court or regular court on your own, or have a lawyer file a lawsuit on your behalf in formal court before the time limit is up. And having a lawyer help you file a lawsuit does not necessarily mean giving over your entire claim for the lawyer to handle. (See Section B, below.)

1. Advantages of Small Claims Court

There are at least three advantages of Small Claims Court over regular, more formal courts.

a. Simple rules

Small claims procedures are set up for people to handle their own cases without lawyers. In several states, lawyers are not even allowed in Small Claims Courts, and in all states the forms, legal jargon and courtroom procedure are kept simple enough for anyone to present a case. In other words, it's the one court where regular folks and plain language are not only tolerated but encouraged.

b.   Low cost

Getting into and through Small Claims Court is inexpensive. The fees for filing court papers are much less than for filing in regular court. Also, you don't have to go through the expensive investigation or preparation required to bring a case to formal court. And you don't have to pay a lawyer to speak for you in court.

c.   Efficiency

Small claims court moves quickly. Unlike formal court cases which can take years, you will get a court hearing in Small Claims Court within a month or two after filing your papers. The hearing itself usually takes no more than 15 minutes, and the judge either announces a decision right there in the courtroom or mails it out within a few days.

2.   Disadvantage of Small Claims Court

The biggest drawback of Small Claims Court is that, as the name indicates, it is for small cases only. Each state puts a dollar limit on how much you can recover in Small Claims Court—from $1,000 to $10,000. This limit means that regardless of how much your claim might be worth, you can only recover the court's dollar limit amount in a Small Claims Court lawsuit. And, once you go to Small Claims Court, your claim is finished. Whatever happens in Small Claims Court will be the final outcome of your entire claim. By going to Small Claims Court to try to collect up to that court's

dollar limit, you forever give up the right to collect any claim value beyond that limit.

Before you can decide whether it makes sense to take your injury claim into Small Claims Court, find out what the dollar limit is in your state, then measure it against what you think your claim is worth.

3.   State Listing of Small Claims Court Limits

The list below gives current dollar limits for each state's Small Claims Court. However, this list is for general reference only. The limit in your state may have changed, or there may be local variances which permit a different limit in certain counties.

Before filing, double-check the latest dollar limits for the Small Claims Court in your county. You will find the court office by looking up Small Claims Court in the government listings of the white pages of your telephone directory. If you do not find a listing for Small Claims Court, call the Justice, Municipal or District Court and ask for the number of the Small Claims Court clerk. When you reach the Small Claims Court clerk, ask what the monetary limit is in your state and county for a Small Claims Court lawsuit.

ALABAMA	$1,500
ALASKA	$5,000
ARIZONA	$1,500
ARKANSAS	$3,000
CALIFORNIA	$5,000
COLORADO	$3,500
CONNECTICUT	$2,000
DELAWARE	$5,000
DISTRICT OF COLUMBIA	$2,000
FLORIDA	$2,499
GEORGIA	$5,000
HAWAII	$2,500
IDAHO	$2,000
ILLINOIS	$2,500
(COOK COUNTY)	$500

INDIANA	$3,000
(MARION & LAKE COUNTIES)	$6,000
IOWA	$2,000
KANSAS	$1,000
KENTUCKY	$1,500
LOUISIANA	$2,000
MAINE	$1,400
MARYLAND	$2,500
MASSACHUSETTS	$1,500
MICHIGAN	$1,500
MINNESOTA	$4,000
MISSISSIPPI	$1,000
MISSOURI	$1,500
MONTANA	$2,500
NEBRASKA	$1,800
NEVADA	$2,500
NEW HAMPSHIRE	$2,500
NEW JERSEY	$5,000
NEW MEXICO	$5,000
NEW YORK	$2,000
NORTH CAROLINA	$2,000
NORTH DAKOTA	$3,000
OHIO	$1,000
OKLAHOMA	$2,500
OREGON	$2,500
PENNSYLVANIA	$4,000
(PHILADELPHIA)	$5,000
RHODE ISLAND	$1,500
SOUTH CAROLINA	$2,500
SOUTH DAKOTA	$2,000
TENNESSEE	$10,000
TEXAS	$2,500
UTAH	$2,000
VERMONT	$2,000
VIRGINIA	$1,000
WASHINGTON	$2,000
WEST VIRGINIA	$3,000
WISCONSIN	$2,000
WYOMING	$2,000

Filing in Small Claims as a Negotiating Tactic

In states with a high dollar limit in Small Claims Court, simply filing a Small Claims Court action and serving the papers on the other side might stimulate the insurance company to raise its settlement offer to you.

If the Small Claims Court dollar limit is significantly higher than what the insurance company has offered, the company has to face the possibility that its insured would lose in Small Claims Court and have to pay you up to the dollar limit. This might prompt a new and higher settlement offer to you. Extra pressure to settle the claim might also come from the insured, who will not be happy about having to go to court.

However, if the Small Claims Court limit in your state is only slightly more than what the insurance company has offered in settlement, a threat to take your claim to Small Claims Court will likely backfire. The only effect of threatening to take the claim to Small Claims Court is that the insurance company will know it doesn't need to offer you anything higher.

4. Will Small Claims Be Worth Your While?

Once you are certain what the Small Claims Court limit is in your state and county, you can decide whether that limit compared with the amount of your claim makes Small Claims Court a practical alternative for you.

Example *If your state's small claims limit is only $1,000 and you believe your claim is worth $5,000, Small Claims Court doesn't make much sense. Since you could only win a maximum of $1,000 if you went to Small Claims Court, you would be forever giving up the remaining $4,000 value of your claim. In this case, it would be wiser to consult an attorney about representing you and perhaps taking your claim to a formal court. (See Section B.)*

Example *If the Small Claims Court limit in your state is $2,000 and the insurance company has offered to settle the claim for $1,800, Small Claims Court probably isn't worth the effort. Small claims court only offers you a chance to get $200 more than the insurance company has offered, and, as with any court, there is the possibility that the judge will award you less than the insurance company's offer, or perhaps nothing at all. And since the insurance company knows that the Small Claims Court limit is $2,000, filing a Small Claims Court lawsuit is not likely to induce it to make a higher offer.*

Example *If the insurance company has offered only $500 in settlement, you believe your claim is worth $1,500, and the limit permitted by your state's Small Claims Court is $2,000, Small Claims Court may be a sensible way to proceed—and more economical than hiring a lawyer or settling for the insurance company's low offer. Plus, simply filing a small claims action may prompt the insurance company to raise its offer. If not, you can go through with your Small Claims Court case and perhaps win the full amount you believe your claim is worth.*

Example *If you believe your claim is worth a bit more than your state's small claims limit—for example, the small claims limit is $2,000 and you think your claim might be worth $2,500—it may make more sense for you to go to Small Claims Court and try for the $2,000 than to settle for an insurance company offer of less than $1,000. Getting $2,000 in Small Claims Court is probably faster, less stressful and more economical than paying a lawyer the customary cut of up to 33% of whatever you wind up getting from the insurance company.*

a. One last look at your odds

Do a final evaluation of your claim. As with any lawsuit, there is always the possibility that in Small Claims Court you will win nothing. Or a judge may award you much less than you think is fair—even less than the insurance company offered to settle your case. Once you take your case through Small Claims Court, you cannot later take the case to another court to try for more money. Nor can you continue negotiations with the insurance company.

Before filing your Small Claims Court case, think once more about how strong your claim is regarding the other party's liability and your own comparative fault. Consider the insurance company's arguments concerning fault and think how those arguments would sound to a judge hearing both sides of the claim in a 15-minute hearing. One way to test your case is to ask a friend or relative to listen to you describe both sides of the story—your claim and the insurance company's response. Your friend or relative can then give you an honest opinion about how your story sounds to someone hearing it for the first time, as a judge will be. And after you have considered the issue of fault, evaluate one more time how much your claim is worth based on the extent of your injuries noted in your medical records.

If you still feel confident that your argument concerning the other party's liability is strong and that your medical records clearly show the injuries for which you are claiming compensation, then Small Claims Court can be a quick and easy place to present your case.

b. Getting tips from a lawyer

The insurance company may have refused to offer you any settlement, or only a small nuisance value amount, claiming that its insured is legally not at all liable for your injuries. If a Small Claims Court judge accepts this argument, you might get nothing at all out of the court procedure and your claim would be finished.

If the insurance company has totally denied your claim, you may want to consult briefly with an experienced personal injury lawyer before taking the case to Small Claims Court on your own. He or she may be able to come up with a good and simple argument why the insured person is liable. If so, you can then decide whether to pay the lawyer for his or her advice and go to Small Claims Court on your own, or have the lawyer represent you in further negotiations or in formal court. (See Section B.)

5. Sources To Help You Through

If you decide to take your claim to Small Claims Court, there are several resources to help guide you through the process. The first is the rules and procedures of the Small Claims Court, available from the Small Claims Court clerk—usually free—and written in straightforward language for non-lawyers.

The second is *Everybody's Guide to Small Claims Court* by attorney Ralph Warner, published by Nolo Press and available in major bookstores or by mail or telephone order. (See the order form at the back of this book.)

Another source of assistance is the Small Claims Court adviser available in some counties. These advisers are court employees who, free of charge, help people use the Small Claims Court process.

But the best way to learn about how Small Claims Court works is to spend a morning or afternoon sitting in Small Claims Court watching other cases. You can learn how the judge runs a particular courtroom. And you can see the effective and not-so-effective ways other claimants present their cases.

Using these resources, the process of getting your claim into court for a judge's decision can be a fast and easy one.

6. Filing and Serving Papers

Before you actually go to Small Claims Court and present your case to a judge, you are required to file with the Small Claims Court clerk a document called a "complaint," in which you as the complaining party are called the "plaintiff." This complaint must name and be delivered to, or served on, the other people you believe were legally responsible for the accident. In the complaint, these people are referred to as "defendants." Along with this complaint, you must serve on the defendants a summons—an official court order to appear in court on the date given to you by the court clerk. This summons and complaint are to be served on the people or businesses actually responsible for the accident, *not* on their insurance company or insurance adjuster.

The rules for how a complaint and summons can be served vary from state to state. Your state's procedures will be spelled out in the official Small Claims Court rules available free from the Small Claims Court clerk's office. As mentioned above, a Small Claims Court adviser may be available free to help explain your local rules about preparing and serving the required papers on the defendant. *Everybody's Guide to Small Claims Court* by Ralph Warner (published by Nolo Press) also provides valuable information.

7. Presenting Your Case

Once you actually go to court, your presentation to the judge can be almost exactly the same as the presentation you made in your demand letter. Small claims courts do not rely on formal rules of evidence like you have seen on television lawyer shows. Instead, a small claims judge will accept as evidence anything that helps to explain what happened in the accident and what your injuries and other damages were.

a. Organizing documents

Because a judge can accept written evidence and will like having things on paper which he or she can refer to, bring with you to court:

- a copy of the demand letter you sent to the insurance company
- a copy of any police report of the accident
- a copy of any rules or laws you believe have been violated
- a copy of any helpful witness statements, or the witness in person if he or she is willing to come to court
- a copy of any photographs of the accident scene or of your injuries or other damages
- copies of all medical billing
- copies of all medical records
- copies of letters or other documents showing any income loss, and
- copies of letters or other documents which show or help explain other losses you suffered as a result of your injuries.

Organize your papers before you get to court. Put all documents concerning liability together, and all documents concerning medical records and billing together, just as you did when you sent them to the insurance company along with your demand letter. Put a cover sheet on top of the papers with a list showing what the documents are and in what order they are presented. This way you will be able to get the document quickly if the judge asks to see it. And if the judge wants copies of the documents, he or she will also be able to locate specific documents quickly.

b.   Preparing an oral statement

In court, judges only want to hear a brief statement of your claim. And some judges take control immediately and pepper you with questions. Your challenge will be to respond to the judge's questions while making sure you emphasize the important points of your case in the short time you are allotted to speak. Plan on presenting your claim in no more than five minutes. In that time, state as simply as possible:

- what kind of an accident you had
- where and when the accident happened

- how and why you believe the accident happened, including why the other person is responsible
- what your injuries were, emphasizing pain and disability caused by the injuries
- what treatment you received
- how long your recovery took
- how much your medical treatment cost, regardless of whether you paid for it yourself or insurance paid for it
- how much income you lost
- any other damages or inconveniences you suffered as a result of the accident, and
- how much compensation you believe is fair and reasonable.

The amount of compensation you ask the judge to award you should be slightly higher than what you believe the case is actually worth, but not as high as you asked for in the demand letter. If the amount you are seeking is higher than the dollar limit for Small Claims Court, explain to the judge what you believe the case is worth and then state that you are aware of the small claims limit, so are asking for the maximum allowed.

Your demand letter is the best place to start to put together your statement to the judge. Take the most important points in your demand letter and jot them down in a list. Then think about how you would simply and briefly state each of the points to the judge, keeping in mind that the judge only wants to hear plain language without any legal jargon. Below is a demand letter (based on Example #1 at the end of Chapter 5, Section G) followed by a statement to a Small Claims Court judge based on the same facts.

Before your court date, practice telling your story several times, using your list of important points as a reference; you'll also be able to refer to the list in court. You might also have a friend listen to the story and ask you questions as you go along, just like a judge might do. And try to visit a Small Claims Court session to see how other people present their cases and to note the kinds of questions the judge asks.

DEMAND LETTER

Dear Ms. X:

As I informed you by letter of January 17, 199X, I was injured in an automobile accident with your insured Matthew White on the afternoon of January 13, 199X in Highgate, Connecticut. I was headed west on Hornsey Lane and stopped at the stop sign at the intersection with Highgate Hill Road. While still stopped, your insured slammed into the back of my car. The force of the blow threw me forward against my shoulder restraints and my head snapped forward and back.

In the middle of that night I woke with a severe headache and extremely stiff neck, so in the morning I went to the Emergency Room of Highgate Medical Center. There I was examined and X-rays were taken of my neck and back. The doctor diagnosed a cervical strain, fitted me with a cervical collar and advised bed rest. Because of the severe pain, he also prescribed pain relief medication.

I was in considerable pain for the next five days, during which I was forced not only to miss work (three days) but also the 50th birthday party in Boston of an old and dear friend. On Monday of the next week I returned to work, but still with pain and stiffness and wearing my cervical collar, which made doing my job very difficult. After another week the doctor advised that I could remove the cervical collar. I continued to have quite a bit of soreness and stiffness for another two weeks, interfering with my sleep and making it impossible to do any recreation or to drive unless absolutely necessary. I continue to suffer occasional stiffness and sleep disruptions, though the more severe pain and discomfort has subsided.

The medical expenses for my treatment, as shown in the enclosed medical and billing records, are:

Highgate Med. Center (emergency room)	$150.00
Highgate Med. Center (x-rays)	90.00
Cervical collar	35.00
Prescription medication	18.00
TOTAL	$293.00

As a result of the accident, I also missed three days of work. As the enclosed letter from the personnel office of Battersea Grocery indicates, my wage loss was $294.00 (24 hours at $12.25 per hour).

Because of the negligence of your insured, I went through a period of extreme pain and discomfort which lasted for several weeks and which still continues to give occasional discomfort. Not only was my normal daily life disrupted, but I was forced to miss the 50th birthday party of a very dear friend whom I rarely get to see. As a result, I demand compensation for my injuries and general damages in the amount of $2,500.

I hope to hear from you soon on this matter.

Very truly yours,

STATEMENT TO COURT

Your Honor,

I was injured in an automobile accident with the defendant Matthew White on the afternoon of January 13, 199x in Highgate, Connecticut.

I was headed west on Hornsey Lane and stopped at the stop sign at the intersection with Highgate Hill Rd. While still stopped, the defendant slammed into the back of my car. The force of the blow threw me forward against my shoulder restraints and my head snapped forward and back.

That night I had severe headache and stiff neck, so in the morning I went to the emergency room of Highgate Medical Center. I had X-rays there and doctor diagnosed a cervical strain. I was given a cervical collar and advised to stay in bed. I was also prescribed pain medication.

I was in a lot of pain for the next five days and had to miss three days of work. I also missed the 50th birthday party in Boston of old and dear friend.

On the next Monday I returned to work, but still with pain and stiffness and wearing my cervical collar. I was sore and stiff for another two weeks, sleeping poorly and unable to do anything but work and lie down.

Even now I still suffer occasional stiffness and sleep disruptions.

The medical expenses for my treatment was $293 and my pay for the time I lost work was $294. I have copies for you here of all the medical billing and records, and a letter from my employer, if you want to see them. I already sent these records to the defendant's insurance company, but I also have more copies here for the defendant.

In sum, Your Honor, because of the negligence of the defendant I went through several weeks of extreme pain and discomfort and I was also forced to miss the 50th birthday party of a very dear friend whom I rarely get to see. Your Honor, I believe that fair and just compensation for my injuries and general damages would be in the amount of $1,500. In addition, I ask that Your Honor also award court costs in this matter.

8. The Day of Your Court Hearing

On the day you are scheduled to have your hearing, get to the courtroom early so that you can watch how the judge conducts other cases. Bring to the court with you three complete sets of your demand letter and all your supporting documents. One set will be for the judge if he or she wants it, one set for the defendant if the judge wants the defendant to have it and one set will be for you to refer to as you present your case.

When your case is called—the name of the case will be "your last name versus the other person's last name" (*Ball v. White* in our example)—move up to the tables which will be in front of the bench where the judge sits. Because you are the plaintiff—the one who filed the lawsuit—you will be asked to speak first. Begin by letting the judge know what kind of case you have—a car accident in which you were injured, an accident in which you fell at the defendant's store and were injured, etc. Then use your prepared statement to describe the accident, your injuries, your treatment, your recovery and your damages. End with a request for a specific amount of damages plus your court costs. If you win in Small Claims Court, in addition to the compensation you are awarded, you are entitled to be reimbursed by the defendant for your costs in bringing the lawsuit: filing fee and the costs incurred in serving the court papers on the defendant. Check your local court rules to see which costs you are entitled to be reimbursed for.

If the judge asks you a question during the course of your statement, answer it as simply and directly as possible. Do not ignore the judge's question and simply return to giving your statement. If a judge asks something, it is usually because he or she thinks it is important to know for the final decision.

If you refer to a document you have brought to court—a police report, a medical record or bill—offer a copy to the judge. You can also tell the judge that you have a complete set of all your documents with a list of contents on the top. If the judge sees that this is an organized set of documents. he or she may be willing to take the whole thing from you. Also let the judge know that you have another set to give to the defendant if the judge wants you to.

After you have finished your presentation and answered the judge's questions. it will be the defendant's turn to speak. He or she may say something you think is wrong or improper, but do not interrupt. Wait until the defendant has finished speaking and then ask the judge for permission to respond briefly to what the defendant has said but with which you disagree. If the judge lets you speak again, make your comments very brief and to the point. Do not repeat what you have said before. Small Claims Court judges want to keep cases moving quickly and they are not pleased when someone in court goes on and on.

Always remain calm and polite with the judge and let your prepared statement do the work for you.

B. Hiring a Lawyer To Work on Your Claim

You might consider consulting with a lawyer if:
- you are not sure enough of your claim to take it into Small Claims Court
- you believe your claim may be worth quite a bit more than the dollar limit of your state's Small Claims Court, or
- if you would just like to get the claim out of your hair and are willing to pay a lawyer to take over major responsibility for it.

Consulting with a lawyer doesn't necessarily mean hiring the lawyer to take over handling your claim completely. It may be possible to briefly discuss your claim with a lawyer to get some ideas about further negotiations on your own with the insurance company, or about how to prepare your case for Small Claims Court.

And consulting with a lawyer doesn't mean just any lawyer. This section discusses how to find the right lawyer to consult with and the different ways you might use a lawyer, including hourly consultation, reduced-fee arrangements and full legal representative.

Small Law Firm Versus Large Law Firm

The size of a law firm does not have much to do with how well the office handles your case.

You may have the idea that a large law office will impress an insurance company into giving you a better settlement, but that is rarely the case. Also, insurance companies know that large law offices often do not put in the time or concern over a small personal injury case that a smaller law office might, and therefore a large office is often easier for an insurance adjuster to settle with at a low figure.

Large law offices tend to be machines set up primarily to crank out money for themselves, and a small personal injury case can easily get lost in the shuffle. Also, large law offices are in the habit of freely spending money on costs and expenses and may too easily use up much of your potential compensation in that way. You are likely to receive more personal attention from a small law office, and many of the best personal injury lawyers choose to work in a law firm with only two or three or four lawyers.

1. Finding and Choosing the Right Lawyer

The practice of law has become specialized over the past couple of decades, and most lawyers know less about handling a personal injury claim than you will after you've read this book. So, your first task is to find a lawyer who has experience representing claimants—called plaintiffs, in legalese—in personal injury cases. You do not want to be represented by someone who has experience in personal injury cases but who has primarily been a lawyer for defendants or insurance companies. Their way of thinking may be too closely tied to the attitudes of insurance companies and they might not fight as hard—consciously or unconsciously—for your claim.

a. Finding experienced lawyers

There are several ways to find referrals to experienced plaintiffs' personal injury lawyers. The best way to proceed is to comparison shop. Get the names of several lawyers and meet with each of them to discuss your claim before you decide to hire any one. And be prepared for rejection. Many lawyers do not take on cases under a certain potential recovery amount, or if a claim is not crystal clear.

Friends and acquaintances   Talk with friends or co-workers who have been represented by a lawyer in their own personal injury claims. If the friend or co-worker says good things to you about that experience with the lawyer, this should at least make you put the lawyer on your list of people with whom to have an initial consultation. But do not make any decision about a lawyer solely on the basis of someone else's recommendation. Different people will have different responses to a lawyer's style and personality, so do not make up your mind about hiring a lawyer until you have met with the lawyer, discussed your case and decided that you are comfortable entering a working relationship.

Other lawyer   Another place to seek a referral to an experienced personal injury lawyer is through another lawyer you may have had contact with.

Lawyers commonly refer cases to one another, and most lawyers will know someone else who handles plaintiffs' personal injury cases. As with referrals from friends or co-workers, however, do not simply take another lawyer's referral as the final word.

Referral service   Most local bar associations have referral services in which the names of lawyers are available, arranged by legal specialty. Call your local bar association referral service and ask for the names of a couple of personal injury lawyers. Unfortunately, bar associations do very little screening concerning the experience of lawyers on their lists. What experience a referral lawyer actually has is a hit-or-miss proposition. Make no decision about a bar referral lawyer until you have met and interviewed him or her.

b. Choosing the right lawyer for you

To find out whether a lawyer is the right one for you, sit down with the lawyer to discuss your claim and possible ways of handling it. Bring copies of all your documents: demand letter, police report, medical records and bills, income loss information and all correspondence with the insurance company. Most personal injury lawyers do not charge anything for an initial consultation about the possibility of representing you and your claim. But before you meet with anyone, find out whether they will charge you for an initial interview. If the lawyer wants to charge you just for discussing whether to take your case, go somewhere else.

General experience   After letting the lawyer know generally what your case is about, there are a few basic things you will want to find out from the lawyer at the outset of your first interview.

- How long the lawyer has been in practice?
- Roughly what percentage of the lawyer's practice involves personal injury cases?
- Does the lawyer most often represent plaintiffs (claimants) or defendants (businesses, insurance companies)?

- If you hired the lawyer, would he or she handle your case or pass it along to another—perhaps less experienced—lawyer in the office? It is normal for more than one attorney in an office to work on the same case, and to have less experienced attorneys handle routine tasks. Find out which lawyer would have responsibility for the case and which lawyer you would be dealing with directly. If there is to be another lawyer directly involved, ask to meet that lawyer, too.

Settlement goal   After you have discussed the facts of your case and the history of your negotiations with the insurance company, you may be able to get some sense from the lawyer about how much he or she thinks your case is worth, and how difficult it may be to get the insurance company to pay that amount. This is when you should let the lawyer know what it is you want him or her to do for you.

- Obtain a certain settlement amount for you with as few costs and as little hassle as possible.
- Obtain any amount more than what the insurance company has offered as soon as possible.
- Obtain as much as possible, no matter how long it takes.
- Some combination of the above.

2. Paying the Lawyer

Disagreements over fees are the most frequent sources of friction between lawyers and their clients, so you may save yourself considerable grief at the end of your case by getting the fee arrangement clear at the beginning.

Hiring a Lawyer for Advice Only

If you are looking to hire a lawyer to give you specific advice which might help you to reopen your negotiations with the insurance company, to prepare and file a lawsuit to protect your rights under the statute of limitations, or to prepare you to take your case to Small Claims Court, you will probably pay the lawyer by the hour. Because lawyers charge anywhere from $75 to $250 per hour, this is only an economical arrangement for you if the lawyer can give you advice on a narrow issue—for example, about how a particular rule or law works concerning liability—which enables you to reenter negotiations or to go to Small Claims Court with some newfound legal authority or a view of the facts you had not considered before.

In this by-the-hour arrangement, the lawyer would not deal directly with the insurance company, put his or her name on court documents, or appear for you in Small Claims Court. You would still be officially handling the matter on your own, armed with whatever advice the lawyer has been able to give you. If you still cannot get a better offer out of the insurance company, you can then return to the lawyer to discuss whether it makes sense for him or her to take on full representation of your claim.

If you decide to use an attorney's services on an hourly basis, agree ahead of time both the hourly fee and the maximum number of hours the lawyer is to spend on your case. Also, know that you will most likely have to pay immediately—the lawyer will not wait until you receive your accident compensation.

a. Get it in writing

A written agreement about fees protects both you and the lawyer in case you have a disagreement later about who gets how much. Most lawyers are careful about putting any fee agreement in writing, and the laws in many states require a lawyer who is likely to charge over a certain amount to put the fee agreement in writing. But it is important to see that your written fee agreement—which both you and the lawyer should sign—accurately and specifically reflects your particular arrangement and is not just a standard office form.

b. Be clear on costs

"Costs" refer to the expenses of conducting negotiations and a lawsuit. Lawyers have a tendency to run up large costs without thinking too much about it. That is a problem for you, because it is the client who must pay those costs out of the settlement amount.

   Some costs are unavoidable. If the lawyer must file a lawsuit to protect your rights under the statute of limitations, the fee for filing that lawsuit is a cost you must bear. If the insurance adjuster on your claim is in another city, you will have to pay the cost of telephone calls back and forth with the lawyer. And, most significantly, if the case does not settle in early negotiations with the insurance company, the lawyer may have to begin what is called "discovery" —the process of questioning you and the defendant under oath, which always involves copying and postage costs at the very least and which sometimes involves examinations of witnesses costing hundreds of dollars.

   Some of the greatest costs of conducting a lawsuit are not always necessary. So make sure that your written fee agreement spells out clearly:

- That costs are to be deducted from your compensation amount *before* the lawyer takes a percentage as a fee. If the lawyer took the percentage fee first, and then costs are deducted,

the lawyer's fee would be higher than the agreed upon percentage. This is an underhanded racket that far too many lawyers pull on unsuspecting clients. Don't get caught by it.
- What specific costs you agree to pay for—such as copying, postage, long-distance telephone, court filing fees.
- What actions involving extra costs the lawyer must get your specific approval for before incurring the costs, such as: depositions, which involve expensive court reporters and transcripts; hiring outside personnel, such as investigators; and ordering official records or reports.

   One simple way to handle the issue is to set a dollar limit on costs, including in your written fee agreement that you must approve in advance any costs beyond that amount.

c. Contingency fee agreements

Because it is difficult for most people to come up with a lot of money in advance to pay a lawyer, lawyers have developed a system of payment in which they require no money from a client to begin a case and instead take a percentage of the client's final settlement or court award as their own payment. This arrangement, known as a contingency fee agreement, can be extremely useful to both clients and lawyers.

   The problem with contingency fee agreements is not the theory but the practice. The amount of the client's compensation a lawyer takes usually runs between 33% to 40%, not counting costs the lawyer has run up processing the lawsuit. This sometimes means that the client winds up taking home less than half of the amount he or she actually won in the case.

Example *You enter a contingency fee agreement with a lawyer in which you agree to pay the lawyer 33% of whatever compensation settlement the lawyer obtains for you after the lawyer has been reimbursed for costs run up processing your case. If the lawyer has spent $750 on* costs and obtains a settlement of $5,000, the $750 would first be subtracted from the $5,000, leaving $4,250. The lawyer would then take 33% of the remaining $4,250, leaving you with only $2,835.

With these kinds of fee percentages, you have to figure out the specific economics of your claim to determine whether it is worth hiring the lawyer on a full contingency fee basis.

If the insurance company has refused to pay you any compensation, or only a token "nuisance value" amount, and the potential damages in your case are fairly large, it is probably worth your while to hire a lawyer on a full contingency basis. You have little to lose and much to gain.

If the insurance company is offering little or no compensation but the total damages your claim would be worth is small—within your state's Small Claims Court limit—it may make equal sense either to hire a lawyer or to take the claim to Small Claims Court on your own. The decision will depend on how comfortable you are going to Small Claims Court, on how technical the insurance company's defense is, and on how confident the lawyer is of getting you a certain amount of money.

If the insurance company has offered you a substantial settlement amount but one which you believe is too low, you must measure what it has offered against what the lawyer could realistically expect to get. If the lawyer can only expect to get an additional 25%, it wouldn't make sense to hire the lawyer and pay him or her 33%; you wind up losing by having hired the lawyer. In that case, a reduced fee arrangement would be the only sensible approach to hiring a lawyer instead of continuing to handle negotiations on your own.

On the other hand, if the lawyer believes he or she can get you enough compensation to overcome the legal fees, hiring the lawyer may be a sensible course of action. If so, try to structure the fee arrangement so that whatever the compensation amount, you are guaranteed no less than you would have received had you just settled with the insurance company on your own.

d.   Reduced contingency fees

If you have already investigated your accident and obtained all the documents pertaining to your claim by the time you consult a lawyer, you have already done much of the work the lawyer would normally have to do. Based on this, some lawyers may be willing to consider accepting a lower percentage contingency fee than normal.

Of course, a lawyer will not be the one to suggest a reduced fee arrangement; you will have to propose it. And most lawyers will be reluctant to agree, in part, of course, because they will make less money. But lawyers are also reluctant because they rarely believe that the work a client has done will be of much value to the case. Bring all your documents to your initial meeting with the lawyer and show the lawyer the organized file you have put together. If you emphasize how much work the lawyer's office will have been relieved of because of your efforts, the lawyer may agree to consider some kind of reduced fee arrangement.

One way to structure a reduced fee would be an agreement that if the lawyer is able to settle the case solely by negotiating with the insurance adjuster— that is, without having to go through any of the litigation process involving the insurance company's lawyers—the lawyer would receive a 25% contingency fee. But the lawyer would receive the standard contingency fee of 33% (40% if the case ultimately goes to trial) if negotiations alone fail to produce a satisfactory new settlement offer. The reason to agree to the larger fee if there is no early settlement is that then the lawyer would have to put in the work of actually litigating the case—filing legal documents beyond the simple complaint (a pre-established form requiring no work), engaging in oral questioning (called "depositions") and written questioning (called "interrogatories") of parties and witnesses.

Another way to structure a reduced contingency fee is to agree that if you receive up to a certain amount—say, $500 or $1,000 more than what you have already been offered by the insurance company —the lawyer will get a basic fee of 25% of the settlement but for everything over the pre-set amount the lawyer will receive 33%. This structure guarantees that you do not wind up getting less by using a lawyer than you would have if you had just accepted the settlement offer the insurance company made to you before you ever met the lawyer.

And still another way to structure a fee arrangement would be to pay the lawyer an hourly fee up to a prearranged limit—say, $500. If the claim cannot be settled within that amount of work, the fee would then switch to a contingency arrangement.

3. Managing Your Lawyer

Certain decisions about the ongoing management of your case should not be left solely to your lawyer's discretion: expenses—whether it is worth it to spend your money on something; your time and hassle, or the time and hassle of someone only peripherally involved in the case, such as a friend or relative witness; finally, the major decision of when to settle your case. None of these decisions can be made in advance. Each depends on how the case is going. And although you must participate in these decisions, you will depend a great deal on your lawyer's advice, which is why it is so important to choose a lawyer who explains what is going on and who listens to what you have to say.

Some of the most important points in a lawsuit at which you should exercise some degree of control over your lawyer are discussed below. Take a few minutes with your lawyer at the beginning of the case and explain that you don't want unnecessarily to limit what the lawyer can do or to tell the lawyer how to do the job. But emphasize that you are concerned about controlling the cost of the lawsuit since the total money involved is not great. If the lawyer is not sympathetic to this problem, perhaps you'd better interview some more lawyers.

a. Deciding when to serve the defendant

A lawsuit technically begins when a complaint, a document setting out the facts and legal basis for your legal action against the defendant, is filed in court. This complaint must be filed within the time limit set by your state's statute of limitations. But the real action of a lawsuit—the part requiring the most work by the lawyer, which runs up both stress and expenses and which you and your lawyer can no longer completely control—does not begin until the defendant and his or her lawyer are brought into the case. And that does not occur until your complaint is served on—or formally delivered to—the defendant.

The decision of when to serve the defendant, and therefore when to start the expensive and stressful activity of a lawsuit, depends on whether settlement negotiations are making any progress. That decision should be made jointly by you and your lawyer.

b. Conducting discovery

The legal process used to get information from the other side in a lawsuit is called discovery. Discovery can involve the relatively simple exchange of written questions and answers called interrogatories, as well as other exchanges of documents. But it can also include expensive procedures called depositions—in which both lawyers get together and question you, the defendant or witnesses in person, while a court reporter records the answers and then prepares a written transcript.

Although depositions are a basic part of most lawsuits, in cases involving small amounts of money they simply may not be cost effective. This is particularly true for depositions of independent witnesses, as opposed to the deposition of the defendant. Make sure that your lawyer bears in mind the expense of taking depositions and does not do so unless really necessary.

The same thing can be said for requests for records and reports. Even though you may have already provided the lawyer with your medical and billing records, lawyers sometimes want to order them again. But the doctor's office will charge again for these records, sometimes a larger fee to a lawyer than to the patient—and the lawyer, in turn, will pass this on to you. Also, lawyers sometimes want to get a doctor to write a report concerning your injuries, but such reports can cost hundreds of dollars. Ask your lawyer—tactfully—not to order any duplicate medical records, or request a medical report, without discussing it with you first.

c.   Independent investigations

It can sometimes be useful for a lawyer to hire an outside investigator—either an expert in accident reconstruction or simply an information-gatherer such as a private investigator—to help piece together what happened in the accident or to dig up information about the defendant. But these outside investigators can get very expensive. Get your lawyer to agree not to use any outside investigators or other outside services requiring extra payment unless you agree to it first.

d.   Using FAX machines and messengers

Lawyers love to use FAX machines and messengers instead of the regular mail. Their love affair with these instant gratification devices comes from the fact that things sometimes move fast in a lawsuit, but it also comes from lawyers' bad habit of leaving things to the last minute. Also, lawyers often take the easiest but most expensive route because they are playing with your money, not their own.

It may seem a petty concern, but using FAX machines and messengers can wind up costing you hundreds of dollars if you don't put a cap on the cost from the beginning. Make a point of asking your lawyer not to charge you for these services unless there is good reason for using them.

e.   Keeping your case moving

Delay is an unfortunate part of the insurance claims business and an even more common part of the lawsuit game. But you have a right to have your lawyer and the insurance company process your claim or lawsuit reasonably promptly. If you have not heard from your lawyer for a while concerning activity on your case, call and find out what is going on and find out when the next event—a response by the insurance company, a letter or document sent by your lawyer—is supposed to take place. Then follow up to make sure it occurs.

A lawyer, like anyone else, does not like to be pestered. On the other hand, you have a right to know what is going on and to make sure that your case is being handled efficiently and not swept under the rug while your lawyer does other things. Be reasonable. Don't call every couple of days and demand to know what has happened in the past 48 hours—and if you are paying the lawyer on an hourly basis, you will be charged for each of these phone calls. But do check in regularly to make sure that something is going on and to get some rough schedule from the lawyer about when the next movement in the case will occur.

f.   Deciding when to settle

The most important decision of all is when to say enough and settle your case. Just as with the decision of when and if to take an insurance adjuster's offer while negotiating by yourself, the decision about when to accept a settlement offer your lawyer has obtained depends solely on whether you are satisfied. The decision should be based upon a balance between what you think the case is worth and the effort and expense it might take to get more than has been offered. And into that hopper you will also throw such facts as how quickly you need the money and how weary you are of the whole process.

Of course, you will want and need your lawyer's advice on this important decision. That is part of what you have hired a lawyer to do. But the decision should not depend on the lawyer's needs—such as the lawyer wanting to settle quickly because he or she needs the money or is busy with other cases, or the lawyer not wanting to settle because he or she wants to go for a jackpot and is willing to take the risk of losing everything. The final decision must be yours.

ACCIDENT CLAIM WORKSHEET

Use this worksheet to help keep track of the information you need to process your accident injury claim. This worksheet is for your personal reference and is not intended to become part of your claim.

LIABILITY

PEOPLE RESPONSIBLE

Name	
Address	
Telephone (work)	(home)
Insurance Company	Policy Number
Auto License	
Other Information	

Name	
Address	
Telephone (work)	(home)
Insurance Company	Policy Number
Auto License	
Other Information	

Name	
Address	
Telephone (work)	(home)
Insurance Company	Policy Number
Auto License	
Other Information	

WITNESSES

Name

Address

Telephone (work)	(home)

Date of First Contact

Written Statement	Yes	No

Other Information

Name

Address

Telephone (work)	(home)

Date of First Contact

Written Statement	Yes	No

Other Information

Name

Address

Telephone (work)	(home)

Date of First Contact

Written Statement	Yes	No

Other Information

Name

Address

Telephone (work)	(home)

Date of First Contact

Written Statement	Yes	No

Other Information

MEDICAL TREATMENT

TREATMENT PROVIDER

Name	
Address	
Telephone	
Date of First Visit	Date of Last Visit
Person Contacted for Medical Records	
Date Requested	Date Received
Person Contacted for Medical Billing	
Date Requested	Date Received
Other Information	

Name	
Address	
Telephone	
Date of First Visit	Date of Last Visit
Person Contacted for Medical Records	
Date Requested	Date Received
Person Contacted for Medical Billing	
Date Requested	Date Received
Other Information	

Name	
Address	
Telephone	
Date of First Visit	Date of Last Visit
Person Contacted for Medical Records	
Date Requested	Date Received
Person Contacted for Medical Billing	
Date Requested	Date Received
Other Information	

INSURANCE

INSURER

Company	
Address	
Telephone	

Insured	Claim Number
Adjuster	
Date Demand Letter was Sent	

Settlement Amount	Date Accepted

COMMUNICATIONS WITH INSURER

Date

Comments

COMMUNICATIONS WITH INSURER

Date

Comments

COMMUNICATIONS WITH INSURER

Date

Comments

COMMUNICATIONS WITH INSURER

Date

Comments

COMMUNICATIONS WITH INSURER

Date

Comments

Index

M

Fight Your Ticket

Attorney David Brown

California 5th Edition

This book shows you how to fight an unfair traffic ticket—when you're stopped, at arraignment, at trial and on appeal.
$17.95/FYT

Collect Your Court Judgment

Gini Graham Scott, Attorney Stephen Elias & Lisa Goldoftas

California 2nd Edition

This book contains step-by-step instructions and all the forms you need to collect a court judgment from the debtor's bank accounts, wages, business receipts, real estate or other assets.
$19.95/JUDG

How to Change Your Name

Attorneys David Loeb & David Brown

California 5th Edition

This book explains how to change your name legally and provides all the necessary court forms with detailed instructions on how to fill them out.
$19.95/NAME

The Criminal Records Book

Attorney Warren Siegel

California 3rd Edition

This book shows you step-by-step how to seal criminal records, dismiss convictions, destroy marijuana records and reduce felony convictions.
$19.95/CRIM

LEGAL REFORM

Legal Breakdown: 40 Ways to Fix Our Legal System

Nolo Press Editors and Staff

National 1st Edition

Legal Breakdown presents 40 common-sense proposals to make our legal system fairer, faster, cheaper and more accessible. It advocates abolishing probate, taking divorce out of court, treating jurors better and a host of other fundamental changes.
$8.95/LEG

BUSINESS/WORKPLACE

The Legal Guide for Starting & Running a Small Business

Attorney Fred S. Steingold

National 1st Edition

This book is an essential resource for every small business owner, whether you are just starting out or are already established. Find out everything you need to know about how to form a sole proprietorship, partnership or corporation, negotiate a favorable lease, hire and fire employees, write contracts and resolve disputes.
$19.95 / RUNS

Sexual Harassment on the Job

Attorneys William Petrocelli & Barbara Kate Repa

National 1st Edition

This is the first comprehensive book dealing with sexual harassment in the workplace. It describes what harassment is, what the laws are that make it illegal and how to put a stop to it. This guide is invaluable both for employees experiencing harassment and for employers interested in creating a policy against sexual harassment and a procedure for handling complaints.
$14.95/HARS

Your Rights in the Workplace

Dan Lacey

National 1st Edition

Your Rights in the Workplace, the first comprehensive guide to workplace rights—from hiring to firing—explains the latest sweeping changes in laws passed to protect workers. Learning about these legal protections can help all workers be sure they're paid fairly and on time, get all employment benefits, and know how to take action if fired or laid off illegally.
$15.95/YRW

How to Write a Business Plan

Mike McKeever

National 4th Edition

If you're thinking of starting a business or raising money to expand an existing one, this book will show you how to write the business plan and loan package necessary to finance your business and make it work.
$19.95/SBS

Marketing Without Advertising

Michael Phillips & Salli Rasberry

National 1st Edition

This book outlines practical steps for building and expanding a small business without spending a lot of money on advertising.
$14.00/MWAD

The Partnership Book

Attorneys Denis Clifford & Ralph Warner

National 4th Edition

This book shows you step-by-step how to write a solid partnership agreement that meets your needs. It covers initial contributions to the business, wages, profit-sharing, buy-outs, death or retirement of a partner and disputes.
$24.95/PART

How to Form Your Own Nonprofit Corporation

Attorney Anthony Mancuso

National 1st Edition

This book explains the legal formalities involved and provides detailed information on the differences in the law among 50 states. It also contains forms for the Articles, Bylaws and Minutes you need, along with complete instructions for obtaining federal 501 (c) (3) tax exemptions and qualifying for public charity status.
$24.95/NNP

The California Nonprofit Corporation Handbook

Attorney Anthony Mancuso

California 6th Edition

This book shows you step-by-step how to form and operate a nonprofit corporation in California. It includes the latest corporate and tax law changes, and the forms for the Articles, Bylaws and Minutes.
$29.95/NON

How to Form Your Own Corporation

Attorney Anthony Mancuso

California 7th Edition

New York 2nd Edition

Texas 4th Edition

Florida 3rd Edition

These books contain the forms, instructions and tax information you need to incorporate a small business yourself and save hundreds of dollars in lawyers' fees.
California $29.95/CCOR
New York $24.95/NYCO
Texas $29.95/TCOR
Florida $24.95/FLCO

The California Professional Corporation Handbook

Attorney Anthony Mancuso

California 4th Edition

Health care professionals, lawyers, accountants and members of certain other professions must fulfill special requirements when forming a corporation in California. This book contains up-to-date tax information plus all the forms and instructions necessary to form a California professional corporation.
$34.95/PROF

S E L F - H E L P   L A W   B O O K S   &   S O F T W A R E

ESTATE PLANNING & PROBATE

Plan Your Estate With a Living Trust
Attorney Denis Clifford
National 2nd Edition
This book covers every significant aspect of estate planning and gives detailed specific, instructions for preparing a living trust, a document that lets your family avoid expensive and lengthy probate court proceedings after your death. *Plan Your Estate* includes all the tear-out forms and step-by-step instructions to let you prepare an estate plan designed for your special needs.
$19.95/NEST

Nolo's Simple Will Book
Attorney Denis Clifford
National 2nd Edition
It's easy to write a legally valid will using this book. The instructions and forms enable people to draft a will for all needs, including naming a personal guardian for minor children, leaving property to minor children or young adults and updating a will when necessary. Good in all states except Louisiana.
$17.95/SWIL

How to Probate an Estate
Julia Nissley
California 6th Edition
If you find yourself responsible for winding up the legal and financial affairs of a deceased family member or friend, you can often save costly attorneys' fees by handling the probate process yourself. This book also explains the simple procedures you can use to transfer assets that don't require probate, including property held in joint tenancy or living trusts or as community property.
$34.95/PAE

The Conservatorship Book
Lisa Goldoftas & Attorney Carolyn Farren
California 1st Edition
When someone becomes incapacitated due to illness or age, a conservator may need to take charge of their medical and financial affairs. *The Conservatorship Book* comes with complete instructions and all the forms necessary to file conservatorship documents, appear in court, be appointed conservator and end a conservatorship.
$24.95/CNSV

software

 WillMaker
Nolo Press
Version 4.0
This easy-to-use software program lets you prepare and update a legal will—safely, privately and without the expense of a lawyer. Leading you step-by-step in a question-and-answer format, *WillMaker* builds a will around your answers, taking into account your state of residence. *WillMaker* comes with a 200-page legal manual which provides the legal background necessary to make sound choices. Good in all states except Louisiana.
IBM PC
(3-1/2 & 5-1/4 disks included) $69.95/WI4
MACINTOSH $69.95/WM4

 Nolo's Personal RecordKeeper
(formerly For the Record)

Carol Pladsen & Attorney Ralph Warner
Version 3.0
Nolo's Personal RecordKeeper lets you record the location of personal, financial and legal information in over 200 categories and subcategories. It also allows you to create lists of insured property, compute net worth, consolidate emergency information into one place and export to *Quicken®* home inventory and net worth reports. Includes a 320-page manual filled with practical and legal advice.
IBM PC
(3-1/2 & 5-1/4 disks included) $49.95/FRI3
MACINTOSH $49.95/FRM3

 Nolo's Living Trust
Attorney Mary Randolph
Version 1.0
A will is an indispensable part of any estate plan, but many people need a living trust as well. By putting certain assets into a trust, you save your heirs the headache, time and expense of probate. *Nolo's Living Trust* lets you set up an individual or shared marital trust, make your trust document legal, transfer your property to the trust, and change or revoke the trust at any time. The 380-page manual guides you through the process step-by-step, and over 100 legal help screens and an on-line glossary explain key legal terms and concepts. Good in all states except Louisiana.
MACINTOSH $79.95/LTM1

GOING TO COURT

Everybody's Guide to Municipal Court
Judge Roderic Duncan
California 1st Edition
Everybody's Guide to Municipal Court explains how to prepare and defend the most common types of contract and personal injury law suits in California Municipal Court. Written by a California judge, the book provides step-by-step instructions for preparing and filing all necessary forms, gathering evidence and appearing in court.
$29.95/MUNI

Everybody's Guide to Small Claims Court
Attorney Ralph Warner
National 5th Edition
California 10th Edition
These books will help you decide if you should sue in Small Claims Court, show you how to file and serve papers, tell you what to bring to court and how to collect a judgment.
National $15.95/NSCC
California $15.95/ CSCC

The Independent Paralegal's Handbook
Attorney Ralph Warner
National 2nd Edition
The Independent Paralegal's Handbook provides legal and business guidelines for those who want to take routine legal work out of the law office and offer it for a reasonable fee in an independent business.
$19.95/ PARA

Getting Started as an Independent Paralegal
(*Two Audio Tapes*)
Attorney Ralph Warner
National 2nd Edition
If you are interested in going into business as an Independent Paralegal—helping consumers prepare their own legal paperwork in uncontested proceedings such as bankruptcy, divorce, small business incorporation, landlord-tenant actions and probate—you'll want these tapes. Approximately two hours in length, the tapes will tell you everything you need to know about what legal tasks to handle, how much to charge and how to run a profitable business.
$44.95/GSIP

Nolo's Partnership Maker
Attorney Tony Mancuso & Michael Radtke
Version 1.0
Nolo's Partnership Maker prepares a legal partnership agreement for doing business in any state. The program can be used by anyone who plans to pool energy, efforts, money or property with others to run a business, share property, produce a profit or undertake any other type of mutual endeavor. You can select and assemble the standard partnership clauses provided or create your own customized agreement. And the agreement can be updated at any time. Includes on-line legal help screens, glossary and tutorial, and a manual that takes you through the process step-by-step.
IBM PC
(3-1/2 & 5-1/4 disks included) $129.00/PAGI1

California Incorporator
Attorney Anthony Mancuso
Version 1.0 (good only in CA)
Answer the questions on the screen and this software program will print out the 35-40 pages of documents you need to make your California corporation legal. Comes with a 200-page manual which explains the incorporation process.
IBM PC
(3-1/2 & 5-1/4 disks included) $129.00/INCI

The California Nonprofit Corporation Handbook
(*computer edition*)
Attorney Anthony Mancuso
Version 1.0 (good only in CA)
This book/software package shows you step-by-step how to form and operate a nonprofit corporation in California. Included on disk are the forms for the Articles, Bylaws and Minutes.
IBM PC 5-1/4 $69.95/ NPI
IBM PC 3-1/2 $69.95/ NP3I
MACINTOSH $69.95/ NPM

How to Form Your Own New York Corporation & How to Form Your Own Texas Corporation
(*computer editions*)
Attorney Anthony Mancuso
These book/software packages contain the instructions and tax information and forms you need to incorporate a small business and save hundreds of dollars in lawyers' fees. All organizational forms are on disk. Both come with a 250-page manual.
New York 1st Edition
IBM PC 5-1/4 $69.95/ NYCI
IBM PC 3-1/2 $69.95/ NYC3I
MACINTOSH $69.95/ NYCM

Texas 1st Edition
IBM PC 5-1/4 $69.95/ TCI
IBM PC 3-1/2 $69.95/ TC3I
MACINTOSH $69.95/ TCM

Neighbor Law:
Fences, Trees, Boundaries & Noise
Attorney Cora Jordan
National 1st Edition
Neighbor Law answers common questions about the subjects that most often trigger disputes between neighbors: fences, trees, boundaries and noise. It explains how to find the law and resolve disputes without a nasty lawsuit.
$14.95/NEI

Dog Law
Attorney Mary Randolph
National 1st Edition
Dog Law is a practical guide to the laws that affect dog owners and their neighbors. You'll find answers to common questions on such topics as biting, barking, veterinarians and more.
$12.95/DOG

Stand Up to the IRS
Attorney Fred Daily
National 1st Edition
Stand Up to the IRS gives detailed stategies on surviving an audit with the minimum amount of damage, appealing an audit decision, going to Tax Court and dealing with IRS collectors. It also discusses filing tax returns when you haven't done so in a while, tax crimes, concerns of small business people and getting help from the IRS ombudsman. This book also includes confidential forms, unavailable to taxpayers, used by the IRS during audits and collection interviewers.
$19.95 / SUIRS

Barbara Kaufman's Consumer Action Guide
Barbara Kaufman
California 1st Edition
This practical handbook is filled with information on hundreds of consumer topics. Barbara Kaufman, the Bay Area's award-winning consumer reporter and producer of KCBS Radio's *Call for Action*, gives consumers access to their legal rights, providing addresses and phone numbers of where to complain when things go wrong, and providing resources if more help is necessary.
$14.95/CAG

Money Troubles:
Legal Strategies to Cope With Your Debts
Attorney Robin Leonard
National 1st Edition
Are you behind on your credit card bills or loan payments? If you are, then *Money Troubles* is exactly what you need. It covers everything from knowing what your rights are, and asserting them, to helping you evaluate your individual situation. This practical, straightforward book is for anyone who needs help understanding and dealing with the complex and often scary topic of debts.
$16.95/MT

How to File for Bankruptcy

Attorneys Stephen Elias, Albin Renauer &
Robin Leonard
National 3rd Edition

Trying to decide whether or not filing for
bankruptcy makes sense? *How to File for
Bankruptcy* contains an overview of the
process and all the forms plus step-by-step
instructions on the procedures to follow.
$24.95/HFB

Simple Contracts for Personal Use

Attorney Stephen Elias & Marcia Stewart
National 2nd Edition

This book contains clearly written legal
form contracts to buy and sell property,
borrow and lend money, store and lend
personal property, release others from
personal liability, or pay a contractor to do
home repairs. Includes agreements to
arrange childcare and other household
help.
$16.95/CONT

FAMILY MATTERS

Divorce & Money

Violet Woodhouse & Victoria Felton-Collins with
M.C. Blakeman
National 1st Edition

Divorce & Money explains how to
evaluate such major assets as family homes
and businesses, investments, pensions, and
how to arrive at a division of property that
is fair to both sides. Throughout, the book
emphasizes the difference between legal
reality—how the court evaluates assets,
and financial reality—what the assets are
really worth.
$19.95/DIMO

The Living Together Kit

Attorneys Toni Ihara & Ralph Warner
National 6th Edition

The Living Together Kit is a detailed guide
designed to help the increasing number of
unmarried couples living together understand the laws that affect them. Sample
agreements and instructions are included.
$17.95/LTK

The Guardianship Book

Lisa Goldoftas & Attorney David Brown
California 1st Edition

The Guardianship Book provides step-by-
step instructions and the forms needed to
obtain a legal guardianship without a
lawyer.
$19.95/GB

A Legal Guide for Lesbian and Gay Couples

Attorneys Hayden Curry & Denis Clifford
National 6th Edition

Laws designed to regulate and protect
unmarried couples don't apply to lesbian
and gay couples. This book shows you
step-by-step how to write a living-together
contract, plan for medical emergencies,
and plan your estates. Includes forms,
sample agreements and lists of both
national lesbian and gay legal
organizations and AIDS organizations.
$17.95/LG

How to Do Your Own Divorce

Attorney Charles Sherman
(Texas Ed. by Sherman & Simons)
California 17th Edition & Texas 4th Edition

These books contain all the forms and
instructions you need to do your own
uncontested divorce without a lawyer.
California $18.95/CDIV
Texas $17.95/TDIV

Practical Divorce Solutions

Attorney Charles Sherman
California 2nd Edition

This book is a valuable guide to the
emotional aspects of divorce as well as an
overview of the legal and financial
decisions that must be made.
$12.95/PDS

California Marriage & Divorce Law

Attorneys Ralph Warner, Toni Ihara &
Stephen Elias
California 11th Edition

This book explains community property,
pre-nuptial contracts, foreign marriages,
buying a house, getting a divorce, dividing
property, and more.
$19.95/MARR

How to Adopt Your Stepchild in California

Frank Zagone & Attorney Mary Randolph
California 3rd Edition

There are many emotional, financial and
legal reasons to adopt a stepchild, but
among the most pressing legal reasons is
the need to avoid confusion over
inheritance or guardianship. This book
provides sample forms and step-by-step
instructions for completing a simple
uncontested adoption by a stepparent.
$19.95/ADOP

JUST FOR FUN

29 Reasons Not To Go to Law School

Attorneys Ralph Warner & Toni Ihara
National 3rd Edition

Filled with humor and piercing
observations, this book can save you three
years, $70,000 and your sanity.
$9.95/29R

Devil's Advocates: The Unnatural History of Lawyers

by Andrew & Jonathan Roth
National 1st Edition

This book is a painless and hilarious
education, tracing the legal profession.
Careful attention is given to the world's
worst lawyers, most preposterous cases and
most ludicrous courtroom strategies.
$12.95/DA

Poetic Justice: The Funniest, Meanest Things Ever Said About Lawyers

Edited by Jonathan & Andrew Roth
National 1st Edition

A great gift for anyone in the legal
profession who has managed to maintain a
sense of humor.
$8.95/PJ

PATENT, COPYRIGHT & TRADEMARK

Trademark: How To Name Your Business & Product

Attorneys Kate McGrath and Stephen Elias,
With Trademark Attorney Sarah Shena
National 1st Edition

This is by far the best comprehensive do-
it-yourself trademark book designed for
small businesses. It explains step-by-step
how to protect names used to market
services and products, and shows how to:
choose a name or logo that others can't
copy, conduct a trademark search, register
a trademark with the U.S. Patent and
Trademark Office and protect and
maintain the trademark.
$29.95 / TRD

Patent It Yourself

Attorney David Pressman
National 3rd Edition

From the patent search to the actual
application, this book covers everything
including the use and licensing of patents,
successful marketing and how to deal with
infringement.
$34.95/PAT

The Inventor's Notebook
Fred Grissom & Attorney David Pressman
National 1st Edition
This book helps you document the process of successful independent inventing by providing forms, instructions, references to relevant areas of patent law, a bibliography of legal and non-legal aids and more.
$19.95/INOT

The Copyright Handbook
Attorney Stephen Fishman
National 1st Edition
Writers, editors, publishers, scholars, educators, librarians and others who work with words all need to know about copyright laws. This book provides forms and step-by-step instructions for protecting all types of written expression under U.S. and international copyright law. It contains detailed reference chapters on such major copyright-related topics as copyright infringement, fair use, works for hire and transfers of copyright ownership.
$24.95/COHA

How to Copyright Software
Attorney M.J. Salone
National 3rd Edition
This book tells you how to register your copyright for maximum protection and discusses who owns a copyright on software developed by more than one person.
$39.95/COPY

LANDLORDS & TENANTS

The Landlord's Law Book, Vol. 1: Rights & Responsibilities
Attorneys David Brown & Ralph Warner
California 3rd Edition
This book contains information on deposits, leases and rental agreements, inspections (tenants' privacy rights), habitability (rent withholding), ending a tenancy, liability and rent control.
$29.95/LBRT

The Landlord's Law Book, Vol. 2: Evictions
Attorney David Brown
California 3rd Edition
Updated for 1992, this book will show you step-by-step how to go to court and get an eviction for a tenant who won't pay rent—and won't leave. Contains all the tear-out forms and necessary instructions.
$29.95/LBEV

Tenants' Rights
Attorneys Myron Moskovitz & Ralph Warner
California 11th Edition
This book explains how to handle your relationship with your landlord and understand your legal rights when you find yourself in disagreement. A special section on rent control cities is included.
$15.95/CTEN

HOMEOWNERS

How To Buy a House in California
Attorney Ralph Warner, Ira Serkes & George Devine
California 2nd Edition
This book shows you how to find a house, work with a real estate agent, make an offer and negotiate intelligently. Includes information on all types of mortgages as well as private financing options.
$19.95/BHCA

For Sale By Owner
George Devine
California 2nd Edition
For Sale By Owner provides essential information about pricing your house, marketing it, writing a contract and going through escrow.
$24.95/FSBO

The Deeds Book
Attorney Mary Randolph
California 2nd Edition
If you own real estate, you'll need to sign a new deed when you transfer the property or put it in trust as part of your estate planning. This book shows you how to find the right kind of deed, complete the tear-out forms and record them in the county recorder's public records.
$15.95/DEED

Homestead Your House
Attorneys Ralph Warner, Charles Sherman & Toni Ihara
California 8th Edition
This book shows you how to file a Declaration of Homestead and includes complete instructions and tear-out forms.
$9.95/HOME

OLDER AMERICANS

Elder Care: Choosing & Financing Long-Term Care
Attorney Joseph Matthews
National 1st Edition
This book will guide you in choosing and paying for long-term care, alerting you to practical concerns and explaining laws that may affect your decisions.
$16.95/ELD

Social Security, Medicare & Pensions
Attorney Joseph Matthews with Dorothy Matthews Berman
National 5th Edition
This book contains invaluable guidance through the current maze of rights and benefits for those 55 and over, including Medicare, Medicaid and Social Security retirement and disability benefits and age discrimination protections.
$15.95/SOA

RESEARCH & REFERENCE

Legal Research: How To Find and Understand the Law
Attorneys Stephen Elias & Susan Levinkind
National 3rd Edition
A valuable tool on its own or as a companion to just about every other Nolo book. This book gives easy-to-use, step-by-step instructions on how to find legal information.
$16.95/LRES

Family Law Dictionary
Attorneys Robin Leonard & Stephen Elias
National 2nd Edition
Finally, a legal dictionary that's written in plain English, not "legalese"! *The Family Law Dictionary* is designed to help the nonlawyer who has a question or problem involving family law—marriage, divorce, adoption or living together.
$13.95/FLD

Legal Research Made Easy: A Roadmap Through the Law Library Maze
2-1/2 hr. videotape and 40-page manual
Nolo Press/Legal Star Communications
National 1st Edition
If you're a law student, paralegal or librarian—or just want to look up the law for yourself—this video is for you. University of California law professor Bob Berring explains how to use all the basic legal research tools in your local law library with an easy-to-follow six-step research plan and a sense of humor.
$89.95/LRME

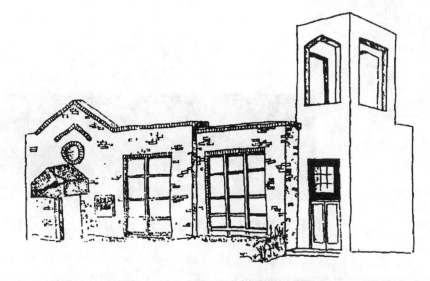

N O L O   P R E S S   /   9 5 0   P A R K E R   S T R E E T   /   B E R K E L E Y   C A   9 4 7 1 0

O R D E R   F O R M

Name

Address (UPS to street address, Priority Mail to P.O. boxes)

Catalog Code	Quantity	Item	Unit price	Total

Subtotal		
Sales tax (California residents only)		
Shipping & handling		
2nd day UPS		
TOTAL		
PRICES SUBJECT TO CHANGE		

SALES TAX
California residents add your local tax

SHIPPING & HANDLING
$4.00   1 item
$5.00   2-3 items
+$.50   each additional item
Allow 2-3 weeks for delivery

IN A HURRY?
UPS 2nd day delivery is available:
Add $5.00 (contiguous states) or
$8.00 (Alaska & Hawaii) to your regular shipping and handling charges

**FOR FASTER SERVICE, USE YOUR CREDIT CARD
AND OUR TOLL-FREE NUMBERS:**
Monday-Friday, 7 a.m. to 5 p.m. Pacific Time
Order line   1 (800) 992-6656
General Information   1 (510) 549-1976
Fax us your order   1 (800) 645-0895

METHOD OF PAYMENT
☐ Check enclosed
☐ VISA   ☐ Mastercard   ☐ Discover Card   ☐ American Express

Account #   Expiration Date

Signature Authorizing

Phone   PICL

N O L O   P R E S S   /   9 5 0   P A R K E R   S T R E E T   /   B E R K E L E Y   C A   9 4 7 1 0

FREE NOLO NEWS SUBSCRIPTION

When you register, we'll send you our quarterly newspaper, the *Nolo News,* free for two years. (U.S. addresses only.) Here's what you'll get in every issue:

INFORMATIVE ARTICLES

Written by Nolo editors, articles provide practical legal information on issues you encounter in everyday life: family law, wills, debts, consumer rights, and much more.

UPDATE SERVICE

The *Nolo News* keeps you informed of legal changes that affect any Nolo book and software program.

BOOK AND SOFTWARE REVIEWS

We're always looking for good legal and consumer books and software from other publishers. When we find them, we review them and offer them in our mail order catalog.

ANSWERS TO YOUR LEGAL QUESTIONS

Our readers are always challenging us with good questions on a variety of legal issues. So in each issue, "Auntie Nolo" gives sage advice and sound information.

COMPLETE NOLO PRESS CATALOG

The *Nolo News* contains an up-to-the-minute catalog of all Nolo books and software, which you can order using our toll-free "800" order line. And you can see at a glance if you're using an out-of-date version of a Nolo product.

LAWYER JOKES

Nolo's famous lawyer joke column continually gets the goat of the legal establishment. If we print a joke you send in, you'll get a $20 Nolo gift certificate.

We promise *never* to give your name and address to any other organization.

Your Registration Card

Complete and Mail Today

HOW TO WIN YOUR PERSONAL INJURY CLAIM **Registration Card**

We'd like to know what you think! Please take a moment to fill out and return this postage paid card for a free two-year subscription to the *Nolo News.* If you already receive the *Nolo News,* we'll extend your subscription.

Name _____ Ph.( ) _____

Address _____

City _____ State _____ Zip _____

Where did you hear about this book? _____

For what purpose did you use this book? _____

Did you consult a lawyer?	Yes	No		Not Applicable		
Was it easy for you to use this book?	(very easy)	5	4	3	2	1	(very difficult)
Did you find this book helpful?	(very)	5	4	3	2	1	(not at all)

Comments _____
_____
_____
_____
_____
_____

THANK YOU PICL

[Nolo books are]..."written in plain language, free of legal mumbo jumbo, and spiced with witty personal observations."

—ASSOCIATED PRESS

"Well-produced and slickly written, the [Nolo] books are designed to take the mystery out of seemingly involved procedures, carefully avoiding legalese and leading the reader step-by-step through such everyday legal problems as filling out forms, making up contracts, and even how to behave in court."

—SAN FRANCISCO EXAMINER

"...Nolo publications...guide people simply through the how, when, where and why of law."

—WASHINGTON POST

"Increasingly, people who are not lawyers are performing tasks usually regarded as legal work... And consumers, using books like Nolo's, do routine legal work themselves."

—NEW YORK TIMES

"...All of [Nolo's] books are easy-to-understand, are updated regularly, provide pull-out forms...and are often quite moving in their sense of compassion for the struggles of the lay reader."

—SAN FRANCISCO CHRONICLE

NO POSTAGE
NECESSARY
IF MAILED
IN THE
UNITED STATES

BUSINESS REPLY MAIL
FIRST-CLASS MAIL PERMIT NO 3283 BERKELEY CA

POSTAGE WILL BE PAID BY ADDRESSEE

NOLO PRESS
950 Parker Street
Berkeley CA 94710-9867